· A HISTORY LOVER'S ·
GUIDE TO
DENVER

A HISTORY LOVER'S
GUIDE TO
DENVER

MARK A. BARNHOUSE

THE
History
PRESS

Published by The History Press
Charleston, SC
www.historypress.com

All cover images by Ryan Dravitz Photography.

First published 2020

Manufactured in the United States

ISBN 9781467142120

Library of Congress Control Number: 2020930492

To Matt Wallington, for everything.

CONTENTS

PREFACE

I have admired Ryan Dravitz's photography for several years, with his frequent posts to DenverInfill.com, the blog chronicling changes to central Denver; it has been a pleasure to work with him on illustrating this volume, and I have greatly appreciated his enthusiasm and willingness to get that perfect shot. Although writing a book is a solitary effort, numerous individuals have contributed with suggestions and encouragement, including Kris Autobee, Alan Golin Gass, Lois Harvey, Leslie Krupa, Thomas J. Noel, Mary O'Neil, Barbara Ormsby, Bob Rhodes, Tom and Laurie Simmons, Judy Stalnaker, Ray Thal and Amy Zimmer. Thanks again to acquisitions editor Artie Crisp and project editor Ryan Finn. As always, thank you, Matt, book widower.

History is all around us in the form of designated historic landmarks. In this volume, landmarks designated by Denver Landmarks Preservation Commission and approved by city council bear the designation "DL" for Denver Landmark or "DLD" for Denver Landmark District. Look for round bronze plaques on landmarked buildings. Sites placed in the National Register of Historic Places, administered by the National Park Service, bear the designation "NR" for National Register or "NRD" for National Register District.

Architects mentioned are Coloradans unless otherwise noted. Personal names are given fully the first time they are mentioned and shortened to first name or initials and last name in later instances.

Geography can be controversial—place names carry meaning. With gentrification having become a political issue, it is important to respect residents who feel that their communities are threatened by development pressures coming from outside. Many neighborhoods have unofficial names, and some residents prefer them to official ones. In this volume, for the sake of clarity, site locations are described based on Denver's established map of "statistical neighborhoods" (available at denvergov.org), with some exceptions, such as "Lower Downtown" for sites below Larimer Street, "Uptown" for what the city map refers to as North Capitol Hill and others.

Sites designated "exterior only" are closed to the public. Please respect the privacy of those who live or work in them. Watch, however, for the Denver Architecture Foundation's annual Doors Open Denver weekend (September), when some may be opened to the public (check denverarchitecture.org).

Introduction

DENVER AND ITS HISTORY

REAL HISTORY

People from the eastern United States might scoff at the notion that a city founded just before the Civil War has enough history, and historical sites, to fill a book. Denver has no Puritan churches, slave plantations or battlefields to visit, no "George Washington slept here" plaques. Yet a rich history need not span four hundred years, and even assuming that Denver's story began with its establishment by white men (ignoring Cheyenne, Arapaho and Ute people who were here long before, as well as other groups that accompanied the whites), Denver's history can fascinate. It bursts with stories of fortune seekers trekking across the Great Plains, captains of industry no less commanding than John D. Rockefeller or Andrew Carnegie, resilient nonwhite pioneers and culture builders and politically minded women who fought so their gender could vote long before their sisters elsewhere could. Denver's history is filled with scoundrels, charlatans and crooks as much as it is with visionaries, saints and progressive city builders.

Denverites have long believed that their story deserved to be told. The Colorado State Historical Society (today's History Colorado) was founded in 1879, three years after statehood and just twenty-one after Denver's birth. Frank Hall published a multivolume *History of the State of Colorado* in 1891. Jerome Smiley followed in 1901 with a 978-page *History of Denver, with Outlines of the Earlier History of the Rocky Mountain Country*, published by the *Denver Times*. Another paper, the *Denver Post*, to commemorate the Pikes Peak Gold Rush centennial, published a 384-page historical supplement in 1959, *This Is Colorado*. Carolyn Bancroft, descendant of pioneer doctor Frederick J. Bancroft, wrote several short books in the 1950s and 1960s, not always historically accurate but entertaining, and Louisa Ward Arps's *Denver in Slices* (1959) opened up Denver's fascinating past to many. Dana Crawford repurposed Larimer Street's 1400 block in 1965 as Larimer Square, showing residents that Denver's past was worth exploring and saving. Denver Landmarks Preservation Commission formed in 1967, and in 1970, concerned citizens established Historic Denver Inc. to safeguard the past. In years since, scores of landmarked buildings and historic districts have contributed to Denverites' pride in its history. The late twentieth and early twenty-first centuries saw the flowering of two prolific historians' careers. Dr. Thomas J. Noel ("Dr. Colorado") and Dr. Phil Goodstein have contributed greatly to Denver's historiography, and scores of other local historians, professional and amateur, have built on their work. Denver's story is indeed rich, well documented and worthy.

UNLIKELY SPOT

Denver's recorded history began on November 1, 1858, when William Green Russell and his party established Auraria, Kansas Territory, on Cherry Creek's western bank where it flows into the South Platte River; they named it for Russell's Georgia hometown, which was itself named for a gold discovery. Earlier, Russell's party had discovered gold in the South Platte at its confluence with Dry Creek in present-day Englewood, and a Lawrence, Kansas party had found gold one mile north of Dry Creek, where party members established short-lived Montana City. These were not the first whites in future Colorado. Zebulon Pike and Major Stephen Long had arrived decades earlier; Long coined "Great American Desert" to describe the arid prairie, presumed incapable of supporting agronomy. In 1850, Lewis Ralston, headed for California, found gold near where Ralston Creek flows into Clear Creek in present-day Arvada; he returned as guide for Russell's party. News of Russell's finds trickled eastward, attracting fortune seekers and setting off the Pikes Peak Gold Rush, named for a famous mountain sixty miles south of the discoveries.

Sixteen days after Russell established Auraria, General William Larimer Jr. and associates founded on Cherry Creek's eastern bank Larimer, a town named for Kansas governor James William Denver. Larimer jumped a claim; in September, William McGaa and John Simpson Smith had established

St. Charles there but had temporarily returned to Kansas. As their only "improvement" consisted of four logs stacked together, Larimer felt entitled to claim it. His party organized Denver City Town Company and platted streets named for themselves (Wynkoop, Blake, Lawrence, Curtis, Welton and others). Larimer and his son waded across the river to found Highland, named for its elevation on a bluff. Highland did not take off immediately, but Denver and Auraria did and soon became fierce rivals. Auraria landed the first newspaper on April 17, 1859, the *Rocky Mountain News*, but Denver won a bigger prize: a stagecoach stop on the Leavenworth and Pikes Peak Express. The gold rush was now in full swing, and the towns were well positioned to supply prospectors headed for the diggings, particularly after John Gregory's reports of rich veins near Black Hawk and Central City.

Concerned that their towns were too far from settled Kansas for effective government, locals, including Larimer and *Rocky Mountain News* publisher William Newton Byers, established Jefferson Territory on October 24, 1859, from parts of Kansas, Nebraska, New Mexico, Utah and Washington Territories. Congress never recognized this creation, instead establishing the Colorado Territory on February 28, 1861, its boundaries identical to the current state. Signing the bill was one of President James Buchanan's last official acts; with Abraham Lincoln's impending inauguration, the United States was just then becoming disunited. Lincoln appointed Missouri lawyer William Gilpin as territorial governor. Denver, Auraria and Highland consolidated into one city on April 6, 1860, the ceremony being held on the Larimer Street bridge. Henceforth, Auraria would be known as West Denver, Highland as North Denver and original Denver as East Denver.

The Civil War shifted the population, with Southerners departing to join their native states' regiments; Denver grew solidly Union. Colorado volunteers fought and won the Battle of Glorieta Pass on March 26–28, 1862, after Texans threatened New Mexico; this doomed the Confederacy's western hopes. In 1864, second territorial governor John Evans ordered Colorado's Third Cavalry, commanded by Colonel John Milton Chivington, to suppress the Cheyennes and Arapahos, two tribes whites greatly feared. Chivington did so brutally, surprise-attacking an encampment on Sand Creek at dawn on November 29, 1864. Ignoring a white truce flag, Chivington's men slaughtered between seventy and five hundred (accounts vary) mostly unarmed Native Americans, of whom about two-thirds were women and children. Initially lauded by Evans and the *News* upon their return, Chivington was eventually subjected to Congressional inquiry. Evans—who had previously founded Evanston,

Illinois, and Northwestern University—remained defensive about Sand Creek for the rest of his life; the massacre remains one of the most inhumane episodes in Colorado history.

The bloody 1860s ended with Denver's population having grown by only 10, from 4,749 in 1860 to 4,759 in 1870. However, the 1870s would decisively put Denver on the map. The first transcontinental railroad, linked in 1868, bypassed the formidable Colorado Rockies, running instead through southern Wyoming, and Denver's leaders feared that Cheyenne would surpass Denver in importance. To prevent this, city boosters—including Evans, Byers, Luther Kountze, Walter Cheesman and others—formed Denver Pacific Railroad and in 1868 began building a line linking Denver with Cheyenne. The first Denver Pacific train arrived at a Wynkoop Street depot on June 24, 1870, and two months later came the first Kansas Pacific train, linking Denver with Kansas City. With these connections, Denver grew rapidly; the 1880 census found 35,629 souls, up 649 percent from 1870.

GREAT BRAGGART CITY

When English traveler Isabella Bird encountered Denver in 1873, she disparaged "the great braggart city" in a letter that she later incorporated into *A Lady's Life in the Rocky Mountains*. Denver was "brown and treeless, upon the brown and treeless plain, which seemed to nourish nothing but wormwood and the Spanish bayonet." In marking Denver's tendency to brag, she correctly ascertained its character. By 1873, Denver was rapidly transforming into a prairie metropolis, and it would soon boast of trees and gardens, with imported seedlings nurtured by water drawn from ditches. Suburbs sprouted, connected to downtown via horsecar with Denver City Railway's 1871 founding. It soon faced rivals, and by the late 1880s, electricity had supplanted animal power. By 1900, Denver boasted of one of America's largest electrified urban rail systems for a city its size, consolidated under Denver Tramway Company and controlled by William Gray Evans, son of John; it would operate streetcars, and later buses, until the 1960s.

Downtown soon took on big-city trappings. Fueled by mining riches, 17th Street grew into the financial hub of not only Colorado (which became the thirty-eighth state on August 1, 1876) but also a larger "Rocky Mountain Empire," the largest and most important city within one thousand miles.

One block away, 16th sprouted department stores and smaller retailers, boasting the main post office, a courthouse and the magnificent Tabor Grand Opera House, built in 1881 by "Silver King" Horace Austin Warner Tabor as a testament to his wealth. On Capitol Hill, mining magnates built magnificent, many-roomed mansions.

The Panic of 1893, an international depression, hit Colorado harder than most places. The state's economy was tied to silver's price, which began falling after Argentina and Brazil stopped buying it. As with the Panic of 1873, the 1893 Panic's initial causes were related to overcapitalized railroads, but the repeal of the 1890 Sherman Silver Purchase Act, which had mandated federal purchases of 4.5 million ounces of silver bullion each month, decimated Colorado's economy. Twelve Denver banks failed, and hundreds of businesses lacked cash. Fortunes that had seemed permanent, including Horace Tabor's, were gone. Thousands went unemployed, and Denver's future seemed bleak.

Yet it survived. Despite civil unrest, including 1894's "City Hall War," when Populist Party governor Davis Waite called up the Colorado National Guard to battle recalcitrant (and corrupt) Denver officials holed up in city hall, prosperity slowly returned. Boosters conceived a multi-day fair, Festival of Mountain and Plain, in October 1895. A kind of Mardi Gras, it featured parades, masked balls and a "Silver Serpent," symbolizing Colorado's ardent wish for federal silver purchase reinstatement. The annual festival continued through 1912. In 1984, promoters revived the name, subtitled "A Taste of Colorado," for Labor Day weekend, and it remains an annual event.

Nearby suburbs, incorporated as independent towns, struggled with post-Panic financial obligations, and residents of the towns of Highlands (west of Larimer's original Highland), South Denver and others voted to merge with Denver, giving it significantly greater population and footprint. By 1902, Denver had become large enough that leaders felt it should fully govern its own affairs, independent of state oversight. Voters approved Article XX to the state constitution, granting Denver a "City and County" home rule government, composed of Denver and adjacent towns, including Elyria, Globeville, Berkeley, Montclair, Valverde and others. These satellites' residents were not given a choice, becoming Denverites whether they wanted to or not. A new city charter proposal, crafted by Progressive reformers, called for open, transparent government, but idealists soon met their match in Boss Speer.

MATURING CITY

Robert Walter Speer had come to Denver in 1878 to recover from tuberculosis. He was a classic machine politician and had built a network from all social classes, from downtown liquor and prostitution interests to utilities and corporations. Voters rejected the Progressives' charter, and the second charter, crafted by corporate interests and machine politicians, won the day. As the first mayor elected (1904) under it, Speer allied himself to Denver's financial elite, protecting their interests and earning enmity from good-government advocates. Chief among these, bolstered by Progressive women's clubs and friend Margaret Tobin Brown, was Judge Benjamin Barr Lindsey. Believing that children in legal trouble should not be judged by adult standards, Lindsey won national renown for establishing America's first juvenile court; disgusted by Denver politics, he published an investigatory polemic, *The Beast*, in 1910, exposing corrupt relationships between Speer and Denver's corporations.

Denverites today tend to forget Speer's political side, instead remembering him for ushering in the "City Beautiful" era. By his 1908 reelection, Denver was fifty years old, and Speer, together with the Denver Country Club set, envisioned transforming Denver from a utilitarian, overgrown town into a first-class city. In their eyes, Denver, with its fine climate and mountain backdrop, was a diamond that simply needed cutting and polishing. The 1893 Chicago World's Columbian Exposition inspired a generation of city builders to re-create their environs along Neoclassical lines, and no mayor was more enthusiastic than Speer, who advocated a grand Civic Center to complement the capitol, with municipal buildings and monuments, landscaped parkways connecting Denver's parks and the Denver Mountain Parks system, allowing city residents (with cars) escape from urban cares and reinvigoration in nature. Fiscal conservatives pushed back, but ultimately Speer's vision largely reached fruition and survives today. Speer's impact on Denver's built environment was greater than any other individual's.

Speer, sensing a shift, opted to not run in 1912, and Denver experimented briefly with commission government. This proved unwieldy, so the prior strong mayor arrangement returned, and in 1916, Speer won a third term, dying two years later. Benjamin Franklin Stapleton, first elected in 1923 with backing from the ascendant Ku Klux Klan, of which he was a member until it was no longer advantageous, worked to complete Civic Center and its western anchor, the 1932 City and County Building. Stapleton served five terms, with an interregnum between the second and third; he oversaw the 1920s boom, the Great Depression and World War II. His most far-sighted act was to push for a municipal airport; city council voted in 1944 to name it for him, and it operated until 1995.

GROWN-UP CITY

Modern Denver was born during World War II and subsequent decades. Before the war, the Works Progress Administration began converting a former tuberculosis sanitarium into an Army Air Corps training facility; this became Lowry Air Force Base. During the war, federal planners considered Denver, far from coasts and borders, to be ideally situated for a potential "second Washington" should the national capital come under attack. After the Soviet Union became the world's second nuclear power, Denver's situation was even more advantageous.

Downtown changed little. A 1947 visitor would have seen a dirtier, grimier version of what had been there in 1927. After the war, merchants modernized and expanded. Out-of-town developers saw Denver's potential, particularly New Yorker William Zeckendorf and two Dallas brothers, Clint and John Murchison; they began remaking what Zeckendorf derided as a "sleepy, self-satisfied town" into something more dynamic, giving Denver its first modern skyscrapers.

Nothing symbolized Denver's new direction better than seventy-seven-year-old Stapleton's 1947 defeat by thirty-five-year-old James Quigg Newton Jr. Over two terms, Newton modernized city government, correctly sensing that Denver would grow, and pushed for infrastructure it would need, including a limited-access freeway, the Valley Highway (today's Interstate 25). Newton also recognized that Speer's Civic Center needed good neighbors and built a new Central Library on its southern border. Newton was aided by a friendly relationship with the "Voice of the Rocky Mountain Empire," the *Denver Post*, helmed by business-boosting editor E. Palmer Hoyt; not since the days of William Byers using his *Rocky Mountain News* to publicize Denver had a newspaper been so vigorous in its boosting.

Denver grew, but not everyone was rising along with the skyline. Racial and ethnic minorities had contributed to Denver life since its first decade, but with the exception of one brief mayoral term by the Jewish Wolfe Londoner (elected 1889), Protestant men had always led the city, often with policies that did not benefit people unlike themselves. As the metropolitan area began sprawling outward from the 1950s through the 1970s, at first within city limits (which grew by annexation) and later in suburbs, parts of Denver grew poorer and less white. African Americans had historically clustered in Five Points northeast of downtown, confined by redlining lenders and racially restrictive real estate deeds in white areas. After World War II, African Americans began moving into adjacent neighborhoods, with whites moving out. Unscrupulous real estate agents hastened the process, encouraging whites to sell before property values declined.

Hispanic people first lived largely on the "West Side," Auraria and adjacent neighborhoods; later, as their population grew, they moved into the "North Side," the former Italian enclave in northwest Denver, and eventually occupied postwar neighborhoods in southwest Denver. Globeville, Swansea and Elyria, near the stockyards, transitioned from largely eastern European to Hispanic, with residents beset by Denver's highest pollution levels from former smelters and elevated Interstate 70, built in the 1960s.

The business class had long ignored tensions between these groups and Denver's white majority, but in the 1960s, activists began gaining prominence. The 1970s saw African Americans elected to city council, the school board, the state legislature and the lieutenant governor's office. After working with Democrats, former boxer Rodolfo "Corky" Gonzales, angered by inaction on issues important to Chicanos, established Crusade for Justice and published *Yo Soy Joaquín*, an epic poem describing the evolution of Chicano culture and his community's struggle for social and economic justice. Concerned about extreme segregation, a judge ordered Denver Public Schools to bus students for better racial balance; anti-busing forces fought the decision to the U.S. Supreme Court. The busing question permeated Denver's politics more deeply than any issue before or since. Not everyone accepted these changes, and violence occurred, including a 1971 bombing that damaged dozens of buses.

Denver embraced urban renewal, voting two to one in 1967 to grant Denver Urban Renewal Authority (DURA) power to acquire and demolish twenty-seven (ultimately reduced to seventeen) downtown blocks, including important historic landmarks, and re-sell them to developers. DURA then demolished the predominantly Hispanic Auraria, for the Auraria Higher Education Center. While the campus came together quickly, the downtown "Skyline" project languished, with vast parking lots negating DURA's promises that developers were lining up. A spike in global oil prices saved Skyline. Suddenly, oil companies clamored for office space, and pundits dubbed Denver "Houston of the North." Skyline boasted gleaming new towers, and other parts of downtown saw historic buildings demolished for skyscrapers. The boom went bust by 1984, and new towers sat empty, derided as "see-through" buildings. Denver became known for America's highest office vacancy rate. By 1987, Denver, and Colorado with it, was seeing negative population growth.

Yet Denver bounced back. In 1983, Mayor William McNichols, holding office since 1968, lost to young Federico Peña, Denver's first Hispanic mayor. Asking voters to "Imagine a Great City," Peña worked to reverse Denver's decline, spearheading a new convention center, a massive addition to the Central Library and, most consequentially, Denver International Airport. It has been as transformative to Denver's economy as anything any mayor has ever done. In the twenty-first century, growth has continued largely unabated. Today's Denver attracts thousands of new residents annually, their continuous arrival straining infrastructure, inflating housing prices and making growth the predominant political issue. The city must grow sustainably, as climate change warms and dries an already-dry Colorado. Denverites are resourceful, however, and will tackle challenges as they have done throughout Denver's history, with determination that a metropolis in such an unlikely spot will continue to thrive.

NIGHTS IN OLD DENVER

Across the prairie they came, lured by promises of instant riches. That they were crossing a vast plain with little water, or that they were invading land that belonged to Cheyenne and Arapaho people, mattered little to men dreaming of fortunes to be had in the Rockies. Some took the well-established Overland Trail across Nebraska, with Pikes Peak Gold Rushers following the South Platte from its confluence with the North Platte. Others chose a southerly route via Smoky Hill Trail across Kansas, following an Indian path along the Smoky Hill River and then blazing across prairie to Cherry Creek's headwaters. From there, it was simple to find Auraria and Denver City. Those who arrived in 1859 or 1860 found little in the way of civilization. Two rival towns divided by a broad, shallow stream offered accommodations of a sort, and food of a sort, but roughness mattered little, for hardly anyone stayed long, so eager were most to leave for the diggings.

Today, everything early travelers encountered is gone, except the two towns' clashing street grids. Pioneer town builders ignored the convention of laying out streets cardinally and instead oriented them toward streams, common in mining towns; they thus avoided oddly shaped blocks, maximizing buildable real estate with simple rectangles. Auraria's founders platted streets paralleling Cherry Creek, which formed its northeastern border, while Denver's decided to align with the South Platte, which ran at an angle to Cherry Creek. The resulting diagonal grids do not quite meet. Ultimately, most of Denver was laid out conventionally, given impetus in 1868 by Henry Cordes Brown's platting of Capitol Hill. This chapter covers those early street grids, the oldest thoroughfares in the city. It takes its title from fundraisers mounted by Historic Denver Inc. in the 1970s called "A Night in Old Denver," held in Larimer Square and Auraria.

AURARIA HIGHER EDUCATION CENTER

Bounded by Speer Boulevard, West Colfax Avenue and Auraria Parkway (Auraria)
(303) 556-2400; ahec.edu

This 150-acre academic campus across Cherry Creek from downtown houses three public institutions: Community College of Denver, Metropolitan State University of Denver and University of Colorado–Denver. Their combined enrollment tops forty-two thousand, served by more than five thousand faculty and staff. The campus was dedicated in 1976, and while most academic buildings date from the late twentieth and early twenty-first centuries, elements of Auraria's earlier history remain.

As Denver grew, Auraria evolved into a mixture of residences and businesses. Many early residents were German, often employed by nearby Milwaukee (later Tivoli-Union) and Zang breweries. Jewish families also lived here. Irish immigrants followed, initially attending services at German-dominated St. Elizabeth's Church on 11th Street. Irish millionaire flour miller John Kernan Mullen helped Auraria's Irish build their own church, St. Leo's on Colfax Avenue at 10th Street (demolished). After 1916, Auraria saw Spanish-speaking newcomers from southern Colorado, New Mexico and Mexico. Not welcome at St. Elizabeth's or St. Leo's, the Hispanic community built St. Cajetan's Church at 9th and Lawrence Streets in 1925, helped by Mullen (his house had previously occupied the corner).

In 1973, DURA began demolishing most of Auraria's buildings for campus construction. Residents and business owners protested, but momentum had been building since 1966, when a committee recommended Auraria for Metropolitan State College. Funding sources (bond issue, federal and state funds) came together, and the project moved forward, opening in phases between 1975 and 1977. Initially, Lawrence and Larimer, one-way streets connecting downtown with Interstate 25, ran through the campus, but Denver built Auraria Parkway in the 1980s, allowing Auraria to cohere into an academic environment. Even though many of Auraria's streets are erased, their ghosts remain thanks to campus buildings' orientation. In recent years, the Displaced Aurarians Association has raised awareness of Auraria's rich past.

Emmanuel Shearith Israel Chapel

1205 10th Street Mall (Auraria)
NR

The oldest extant church building in Denver, this chapel dates to 1876. Built by Episcopalians, eastern European Jewish immigrants bought the rhyolite Gothic Revival church in 1903, forming Shearith Israel, an Orthodox congregation that met here until 1958. It was also called Tenth Street Shul. Today, it houses a gallery for Auraria's art students.

Golda Meir Center

1146 9th Street (Auraria)
(303) 556-3291; msudenver.edu/golda; call for tour

A duplex originally located at 1606–8 Julian Street, Golda Meir Center honors Israel's first female prime minister, who served from 1969 to 1973. Meir, born in Russia in 1898, immigrated to America with her parents in 1906, settling in Milwaukee. In 1913 she came to Denver to live with her sister, Sheyna; brother-in-law, Sam Korngold; and niece, Judith, in this duplex, attending North High School and learning about Zionism at home. In her 1975 autobiography, she wrote, "To the extent that my own future convictions were shaped and given form, and ideas were discarded or accepted by me while I was growing up, those talk-filled nights in Denver played a considerable role." In 1981, researchers determined that this house had been her home; it had been slated for demolition. It was moved twice before its final placement on campus in 1988. The museum, restored to resemble its appearance when she lived here, is on the right side. The basement houses Golda Meir Center for Political Leadership, operated by Metropolitan State.

Ninth Street Historic Park

9th Street between Champa and Curtis Streets (Auraria); exteriors only
NRD

Saved from demolition by Historic Denver Inc., this block boasts some of the oldest houses in Denver. Impetus came from Don Etter's photographic history, *Auraria: Where Denver Began* (1972). Rescuing fourteen structures proved a monumental undertaking, but Historic Denver raised funds from thousands of contributors and obtained *pro bono* help from architects, contractors and passionate amateurs; the park, its asphalt street replaced by lawn, was dedicated on August 1, 1976, Colorado's centennial. The buildings provide space for campus use, mostly housing scholastic departments. Several are "Territorials," built prior to statehood.

The most interesting house is the oldest, at 1020, the Smedley-Cole House, built in 1872 by dentist William Smedley at prairie's edge. In 1933, Ramon and Carolina Gonzalez bought it, and in 1948, they opened the Casa Mayan restaurant, which became known for authentic Mexican food. Casa Mayan hosted not only Denver diners but also famous people passing through, including President Harry Truman in 1948. It served as a social center, with music, dance and Spanish language lessons; the Gonzalez family also aided Mexican immigrants and provided meals to homeless people. The Auraria Casa Mayan Heritage organization's website (acmh.cfsites.org) has more history.

Also notable is the Stephen Knight house at 1015, an 1885 Second Empire design that Etter called "perhaps the most perfectly proportioned and tastefully embellished Victorian house in Denver." Next door, the

The Smedley-Cole House, later Casa Mayan, at Ninth Street Historic Park. *Photograph by author.*

1885 Witte house at 1027 features a dome. In 1890, Milwaukee Brewery bookkeeper William Schultz built the "double" at 1045–47. Eugene Madden, owner of Madden's Wet Goods on Larimer Street, lived in 1047, representing southwest Denver on city council. Charles Roger Davis, father-in-law to Stephen Knight, owned Eagle Flour Mill at 8th and Curtis, living in an 1873 Carpenter Gothic at 1068. Frederick Carl Eberley designed 9th Street's only commercial structure, the two-story 1906 Groussman Grocery at 1067. Russian Jewish immigrant Albert Groussman lived upstairs.

St. Cajetan's Center

1190 9th Street (Auraria); exterior only
DL

This 1926 Spanish Colonial Revival church designed by Robert Willison, built partly with labor donated by congregants, dominates the southwestern end of the Larimer Street pedestrian mall. For Auraria's Hispanic community, this was the center of their lives; the church, whose congregation moved in 1975

St. Cajetan's Church, now St. Cajetan's Center, Auraria.
Photograph by author.

to southwest Denver, operated a school, credit union, health clinic and other services. Campus managers remodeled the interior as a performance space and renovated the exterior.

St. Elizabeth of Hungary Church

106 St. Francis Way (Auraria)
(303) 534-4014; stelizabethdenver.org
DL, NR

Unlike St. Cajetan's congregation, St. Elizabeth's remains on site, with regular services and a daily sandwich line for the poor. Dating to 1898, its Romanesque Revival design by Father Adrian is built of rhyolite stone quarried in Castle Rock. Due to the different angles of the downtown and Auraria street grids, the 162-foot corner tower terminates the Arapahoe Street vista from downtown, although the church is actually on Curtis Street. The congregation, initially predominantly German, dates to 1878; the present building replaced an earlier church. Brewer Philip Zang contributed funds for one of its bells with the understanding, encouraged by Father Francis Koch, that it would ring "*zang! zang!*" rather than "*clang, clang.*" On February 23, 1908, Father Leo Heinriches, while celebrating Communion, was assassinated by an Italian man, a crime that briefly garnered national notice. The attached Gothic-style friary, built in 1936, was designed by Jules Jacques Benoit Benedict and funded by the May Bonfils Trust.

Tivoli Student Union

900 Auraria Parkway (Auraria)
DL, NR

Built over the course of a century, the former Tivoli-Union Brewery is all that remains of Auraria's industrial sector. Moritz Sigi constructed the oldest portion, Sigi's Hall, in 1870 as Sigi's Brewery. Sigi died in 1875; Alsatian immigrant John Good bought it and renamed it Colorado Brewing Company. Max Melsheimer later bought it from Good, renaming it Milwaukee Brewery, and under his management the brewery grew. In 1882, Melsheimer built the

St. Elizabeth of Hungary Church, Auraria. *Photograph by author.*

Harold Baerresen–designed Turnhalle for West Denver Turners, a German social organization. Melsheimer commissioned Frederick Eberley for the seven-story tower facing 10th Street. Built in 1890, the Good-funded expansion gave Melsheimer a 600,000-barrel capacity, but the Panic of 1893 put him in arrears. Good foreclosed in 1900, renaming the brewery Tivoli, for the Copenhagen gardens. He merged it in 1901 with Union Brewery, forming Tivoli-Union.

Colorado's 1916 early adoption of Prohibition forced Tivoli-Union to create "Dash," a near beer touted as a health drink. After Prohibition's end in 1933, Tivoli-Union resumed brewing beer; by the end of World War II, it was producing 150,000 barrels annually. In 1961, Tivoli introduced Hi-En Brau, a stronger beer inspired by hard-to-find German imports. Good's last heir died in 1964, and in 1965, Carl and Joseph Occhiato bought Tivoli-Union, shortly before the June 16, 1965 South Platte flood deluged it with seven feet of water. The Occhiato brothers soldiered on, introducing Denver Beer and Aspen Gold. A six-week 1966 labor strike resulted in Tivoli losing tavern accounts, and it never recovered; operations ceased in 1969.

Preservationists fought to save the historic brewery from demolition. It sat empty even as the campus sprouted up around it. In 1985, after renovation and a 100,000-square-foot addition, a private developer opened Tivoli Denver, for shopping and entertainment. The tower's multilevel brew house with its huge copper kettles and downtown view became the Rattlesnake Club, briefly Denver's hottest restaurant. Tivoli Denver struggled, and in 1991, students voted to convert the Tivoli into a student union, which opened in 1994. In 2015 brewing returned, with a new Tivoli Brewing Company, complete with taproom (tivolibrewingco.com). Crafting modern and historical styles, including Sigi's Wild Horse Bock, as well as a version of Hi-En Brau, Tivoli partners with Metropolitan State University's brewing program in teaching the art and business of beer.

CONFLUENCE PARK

2250 15th Street (Downtown)
denvergov.org/content/denvergov/en/denver-parks-and-recreation/parks/find-a-park

Confluence Park, where Cherry Creek flows into the South Platte, is near St. Charles Town Company's 1858 claim and, thus, the foundation point of Denver; the Russell Party also panned for gold here briefly.

The confluence was disregarded as the river evolved into an industrial waterway. After the devastating 1965 flood, however, Denverites woke up to the river's potential. State senator Joe Shoemaker formed Platte River Greenway Foundation in 1974 to clean up the waterway and build a recreational trail along its length within city limits. By Labor Day 1975, Confluence Park, the Greenway's centerpiece, was complete. On the west bank, the trail passed by a plaza (named for Shoemaker) jutting into the river; this connected to Cherry Creek's south bank via concrete bridge. In between, kayakers rode man-made rapids. More recently, the park has expanded to encompass a triangle on the north bank, and Denver has completely rebuilt Shoemaker Plaza.

LARIMER SQUARE

1400 block of Larimer Street; both sides (Downtown)
(303) 534-2367; larimersquare.com
DLD, NRD

In November 1858, William Larimer built his log cabin, Denver's first domicile, at the future corner of 15th and Larimer Streets. In 1963, Dana Crawford encountered this block and embarked on a nationally recognized feat of preservation. The block, part of Larimer Street's long "skid row," was included within DURA's proposed Skyline plan. Crawford had loved Cambridge's Harvard Square in her Radcliffe College days and had studied St. Louis's Gaslight Square and San Francisco's Ghirardelli Square. She believed that Denver needed something similar, a human-scaled historic district, where people could shop, dine and enjoy city life. Skyscrapers and bigness were ascendant; Crawford, like urban theorist Jane Jacobs, knew that people crave intimacy and smallness. The block's historical associations and architecture called to her.

With husband John and several friends (including future congresswoman Patricia Schroeder), Crawford formed Larimer Square Inc. and began buying buildings with no guarantee that DURA would not condemn them. Crawford gained control of sixteen structures (of eighteen on the block) and hired Langdon Morris to plan the project. He created courtyards and mid-block passages, with something interesting around every corner. Work commenced, and Crawford began signing tenants to show DURA that the block no longer suffered from disinvestment; in late December 1965,

Larimer Square. *Photograph by Ryan Dravitz.*

the first business, the beer hall Your Father's Moustache, opened at 1433. Newspapers covered Larimer Square's progress, publicizing Crawford's work and inspiring preservation-minded citizens. Crawford sold Larimer Square in 1986. Today, it houses restaurants and upscale retailers; offices fill upper floors. Some of Morris's open spaces have been in-filled with new structures. In 2018, Larimer Square's owner announced plans for high-rise towers, demolishing alley-facing portions of historic buildings to accommodate them; public outcry ensued. As of this writing the owner has backed away from the plans.

Granite Building

1456–60 Larimer Street

The third structure built here (the first was Larimer's cabin), and Larimer Square's tallest building at four stories, dates from 1883. Landowners George Washington Clayton and his brother, William M. Clayton, built it for department store impresario Michael J. McNamara, a popular and successful Irish immigrant. Architect John W. Roberts specified mostly Colorado building materials, including gray rhyolite, granite and red sandstone. After

McNamara Dry Goods relocated, it became the Granite Hotel. It was from here, in February 1908, that Pinkerton Agency detective James McParland kidnapped hotel guest William "Big Bill" Heywood, Western Federation of Miners' leader, for extradition to Idaho to stand trial for conspiracy to murder Governor Frank Steunenberg. Defended by Clarence Darrow, Heywood was acquitted and defected to the Soviet Union, and his body resides in Moscow's Red Square.

Kettle Arcade

1426 Larimer Street

The 1873 Kettle Block, now Arcade, is one of Larimer Square's oldest structures. Butcher George E. Kettle purportedly saved money in its construction by erecting only front and back walls, relying on neighboring buildings for support, or so the story goes (buildings on either side are actually younger). The arcade leads to the Court of the Bull and Bear, created by Morris. It is named for red sandstone carvings salvaged from the 1963 demolition of the Mining Exchange Building at 15th and Arapahoe Streets, flanking the left-hand arched opening. The courtyard's bronze cherub–topped granite monument honors Richard Pinhorn, owner of the Manhattan Restaurant at 1635 Larimer. Pinhorn died in 1922, leaving the business to employees, and to honor him, they erected a drinking fountain, serving both humans and animals; this monument once formed the fountain's centerpiece. Crawford obtained it in 1971 after DURA leveled the restaurant. Prior to Kettle's building, the site hosted an 1859 log cabin occupied by self-anointed "Count" Henri Murat, one of early Denver's more colorful characters, spinning tall tales while cutting hair and moonlighting as a bartender.

Miller Block

1401 Larimer Street

Once the Lanktree Hotel, for many decades this 1889 three-story red brick structure housed Gahan's Saloon, operated by City Councilman William Gahan and later by his son, John. With Denver's old city hall directly across

14th Street, this was the liquid epicenter of Denver's political scene, its bar popular with politicos and those who would influence them, as well as policemen and firemen, headquartered in city hall. After Colorado enacted Prohibition, it became Gahan's Soft Drinks, but downstairs, John Gahan operated a speakeasy, knowing that the Denver Police Department would never raid its favorite watering hole.

Lincoln Hall

1415 Larimer Street

With this two-story building, possibly dating to the 1860s or 1870s, the mansard-roofed third floor came later, housing a dance floor suspended from cables, giving dancers "extra bounce." The dance hall acquired a notorious reputation, often raided by police. From 1891 until Dana Crawford's 1965 purchase, it housed a leading saddlery, Fred Mueller Saddle and Harness, owned by his employees in later years.

Apollo Hall

1425 Larimer Street

Also called the Congden Building, for Larimer Square investors Tom and Noel Congdon, this 1870s building replaced two earlier structures. In July 1859, Libeus Barney of Vermont opened Apollo Hall, a two-story wood-frame building with a saloon downstairs and large room upstairs, rentable for parties, balls and meetings; later that year, Apollo Hall hosted Denver's first theatrical performance, a traveling company from Chicago. Downstairs, drunken miners were apparently careless enough with their currency, gold dust, that Barney made handsome profits through careful sweeping after last call. In 1860, Apollo Hall hosted a "People's Government of Denver" and "People's Court" organizing committee to combat frontier crime. Next door was El Dorado Hall, where in 1859 citizens created Jefferson Territory, and while this extra-legal entity existed, the lower half its legislature met here.

Gallup-Stanbury Building

1445–53 Larimer Street

Fifty feet high and fifty feet wide, Gallup-Stanbury's spiky cornice minarets give it a jaunty air. In 1865, Andrew M. Stanbury opened the Tambien saloon on the site, and it soon became notorious; a year later, he closed it for renovations, posting a notice in the *Rocky Mountain News* that regular patrons who owed him money would be welcome to drop by to help fund repairs. In 1873, he partnered with Avery Gallup to demolish the saloon and erect this building, partly to house Gallup's posh shop, the Bazaar. Lawyers, doctors, dentists and fine dressmakers leased upstairs rooms. Later, as Larimer Street declined, these became the Antlers Hotel.

LOWER DOWNTOWN HISTORIC DISTRICT

Cherry Creek to 20th Street, Larimer/Market alley to Wynkoop Street (Lower Downtown)
(303) 605-3510; lodo.org
DLD

When city council approved this twenty-two-square block historic district in 1988, some landowners were convinced their property rights had been stolen. They have since learned otherwise, as the district has succeeded hugely, with corresponding land value growth. A largely intact collection of brick-construction nineteenth- and early twentieth-century commercial buildings, LoDo, as *Denver Post* columnist Dick Kreck christened it in the 1980s, escaped demolition waves that transformed other parts of downtown. Few were interested in the area so far from downtown's center. More than once city planners envisioned complete demolition, even routing a proposed freeway through it, but nothing came of those schemes. Dana Crawford's Larimer Square transformed expectations when she demonstrated that preserving old buildings could be profitable.

Beginning in the 1870s, downtown below Larimer Street evolved into a warehouse district. Most warehouses were five or six stories tall, and on Wynkoop Street, elevated sidewalks facilitated easy goods transfer from boxcars parked on sidings in front. This was a major employment center, with grocery wholesalers, agricultural implement dealers, saddle and western wear manufacturers and moving and storage warehouses. After the mid-twentieth century, warehousing predominated, as wholesalers and manufacturers moved closer to freeways and Colorado's economy transitioned away from agriculture and ranching. The solid, dignified buildings remained, forgotten by those who never ventured past Larimer. Yet some admired them; Frank Lloyd Wright visited Denver in 1948 and told a reporter that the most impressive view in the city was the wall of brick warehouses along Wynkoop Street that greeted him as he stepped out of Union Station. Most of that "Wynkoop wall" remains intact. LoDo is downtown's center once again, thanks to Union Station's 2014 conversion to a multimodal transportation hub, as well as new construction in former railyards behind it. Its streets hum with pedestrians; its historic buildings are filled with offices, loft condominiums, shops, restaurants and galleries; and its urban fabric is knit back together with infill buildings complementing old ones. A design review board, combined with the landmark district, ensures that LoDo will maintain its human scale.

Barney L. Ford Building

1514 Blake Street
DL, NR

Born into slavery in Virginia in 1822, Barney Lancelot Ford, son of a white plantation owner and an enslaved African, escaped his bonds in 1848 and went to Chicago via the Underground Railroad. He came to Colorado in 1860 seeking gold but was barred from staking a claim due to his race. He moved to Denver in 1862 and opened a restaurant at this site. It burned down in Denver's 1863 great fire, and Ford quickly rebuilt in brick, with two stories (the third dates to 1889). Here he operated People's Restaurant on the ground floor, a barbershop and ladies' hair salon in the basement and, upstairs, a saloon. Ford also built the Inter-Ocean Hotel down the block and another Inter-Ocean Hotel in Cheyenne. Ford died in 1902 and is memorialized in stained glass in the Colorado Capitol's House Chamber. After seeing various uses during the twentieth century, the building underwent renovation in 1983 to its current use, ground-floor restaurant/retail space and offices upstairs. The parking lot across Blake Street was the site of Constitution Hall, an 1865 structure where delegates drafted Colorado's constitution in 1876; an arsonist destroyed it in 1977.

Barteldes Hartig Building

1600 Wynkoop Street; exterior only

Designed by Aaron Gove and Thomas F. Walsh for Kansas-based Barteldes, Hartig & Company, this 1906 seed warehouse with widely spaced windows supports six hundred pounds per square foot, seeds being very heavy by volume. On the 16th Street façade, a grand arched entry to the second floor, framed in red sandstone, leads to thin air; this originally connected with the now-demolished 16th Street viaduct, built to cross railroad tracks behind Union Station. It became loft condominiums in the 1990s.

Barth Hotel

1514 17th Street; exterior only
seniorhousingoptions.org
DL, NR

Designed in 1882 by Frederick Eberley as a warehouse for liquor wholesaler Moritz Barth, this four-story red brick edifice was converted to the Union Hotel by 1890, and in 1905, it was the Elk Hotel (the name still evident in the sidewalk). New owner M. Allen Barth, son of Moritz, renamed it in 1930, and it continued operating for five decades. In 1980, Senior Housing Options bought it, restoring it and creating affordable residences for seniors displaced by the oil boom era's frequent development-related building demolitions. It has since become assisted living for people with disabilities and undergone further restoration.

Brecht Candy Company Building

1616 14th Street; exterior only

Still retaining signage of later occupant Acme Upholstery, this 1909 red brick factory terminates the southwestern view down Wazee Street similar to Coors Field's capping of its northeastern end. Gustavius A. Von Brecht commissioned it for his candy manufactory; he had chosen Denver for easy access to beet sugar and for its dry climate, as candy making is easier in low humidity. A ghost sign on the rear reads "Brecht Candies 'make Life Sweeter.'" In 1994, Dana Crawford's development team renovated it into residential lofts.

Colorado Saddlery Building

1631 15th Street

Irish immigrant Michael J. O'Fallon commissioned this five-story, 1908 red brick warehouse for his plumbing supply company, and ghost signs advertising his wares still run vertically along the Wynkoop Street façade, preserved during renovation. From 1945 to 2005, it housed Colorado Saddlery, and when it moved out, it was the last remaining saddle manufacturer in Lower Downtown, which once boasted at least five. Pershing Van Skoyk and three others founded Colorado Saddlery after The Denver Dry Goods Company bought their former employer, pioneer saddlery Herman H. Heiser Company; Colorado Saddlery's early designs for saddles, holsters and other leather goods were similar to Heiser's. It gained a reputation for excellent workmanship, attracting customers from Hollywood stars including John Wayne, for whom it built a custom eighteen-inch saddle; Lorne Greene; and Ken Curtis. In 2010, it was renovated as offices with ground floor retail/restaurant space.

Denver City Railway Building

1635 17th Street
DL, NR

Denver City Railway, founded as a horsecar line in 1871, grew so quickly that a decade later that it required a massive car barn and stables for horses, and it hired Harold and Viggio Baerresen to design this eclectic red brick structure. The first-floor car barn connected directly with tracks on 17th Street, while horses' stalls filled second and third levels, their fodder being stored on the fourth. Ten years later, with electric streetcars replacing animal-powered ones, the architects converted it to a manufacturing and warehousing facility, giving the 17th Street façade a new face. Mining equipment manufacturer Hendrie and Bolthoff, founded by Charles Hendrie in Central City in 1861, joined by Henry Bolthoff in 1874 and one of the world's largest such firms in its heyday, occupied it for seven decades beginning in 1902. Today called Streetcar Stables, it houses restaurants and shops at street level, with loft residences above.

Elephant Corral

1444 Wazee Street

The original Elephant Corral was built of cottonwood logs in 1858–59 by Charles Blake and Andrew Williams and destroyed in Denver's great 1863 fire. In its original incarnation, it served as hub for new arrivals, with a hostelry (Denver House) and facilities for buying and selling cattle, oxen, horses and mules—but no pachyderms. The name derived from gold seekers coming west to "look for the elephant"—metaphorically something rare and exciting. A two-story brick building replaced the burned structures, housing Union Hall, a meeting place also used for dances, the *Denver Daily Gazette* and the Colorado Military District; the first floor continued as horse stables. In 1902, a new owner demolished it and built the current assemblage, with its large courtyard facing Wazee Street; horse-trading continued here at least until 1910. A new owner converted the complex to office space in 1981.

House of Mirrors

1942 Market Street; exterior only

Holladay Street's 1900 block was once so synonymous with prostitution that relatives of its namesake, stage line operator Ben Holladay, asked Denver to change it; the city adopted Market, alluding to wholesale food businesses or, some have maintained, to "flesh markets" on this and nearby blocks. Market Street acquired such notoriety that legitimate businesses on its southwestern and northeastern stretches petitioned to have those blocks renamed Walnut Street. This William Quayle–designed house, built by the reigning "Queen of the Row," the madam Jennie Rogers, was Market's best-known brothel from its 1889 opening until its closure in 1915 or 1916. Originally bedecked with stone carvings depicting faces and phallic symbols, some exterior ornamentation was lost when a later owner applied stucco to the façade. Rogers decorated opulently, with massive rich woodwork and furniture, crystal chandeliers and mirrors on the reception room's walls and on ceilings. Fifteen rooms for "boarders," as they were called, were upstairs, reached by a carved walnut staircase. The house entertained legions of businessmen, politicians and conventioneers, and Rogers acquired the building next door (1946 Market) to create a Turkish harem experience. In 1908, Rogers sold the house to Market Street's other reigning queen, Mattie Silks, who operated it until reformers prevailed on city hall to shut down the remaining fleshpots. The building later housed Tri-State Buddhist Church before conversion to a warehouse; all original interior details are gone. Walk across 20th Street to view 2009 Market Street, another onetime brothel owned at different times by both Rogers and Silks.

J.S. Brown Mercantile

1634 18th Street
DL, NR

Although John Hickenlooper was not LoDo's earliest building renovator, the 1988 opening of his (and partners') Wynkoop Brewing Company, Denver's first brewpub, put the neighborhood "on the map" for locals and visitors and made Hickenlooper so well known that after selling out, he served two terms as Denver's mayor, followed by two as Colorado's governor. "Hick," as he is nicknamed, chose the John Sidney Brown Mercantile for his brewery. Brown opened his business in 1861, growing it into one of Colorado's largest grocery wholesalers. He stood with other city leaders to put Denver on the map by incorporating Denver Pacific Railroad. By 1899, Brown's bustling business necessitated commissioning Gove and Walsh for this red brick structure. Its rusticated stone base, arched windows and fancy masonry cornice make this one of LoDo's handsomest buildings. The brewpub's interior retains original tin ceilings and golden oak woodwork.

Littleton Creamery

1801 Wynkoop Street
DL, NR

Constructed in stages between 1903 and 1916, this resembles no other Denver building. Gove and Walsh designed the 1903 portion on the 18th Street corner for dairy products purveyor Littleton Creamery. They made the largely windowless structure noteworthy with polychrome brickwork, featuring horizontal light and dark stripes on floors two through four, with a lattice and diamond pattern above. Beatrice Foods bought Littleton Creamery in 1912 and hired architects Frederick E. Mountjoy and Park M. French for an eight-story wing with its own spectacular brickwork; in 1916, the pair designed a five-story wing for ice making. Beatrice utilized cork insulation, and their 1.3-million-cubic-foot cold storage facility became profitable in its own right as they leased space to other companies. At its peak, Beatrice produced up to thirty thousand pounds of butter here daily. Beatrice sold it after ceasing operations in 1979. Defrosting took months, with ice well protected by cork. Dana Crawford renovated it, opening in 1986 the Ice House Design Center, a to-the-trade collection of furnishings showrooms. It eventually lost tenants and was converted to residential lofts in 1997.

Market Center

1350 17th Street and adjacent buildings along Market Street

Six adjoining edifices constructed before 1893 and renovated together as one project in 1981, Market Center hints at early Lower Downtown's diverse economy. At 1620 Market, Reverend Horace Hitchings, rector at St. John's Episcopal Church, built the four-story, buff brick Hitchings Block; he later served at New York's Trinity Church. At 1624, fruit and flower wholesaler Gustavus Liebhardt built a four-story red brick block; in 1937, meatpacker Lindner Packing and Provision Company took over the property, known today as the Liebhardt-Lindner Building. Continuing down the row are three additional three-story buildings, each once home to wholesale traders: Napoleon McCrary at 1634–38; Waters at 1642; and Bockfinger-Flint Mercantile at 1644–50. Holding the 17th Street corner, the four-story Columbia Hotel began in 1880 as an office building constructed by James

Duff, a Scot representing London investors. After remodeling, the Columbia opened in 1892, with ninety guestrooms and hot and cold running water. From this respectable beginning, it devolved into a flophouse after train travel declined, before coming back to life as an office building once again.

Mercantile Square

1600 Block of 16th Street (southwest side)

Mercantile Square is named for its onetime owner, C.S. Morey Mercantile. Chester Stephen Morey came to Denver in 1872 for his health and, in 1884, founded his firm, which would reign as Colorado's largest wholesale grocer until 1956. In 1896, demonstrating faith in Denver following the 1893 Panic, he hired Gove and Walsh to design Denver's first major post-crisis warehouse. The architects departed from Wynkoop's red palette, opting for buff-colored brick. Like the Bartheldes Building opposite, a second-floor door once served as grand entrance to Morey's executive offices off of the 16th Street viaduct. The Henry Lee Building anchors the Wazee corner. Lee, a pioneering agriculturalist, demonstrated in 1864 that onions could

The 1500 block of Wynkoop Street, showing Mercantile Square. Note the ornate second-floor "entrance." *Photograph by author.*

thrive in Colorado, later founding a farm implement business that filled this building. In 1907, Morey bought Lee's building and erected two alley-spanning bridges, one for goods and the other for his personal office. Morey Mercantile used both buildings to manufacture and package its ubiquitous line of food products bearing red "Solitaire" labels; Solitaire's logo remains a ghost sign above the cornice. Morey also devoted years to Denver Public Schools; a Capitol Hill middle school bears his name. Generally even-tempered, Morey was beside himself when he thought he saw a body drop down the open elevator shaft. He dismissed the swashbuckling office boy who pulled the stunt of sliding down the cable, a young Denverite named Douglas Fairbanks, who later moved to Hollywood.

Mercantile Square's redevelopment came together when John Hickenlooper learned that Joyce Meskis, Tattered Cover Book Store's owner, needed space for back-of-house operations, having outgrown her Cherry Creek store. As LoDo grew busier, Hickenlooper and Meskis partnered with developer Charles Woolley and others to create a project to house a second Tattered Cover, restaurant/retail space and, on upper floors, income-qualified loft apartments for downtown workers. DURA assisted in financing, and it qualified for historic tax credits and grants.

The Oxford Hotel

1600 17th Street
(303) 628-5400; theoxfordhotel.com
DL, NR

Strategically sited near Union Station, the Oxford opened in 1891 and remains Denver's oldest operating hotel. Original investors Adolph Zang, Philip Feldhauser and William Mygatt commissioned Frank E. Edbrooke to design the five-story red brick hotel, which catered to travelers with means. In 1902, Edbrooke designed a matching addition along Wazee Street, and in 1912, the hotel bridged the alley with a Montana Fallis–designed, Beaux Arts–style, white glazed terra cotta–tiled annex, now an office building. In 1933, the Oxford commissioned an Art Deco makeover by Gilbert Charles Jaka, and his Cruise Room bar, patterned after an RMS *Queen Mary* lounge, remains intact, its interior illuminated in red neon, with bas-relief portraits of drinkers from foreign countries adorning walls. During World War II, the hotel billeted servicemen about to ship out by train. The Oxford survived train travel's 1960s collapse by booking entertainment in the corner bar, including folk singers, melodrama troupes and the Queen City Jazz Band. In 1979, Charles Callaway bought it and partnered with Dana Crawford in 1980. They closed the hotel, reopening it in June 1983 after major renovations. Their success at bringing people to an otherwise down-at-heel area positively influenced city council when it voted to landmark the historic district.

Spratlen & Anderson Wholesale Grocery

1450 Wynkoop Street
NR

Frank Edbrooke designed this restrained building for grocery wholesaler Spratlen & Anderson Mercantile Company in 1906. Initially four floors (with a fifth added during construction), a sixth came later; both upper floors boast distinctive roundels between arched windows. After Spratlen & Anderson went out of business in 1923, a drug wholesaler bought it, and in the 1960s and 1970s, it was a furniture factory. In 1990, Dana Crawford converted it to Edbrooke Lofts. As with Larimer Square and the Oxford, Crawford saw potential here when few others did and faced obstacles in financing Denver's first large-scale loft condominium; the 15th Street viaduct had not yet been demolished, and hardly anyone lived in Lower Downtown. However, by the project's completion, all units had been sold, inspiring dozens of other loft conversions across downtown.

The Sugar Building

1530 16th Street
NR

By the time German immigrant Charles Boettcher traveled back to his native country to discover a thriving sugar beet industry, he had already made a fortune from Colorado enterprises, including a chain of hardware dealers and a blasting power factory. On his German sojourn, he realized that Colorado's climate was ideal for sugar beet cultivation and emptied his wife's steamer trunk, filling it with sugar beets and seeds. He convinced

The Oxford Hotel. *Photograph by author.*

The Spratlen & Anderson Building, now Edbrooke Lofts. *Photograph by author.*

farmers to grow the crop, and an industry soon took off, with sugar beets dominating the state's agriculture for decades. To process beets, he built and bought refineries, eventually merging them to form Great Western Sugar Company. In 1906, he commissioned Gove and Walsh for a headquarters facing 16th Street and, around the corner on Wazee, a warehouse for the finished product. The architects employed buff-colored brick, with red brick for the warehouse. The building's botanically inspired ornamentation is influenced by Chicago architect Louis Sullivan, whose work also informs its overall composition. Fully renovated, the Sugar Building still boasts its open-cage elevator, a rarity anywhere, as well as Great Western's logo in terrazzo at the entry.

Wells Fargo Depot

1338 15th Street
DL

When the only way to get to Denver was by stage, it was at the 15th and Market corner (then F Street and Holladay) where passengers alit from coaches and first set foot in its dusty streets. In 1866, Ben Holladay bought a two-story brick building, originally a bank, to serve as depot for his Overland Stage Lines. Later that year, he sold out to Wells Fargo and Company, which ran passenger service until 1869, continuing thereafter with freight only. Wells Fargo or a later owner remodeled, giving it distinctive Gothic arches on the 15th Street side, matching the 1874 Tappan Block, three stories high, next door. After World War II, upper floors of both buildings were deemed structurally unsound and were removed, and in 1973, the Wells Fargo Depot was renovated and leased as retail space, the landlord no doubt influenced by nearby Larimer Square.

Wynkoop Street Railroad Bridge (Manny's Bridge)

Wynkoop Street and Cherry Creek

This steel truss bridge, built by Pennsylvania Steel Company in 1908, once allowed trains operated by Denver and Rio Grande Western Railroad to move freight cars along Wynkoop Street, serving its warehouses. It is one of several still spanning Cherry Creek, a reminder that before the land behind Union Station became a twenty-first-century forest of commercial and residential buildings, it hosted a vast railyard for both passenger and freight trains. The bridge is officially named "Manny's Bridge" for Dr. Manny Salzman (1918–2018), who as neighborhood association president was instrumental in saving it from demolition and restoring it for pedestrians and bicyclists, linking LoDo with Cherry Creek Trail. Salzman and his wife, Joanne, were LoDo pioneers, in 1976 buying and renovating the Gove and Walsh–designed Spice and Commission Warehouse at 1738 Wynkoop Street. Above ground-floor retail and middle-floor office space, their top-floor residence was one of the first lofts in Denver. Salzman was also instrumental in convincing city council to designate the Lower Downtown Historic District in 1987.

THE REAL WEST

eople often carry mental images of the American West based on movies, television shows, novels, paintings and sculptures. They know, or think they know, about cowboys and Indians, gold and silver rushes, prostitutes and bordellos. Denver is portrayed as a wild town, and perhaps in the 1860s it was. Once the railroad arrived, however, Denver grew into the hub of civilization for a vast hinterland, and elements of the "Old West" evolved into big businesses. The biggest, by the turn of the twentieth century, was agriculture. Although the "Great American Desert" is not an easy place to grow crops, farmers found ways, and Denver developed a large flour milling industry, with John Mullen's Auraria operations employing hundreds. Chicago and Omaha may have been major meatpacking towns, but Denver was not far behind. In 1886, Denver Union Stock Yard Company opened north of town adjacent to the South Platte and multiple rail lines, and by 1905, stockyards were sprawled across 105 acres and annually processed approximately 240,000 head of cattle, 116,000 hogs, 300,000 sheep and 23,000 horses and mules. Associated odors gave impetus to the derisive term "cow town" to describe Denver, a moniker still used after meatpackers closed and stockyards lay dormant except for two weeks in January. This chapter explores both the mythical aspects of the American West—as popularized by the likes of entertainer William F. "Buffalo Bill" Cody, painter Charlie Russell and clothing manufacturer Jack Weil—as well as the more prosaic world of hardscrabble farmers, innkeepers and canal builders. Its title derives from a landmark 1996 exhibition exploring similar themes, staged jointly by Denver Art Museum, Denver Public Library and Colorado Historical Society.

AMERICAN MUSEUM OF WESTERN ART

1727 Tremont Place (Downtown)
(303) 293-2000; anschutzcollection.org; admission fee
DL, NR

Occupying upper downtown's oldest building, this museum displays the personal collection of Philip Anschutz. The Frank Edbrooke–designed building opened in 1880 as Brinker Collegiate Institute, for wealthy girls. Proprietor Joseph Brinker died around 1886, and in 1889, new owners converted it into a "gentleman's club," the Richelieu. Six months later, they lost it in a card game to notorious gambling kingpin Ed Chase and his partner, Vaso Chucovich. They renamed it the Navarre, for France's King Henry IV, Henry of Navarre, a notorious womanizer, and offered to their clientele public dining, private gambling and even more private activities with discreet ladies upstairs.

When the Brown Palace was built across Tremont Street in 1892, its construction included a tunnel connecting to the Navarre. Legend says that Brown guests used this to pass into the Navarre for illicit pleasures, but in reality, it had a very low ceiling and was utilized to share coal—anyone using it to return from the Navarre would surely emerge smudged with telltale black dust. Gambling and prostitution ended after 1904 when Robert Speer became mayor and bowed to public pressure to close down the vice houses—this despite his close association with such houses and his friendship with Chucovich.

The Navarre continued as a restaurant for several decades under owner Johnny Ott after 1946, when it was one of Denver's finest. In 1964, clarinetist Peanuts Hucko converted it into a jazz club, which eventually closed. It sat empty until 1983, when cattleman William Foxley bought it, spent significant sums on renovation (including reconstructing the cupola and porch) and opened the Museum of Western Art. That gallery closed in 1997, with its art sold. Anschutz then bought it to privately display his collection for family and friends; he opened it to the public in 2012.

The Navarre, now the American Museum of Western Art. *Photograph by Ryan Dravitz.*

The museum is open three days per week; pre-reserved tour tickets are recommended. More than six hundred works fill galleries on three floors, displayed salon-style. Its holdings cover the full range of western art, from George Catlin through the Santa Fe and Taos schools and twentieth-century Modernism.

THE BUCKHORN EXCHANGE

1000 Osage Street (La Alma–Lincoln Park)
(303) 534-9505; buckhorn.com
DL

Founded in November 1893 as the Rio Grande Exchange by Henry H. "Shorty Scout" Zietz, the Buckhorn is Denver's oldest restaurant and bar. In 1875, ten-year-old Zietz met Buffalo Bill and joined his shows; the great Lakota leader Chief Sitting Bull, who was also part of Cody's show, gave him his "Shorty Scout" nickname for his height. The Buckhorn, sited directly across Osage Street from Denver and Rio Grande Railroad's Burnham Yards, gained fame for Zietz's hospitality, attracting notable visitors. When President Theodore Roosevelt stopped in Denver in 1905, Zietz escorted him to western Colorado to hunt big game; four other presidents have also dined at the Buckhorn, including Franklin Roosevelt, Dwight Eisenhower, Jimmy Carter and Ronald Reagan. At Prohibition's 1933 repeal, Colorado granted the Buckhorn Liquor License No. 1, which it still holds. Zietz died in 1949, his family continuing to operate the Buckhorn until 1978, when they sold it to a local group that promised to retain Zietz's spirit. Visiting the Buckhorn today, diners gape at the restaurant's 575-piece collection of taxidermy adorning the walls (be sure to look for the exceedingly rare jackalope), as well as a 125-piece gun collection. The menu is "Old West"—big on meats, including bison and game, along with beef. Reservations are recommended.

BUFFALO BILL MUSEUM AND GRAVE

987½ Lookout Mountain Road (Jefferson County/Denver Mountain Parks)
(303) 526-0744; buffalobill.org; admission fee (museum)

The most famous showman of his time, William F. Cody, better known as Buffalo Bill, chose Lookout Mountain for his final resting place. Gaining notice in youth as a buffalo hunter, a scout and the hero of a Ned Buntline dime novel, Cody jumped into show business in the 1870s, performing in Wild West shows. After forming Buffalo Bill's Wild West in 1883, an outdoor event with hundreds of performers, he toured America and Europe repeatedly, performing for Queen Victoria during her Golden Jubilee year and becoming as famous in Europe as he was at home. Cody held progressive views, paying female employees (including sharpshooter Annie Oakley) the same as men and supporting suffrage. On show posters, he referred to Lakota performers not as "Indians" but as "Americans," promoting their culture as something to be preserved. Cody died in January 1917 at sister May Cody Decker's home at 2932 Lafayette Street. After lying in state in the capitol, his funeral took place at the 14th and California Street Elks Lodge; interment had to wait for ground to thaw, and he was buried in June. Cody, Wyoming, which he had founded, and North Platte, Nebraska, where he had lived, both vied for his burial site, but his wife, Louisa; sister; daughter; and priest all confirmed his choice of Lookout Mountain. After Louisa died in 1921, she was interred beside him; to prevent rival claimants from absconding with Buffalo Bill's body, thick concrete was poured on top.

The museum, established in 1921 by Cody's friend Johnny Baker, exhibits artifacts once owned by Cody; the present building dates to 1978. Between museum and grave, the 1921 Pahaska Tepee, named for Cody's hunting lodge near Yellowstone National Park, houses a gift shop and café.

CHATFIELD FARMS

8500 West Deer Creek Canyon Road (Jefferson County)
(720) 865-3500; botanicgardens.org/chatfield-farms; admission fee
NR (Hildebrand Ranch)

In 1866, German immigrant Frank Hildebrand bought property on Deer Creek near its emergence from the foothills. He built irrigation ditches to water 200 acres for wheat and other crops, built up a herd of six hundred head of Hereford cattle and lived self-sufficiently, learning the vagaries of Colorado's dry environment. Ultimately, his descendants owned what grew into 2,000-acre Hildebrand Ranch into the 1970s. After the 1965 South Platte flood, the U.S. Army Corps of Engineers condemned the ranch to build Chatfield Reservoir. Denver leased about 750 acres the Corps did not need and turned over a portion—with the Hildebrand Ranch farmhouse, summer kitchen, bunkhouse, barns, sheds, granary, icehouse, blacksmith shop and schoolhouse—to Denver Botanic Gardens. Today, Chatfield Farms offers visitors restored ranch buildings, gardens and a natural area with 2.5 miles of trails. The DBG uses acreage south of the creek for Community Supported Agriculture and Chatfield Farms Veterans programs. In autumn, visitors enjoy the corn maze and ten-acre pumpkin patch, and during December, ranch buildings become Santa's Village, complete with live reindeer. Docent-led tours are available with advance booking for groups of ten or more (extra fee).

DELANEY FARM HISTORIC DISTRICT

170 South Chambers Road (Aurora)
(303) 739-6666; dug.org/about-delaney-community-farm
Aurora Landmark, NR

Surrounded by subdivisions and bordered by the High Line Canal, DeLaney Farm, with its historic buildings constructed between 1866 and 1945, spreads across 158 acres. Among the buildings are DeLaney Round Barn, built as a grain silo and converted to a two-story barn, the only surviving round barn in Colorado; John Gully Homestead House, Aurora's oldest surviving home, moved here in 1982; and Coal Creek Schoolhouse, built around 1928. The restored round barn features exhibits on farming. Beginning in 1997, Denver Urban Gardens (DUG) partnered with Aurora, which owns DeLaney Farm, to grow food using sustainable methods. In 2017, DUG formally partnered with Project Worthmore to repurpose it for Aurora's refugees, allowing them to grow organic food and integrating them into the larger community.

THE FORT

19192 Colorado 8 (Morrison)
(303) 697-4771; thefort.com
NR

Created by Sam Arnold and his first wife, Elizabeth, The Fort restaurant opened in 1963, occupying an adobe fort they built after becoming fascinated with Bent's Fort, built on the Santa Fe Trail near present-day La Junta in 1833. After discovering Lieutenant James Abert's 1845–46 drawings of it and visiting the site, then a ruin, to take measurements, Arnold engaged William Lumpkins to design what he intended as a family home. Arnold hired Taos, New Mexico's Dalton Montgomery, an adobe expert, and his crew leveled part of an outcropping at the seven-acre site and began fabricating approximately eighty thousand adobe bricks from the resulting soil.

After construction began, the Arnolds decided to open it as a restaurant, with family quarters upstairs, after they realized how expensive their dream house had become. Arnold traveled to New Mexico to find artisans for tin light fixtures and carved pine doors, tables and Padre Martinez chairs and spent hours researching the food that travelers would have eaten at Bent's Fort. The resulting menu, still served today, included bison, elk, quail and Rocky Mountain oysters (for the uninitiated: bull testicles), along with more conventional fare. Arnold went on to write deeply researched cookbooks, becoming a premier authority on Old West foods. In 1997, Arnold hosted President Bill Clinton, First Lady Hillary Clinton and other world leaders in Denver for Summit of the Eight, serving bison, trout and fried squash blossoms filled with wild mushrooms and rattlesnake meat. In 2000, Arnold established the nonprofit Tesoro Foundation, dedicated to educating adults and children about the West's cultures and traditions (tesoroculturalcenter. org). The Arnolds' creation impressed the National Park Service, which reconstructed Bent's Old Fort on its original site, consulting with Arnold on adobe design and construction (nps.gov/beol/index). The Fort offers group tours by reservation.

FOUR MILE HISTORIC PARK

715 South Forest Street (Washington Virginia Vale)
(720) 865-0800; fourmilepark.org; admission fee
DL, NR

Located four miles southeast of Denver's original boundaries, Four Mile House is Denver's oldest building, its original section dating to 1859. Jonas and Samuel Brantner built it near Cherry Creek as Samuel and his wife Elizabeth's homestead. In 1860, the brothers moved on, selling it to widow Mary Cawker, mother of two teenage children. She opened a stop for stages journeying to Denver along the Cherokee Trail, and the original log cabin portion is furnished to show what travelers would have

Four Mile House. *Photograph by author.*

encountered. After the 1864 Cherry Creek flood, Cawker decided to sell to Levi and Millie Booth, who operated the stage stop into the 1870s. They bought land on both sides of Cherry Creek, eventually totaling 640 acres; Millie kept bees, and one year she produced more than four thousand pounds of honey. The Booths added onto the original log cabin (covering it with clapboard siding) in 1883, and the parlor, office and kitchen contain many original furnishings. Booth descendants owned the property into the 1940s, and in 1975, Denver bought it to create the twelve-acre historic park, opened in 1978. Besides the house, additional buildings include a reconstructed bee house, a summer kitchen, a root cellar, a three-seat privy (nonfunctioning), a tipi and farm animals, including chickens and Angora goats.

HIGH LINE CANAL

From Waterton Canyon in Douglas County to Green Valley Ranch in Denver
(720) 767-2452; highlinecanal.org
National Landmark Trail

Completed in 1883, the High Line follows a serpentine, seventy-one-mile path from the South Platte to open fields near the airport. President Ulysses Grant had called in 1873 for a canal to irrigate parched prairies in eastern Colorado, and farmers agitated for one to follow the natural contour of high ground south and east of Denver. When railroad baron Jay Gould gained control over the Kansas Pacific, it came with 100,000 acres of formerly public land. Gould alerted London banker Lord James Barclay, who set up companies (collectively, "the English Company") to market the land and make other investments. He sent out James Duff as his local agent. Duff set up Northern Colorado Irrigation Company, which in 1879 began excavation, engineered by Edwin Nettleton, using horses. Unfortunately for their effort, by then eighty-seven other entities had already claimed water rights, and since water is allocated by seniority, from its beginning the canal often ran dry; when water flowed, much seeped underground. Ultimately, it irrigated about 20,000 acres of farmland, far below initial expectations, at a cost of $650,000, but Duff, Barclay and Gould still profited by land sales. In 1924, Denver Water bought the canal, and after decades of forbidding public access, in 1970 it opened the canal and its cottonwood-lined path to recreational use.

Today, more than 350,000 people reside within one mile, and many more enjoy it by hiking, bicycling and horseback riding. In 2014, "a passionate coalition of private citizens" formed High Line Canal Conservancy to protect and enhance the canal.

NATIONAL WESTERN STOCK SHOW

4655 Humboldt Street (Elyria)
(303) 296-6977; nationalwestern.com

Held every January but one since 1906, National Western Stock Show and Rodeo, "the Super Bowl of livestock shows," epitomizes Denver's western heritage. Today attracting nearly 700,000 visitors across sixteen days, its first run, held in a Sells-Floto Circus tent near Denver Union Stockyards, drew about 15,000. Stockmen traveled from ranches, and Denver residents, owning no livestock, came too—this trade show has always attracted urbanites curious about rural life and the animals that are traded and win prizes here. In 1907, organizers introduced horse shows. The 1931 twenty-fifth anniversary brought the first rodeo; in 1935 came Catch-a-Calf, and in 1975 the National Sheep Shearing Contest joined the show. In 1995, it added Mexican Rodeo and, in 2006, the Martin Luther King Jr. African American Heritage Rodeo. Kicking off festivities, National Western stages a downtown parade of Texas Longhorn cattle, cowboys and cowgirls, horseback riders, marching bands and floats, reminding Denverites "it's Stock Show time again."

In 1909, National Western, aided by meatpackers Swift and Armour, built its first permanent structure, the six-thousand-seat National Amphitheater and Livestock Pavilion, still in use today (DL). It was Denver's first enclosed arena; exterior pilasters featured flagpoles for twelve western states. National Western added barns and other buildings but always struggled for space. After World War II, organizers prioritized a new arena, working with the city to build Denver Coliseum, approved by voters in 1947; it opened in 1952, a massive concrete building (the roof weighs 5,400 tons) that doubles as concert and event venue. National Western built the Hall of Education in 1973 and additional facilities in 1987, 1991 and 1995.

The next step is National Western Center. This will be collaborative between National Western, the city, Colorado State University, Denver Museum of Nature and Science and History Colorado to reimagine the 250 acres that

National Western Stock Show's National Amphitheater and Livestock Pavilion, now the Stadium Arena. *Photograph by author.*

comprise the stock show and adjoining historic stockyards. It resulted from National Western nearly moving to Aurora; deciding that Denver could not afford to lose the event, the city and private groups teamed to create a plan to keep the show in place. National Western Center will include new stock show buildings, educational facilities focused on sustainable agriculture, a restored South Platte waterfront and new streets. It will preserve history by renovating and reusing the 1898 Livestock Exchange Building, the 1917 Armour & Company Administration Building (DL) and water tower and the livestock bridge across the river. The master plan suggests that "western heritage artifacts and educational pieces" will be integrated throughout.

PLAINS CONSERVATION CENTER

21901 East Hampden Avenue (Aurora)
(303) 326-8380; botanicgardens.org/beyond/plains-conservation-center; aurora.gov

Managed by Aurora's parks department with programs by Denver Botanic Gardens, this 1,100-acre remnant of Colorado high plains, surrounded by development, replicates nineteenth-century short grass prairie life.

The Cheyenne Camp, with four Cheyenne tipis, portrays seminomadic Indian life prior to Euro-American settlement, while Wells Crossing Farm includes two homesteads, a schoolhouse, a blacksmith shop and a barn. Visitors learn how, lacking wood, early homesteaders cut sod to make "bricks" to build their homes. A nature center displays exhibits about the site's ecosystem, and trails leading from it may reveal prairie dogs, pronghorns, coyotes, red-tailed hawks, bald eagles and occasional rattlesnakes. Prairie wagon group tours (fee; reservations required) follow these routes, educating participants along the way.

ROCKMOUNT RANCH WEAR AND MUSEUM

1626 Wazee Street (Lower Downtown)
(800) 776-2566; rockmount.com

Bob Dylan, Eric Clapton, Robert Plant and the Avett Brothers have shopped here. Elvis Presley, David Bowie and President Reagan were fans. The lone "Western" business in a neighborhood that once boasted many, Rockmount Western Wear and Manufacturing Company dates to 1946, when Jack A. Weil, "Papa Jack," founded it. Weil rode the post–World War II western wear boom by inventing snap-button shirts and popularizing the bolo tie; as his descendants say, "He is to Western wear what Henry

Rockmount Ranch Wear. *Photograph by author.*

Ford is to the car." Rockmount's "Sawtooth" pocket and "Diamond" snap design represent America's longest continuously made shirt model. Son Jack B. Weil joined in 1954, introducing western fashions to the eastern United States. Grandson Steve Weil, who began selling to the public from this store in 2001, and great-grandson David Oksner, represent third and fourth generations in Rockmount, which sells wares internationally. When he died at 107, still working every day, Jack A. Weil was the "world's oldest CEO." Rockmount shirts have been featured in films, clothing Robert Redford in *The Horse Whisperer*, Clark Gable and Marilyn Monroe in *The Misfits*, Nicholas Cage in *Red Rock West*, Woody Harrelson in *The Cowboy Way* and Meg Ryan and Dennis Quaid in *Flesh and Bone*. Rockmount shirts figured prominently in Ang Lee's *Brokeback Mountain*, particularly in its moving final scene. Museums have collected Rockmount pieces, including the Smithsonian and the Autry Museum. The store, occupying a 1909 warehouse designed by William E. and Arthur A. Fisher, hosts a museum of vintage Rockmount designs and memorabilia.

WORKING CITY

Historians have long recognized transportation's importance to Denver: with the Continental Divide blocking westward routes, Denver would have died without the railroad and, later, with the advent of aviation, would have remained isolated but for boosters' efforts to make Denver an air hub. On the local scale, beginning with a single horsecar line, by the 1890s Denver boasted an extensive electrified streetcar network that bound neighborhoods to downtown through World War II, after which, as with most cities, private automobiles driven on new freeways became Denverites' favored mode.

Although Denver never industrialized on the scale of Pittsburgh or Cleveland, the young city required manufactories to provide goods for consumers and businesses, and most of these arose near railroad lines or rivers. Denver attracted workers seeking better lives, many of them immigrants from other continents or other parts of the United States, and the cultures they brought with them diversified what had begun as a mostly white, Protestant town. It was not only those who worked with their hands who came but also clerks, bank tellers, accountants, journalists, firemen and myriad other professions and trades that make up a city. Industrial titans used to capture most historians' attention, but in recent years, the roles played by their workers have come to the fore. This chapter explores the places they worked and the things they did.

COLORADO RAILROAD MUSEUM

17155 West 44th Avenue (Golden)
(303) 279-4591; coloradorailroadmuseum.org; admission fee

The fifteen-acre Colorado Railroad Museum's one-hundred-plus-piece collection ranges from narrow- and standard-gauge steam and diesel locomotives to boxcars, passenger cars, cabooses, specialized equipment, a G-scale garden railway, a working water tank and other features. The museum's roots lie in Alamosa, where in 1950 founder and narrow-gauge (three-foot spacing) rail enthusiast Robert W. Richardson bought Denver and Rio Grande Railroad's locomotive no. 346 to attract customers to his Narrow Gauge Motel. Together with Cornelius "Corny" Hauck, another rail fan and collector, he founded the museum in 1959, constructing its 1880s-style "depot" for exhibits and offices the same year. This is painted yellow and brown, the Denver and Rio Grande's livery, and in its basement Denver Model Railroad Club built "Denver and Western," an elaborate HO- and HOn3-scale model train layout. In 2000, the museum completed the five-stall Cornelius Hauck Roundhouse, where volunteers restore rolling stock, aided by a working Armstrong turntable. The 1997 Robert W. Richardson Library archives more than ten thousand books and thirty-four thousand other items, including photographs, documents and artifacts. Check the website for events, including train rides around a one-third-mile loop (extra ticket required).

COORS BREWERY TOUR

13th and Ford Streets (Golden); parking lot
(303) 277-2337; millercoors.com/breweries/coors-brewing-company/tours; admission fee

Visiting the world's largest single-site brewery has been popular for generations. Lasting about thirty minutes, tours are self-guided, following a route and augmented with hand-held personal listening devices, above malting, brewing and packaging departments. Along the route, Coors displays company memorabilia and historical photographs. The tour ends in the Hospitality Lounge, with three eight-ounce beer samples (must be twenty-one, valid identification required) and a souvenir glass.

Founder Adolph Herman Joseph Coors was a twenty-six-year-old Prussian immigrant who, with a partner, bought the former Golden City Tannery on Clear Creek in 1873 and began brewing; Coors later became the sole owner and brought his children and grandchildren into the operation. Coors survived Prohibition by manufacturing porcelain, malted milk and Manna, a near beer. Adolph's grandson Bill Coors pioneered two-piece cans made with recyclable aluminum, now the industry standard. Cold filtered instead of pasteurized, Coors became a novelty outside its original eleven-state distribution area in the 1960s. *Smokey and the Bandit*'s (1977) plot follows a bootlegged Coors shipment from Texarkana to Atlanta. The beer has been available nationwide since Coors built an eastern packaging plant in the mid-1980s.

The Coors family has been newsworthy since 1960, when CEO Adolph Coors III was murdered during a botched kidnapping. From the 1960s through the 1980s, his brother and successor Joseph Coors's conservative politics generated headlines; he cofounded and bankrolled the Heritage Foundation and frequently advised President Reagan as a member of his "Kitchen Cabinet." Several groups boycotted Coors, based on its anti-union stance and hiring discrimination toward women and the African American, Hispanic and LGBTQ communities; these boycotts resulted in reforms. In 2005, Coors merged with Canada's Molson, forming Molson Coors Brewing Company.

DENVER CITY CABLE RAILWAY COMPANY BUILDING

1215 18th Street (Downtown)
DL, NR

Denver City Cable Railway, formed in 1889 by Denver City Railway's owners, built this two-story, Romanesque Revival powerhouse and car barn. It came late to cable car technology, Denver Tramway Company having beaten them to it. Streetcars powered by overhead wires, invented that year, shortly made cable cars less attractive, and they would disappear from Denver streets by 1900. The building's ornate brickwork suits its downtown location, belying its original industrial use, and its impressiveness factored into its 1973 salvation. Slated for demolition under DURA's Skyline project, Gus Dessin, a Portland, Oregon restaurateur who had created family eatery Old Spaghetti Factory, discovered it when scouting for a Denver location, deeming it perfect. Learning of its impending demolition, he contacted Historic Denver Inc. Its president,

E. James "Jim" Judd, recognized the building's worth. Judd developed a renovation plan, acquired the building from DURA and obtained funding from Colorado National Bank, whose president, Bruce Rockwell, served on HDI's board. He cleaned the brick, including the 110-foot smokestack, and renovated the upstairs into office space. On the ground floor, Old Spaghetti Factory served generations of Denver diners from 1973 until 2018. In 2019, Urban Putt, a Denver-themed "experiential" putt-putt golf course and restaurant, opened. It continues to house, as Old Spaghetti Factory had, Denver City Cable Railway's car no. 54, along with an antique bar once owned by boxer and Colorado native Jack Dempsey.

DENVER FIREFIGHTERS MUSEUM

1326 Tremont Place (Downtown)
(303) 892-1436; denverfirefightersmuseum.org; admission fee
DL, NR

This museum occupies Denver Fire Department's second Station One (1909), a Neoclassical design by Glen Huntington. Initially, horse stalls lined first-floor walls, with a hayloft upstairs; these disappeared when DFD converted to motorized firefighting. In 1975, Station One moved to Colfax Avenue and Speer Boulevard, and Chief Myrle Wise, seeing the firehouse's potential value as a firefighting museum, applied for landmark status and turned to

The Denver Firefighters Museum. *Photograph by Ryan Dravitz.*

volunteer group Denver Fire Reserves to begin the transformation. In 1979, civic leaders formed a governing body, and the museum opened in 1980. The ground floor is packed with exhibits documenting Denver's firefighting history, including nineteenth- and twentieth-century hook-and-ladder, pumper and engine carriages and trucks, along with dispatching systems, uniforms and displays on historic Denver fires. Upstairs are the firemen's locker room, the chief's private quarters, a steel fragment from New York's World Trade Center and changing displays. Volunteer docents, usually retired firefighters, offer a wealth of information to civilians unfamiliar with the science and art of firefighting.

DENVER GAS & ELECTRIC LIGHT COMPANY BUILDING

910 15ᵗʰ Street (Downtown); exterior only
DL, NR

Designed by Harry W.J. Edbrooke under his uncle Frank Edbrooke's supervision, this ten-story building opened in 1910 as Denver Gas and Electric Light Company's headquarters. This firm, product of an 1889 consolidation of electricity providers, had come under fire in 1906 for rigging an election to win an exclusive franchise, and its president, Henry L. Doherty, was briefly jailed by crusading judge Ben Lindsey. Doherty's Cities Service Company owned Denver Gas & Electric until 1943; in 1923, it changed its name to Public Service Company of Colorado. The building was remarkable in 1910 for its exterior lighting, showcasing Denver G&E's primary product: electricity. Nearly thirteen thousand lightbulbs create geometric patterns and outline tenth-floor arched windows. By day, its Louis Sullivan–style glazed white terra-cotta tile façade gleams brightly. After Public Service left for new quarters, in 1963 two local men converted it to the Insurance Exchange Building, and in 1985, after more than two decades spent in darkness, a new owner restored the exterior lighting. It currently houses "a telecom hotel and content delivery network center," closed to the public.

Denver Press Club

1330 Glenarm Place (Downtown)
(303) 571-5260; denverpressclub.org
DL, NR

As America's oldest press club (founded in 1867), Denver Press Club's mission supports journalism, but for its members, it has always served as a good place for a drink (except, officially at least, during Prohibition). Its founders, working for the *Rocky Mountain News* and competing papers, first met in the basement of grocer and later Denver mayor Wolfe Londoner's Larimer Street shop, where they kept a barrel of Taos Lightning (early Denver's elixir of choice), played poker and swapped stories. The club, formally organized in 1877, moved to a succession of hotel bars, where members typically clashed with management over rowdy behavior. In 1925, directors built this permanent clubhouse. Designed by Merrill and Burnham Hoyt, the two-story Tudor Revival building includes a bar and dining room on the main floor, with an event space upstairs. The Pulitzer Room showcases members' Pulitzer Prizes. The basement Poker Room boasts a 1945 Herndon Davis

The Denver Press Club. *Photograph by author.*

mural with faces of notable members. Membership was restricted to men until the 1960s. Notable members have included Eugene Field, Lowell Thomas, Burns Mantle, Damon Runyon, Gene Fowler, Byron White, William E. Barrett, Pat Oliphant, Sandra Dallas, Paul Conrad, Frederick Gilmer Bonfils, Lee Taylor Casey, Harry Mellon Rhoads, Reynelda Muse, Gene Amole, Carl Akers, "Stormy" Rottman, Thomas Hornsby Ferril, Palmer Hoyt, Gene Cervi, Cynthia Hessin, Don Kinney, Tom Gavin, Sam Lusky, Holger Jensen, Greg Lopez, Bob Palmer and Starr Yelland. Annually, it bestows the Damon Runyon Award to a journalist "whose career has embodied the style and verve" of the legendary newsman and short story writer. Club programs, including lectures and author appearances, are open to the public. In 2008, the Society for Professional Journalists designated the club as a "significant historical place in journalism."

DENVER TRAMWAY COMPANY BUILDING

1100 14th Street (Downtown)
(303) 228-1100; hotelteatro.com
DL, NR

By 1900, Denver Tramway Company, after winning Denver's streetcar wars, had bought all competitors and consolidated them into one operation with 160 miles of lines. Later, fresh from the 1906 election that let DTC retain its franchise, company president William Gray Evans centralized operations. The ideal site at 14th and Arapahoe Streets had been in his family since his father, John, had built his home there decades earlier, when it was "Millionaire's Row." It was a half block from DTC's Central Loop, where many lines converged, and from Interurban Loop, operated by DTC's sister company, Denver and Interurban Railroad. Evans bought additional properties along Arapahoe down to 13th and hired William and Arthur Fisher to design an eight-story headquarters and attached multilevel car barn. Their Renaissance Revival design utilizes dark-red brick, contrasting with white glazed terra-cotta trim. The frieze features large "T" symbols, for "Tramway." The 1910 headquarters boasted an elegant lobby, with pink Tennessee marble floors, Vermont green marble baseboards and white Arizona marble wainscoting. It was customary for new structures' builders to boast of Colorado materials used, but DTC, a monopoly, no longer needed to curry favor after the 1906 election.

The attached Central Division Carhouse utilized the site efficiently, with lower-level entry on 13th Street and upper-level entry on Arapahoe, made possible by Arapahoe's steep slope. By storing cars downtown instead of in scattered car barns, DTC made better use of rolling stock. A partial third floor housed facilities for conductors and motormen, including an auditorium, gymnasium, locker room with showers, bowling alleys, reading room, billiard room and barbershop. After a 1920 strike, DTC eliminated these perks.

In 1957, seven years after streetcars ceased operating, DTC sold the complex to University of Colorado for its Denver Extension Center (ancestor to today's UCD). The university used it for classrooms and faculty offices until 1987, selling the car barn to Denver Center Theatre Company to house costume and set construction shops and rehearsal spaces. In 1999, the restored tower reopened as the 110-room Hotel Teatro, a boutique property with a theatrical theme, reflecting its location across from Denver Performing Arts Complex. Its restaurant, The Nickel, nods to DTC's history in its name: for decades streetcar fare was five cents.

DENVER TRAMWAY COMPANY POWER HOUSE

1416 Platte Street (Highland)
(303) 756-3100; rei.com/stores/denver
DL

Overlooking the South Platte's confluence with Cherry Creek, the Denver Tramway Company Power House generated electricity for Denver's once-extensive streetcar system. After DTC's consolidation, it hired Denver engineering firm Stearns Rogers to build this central power plant, replacing scattered ones inherited from predecessor companies. Although built for industry, beauty was not ignored, and the 286-by-102-foot structure includes many handsome design elements. It opened in 1901, reaching full power in 1902; in 1911, DTC expanded it. Inside the cavernous structure, with its 42-foot ceiling, nineteen boilers, cooled by river water, generated 9,500 kilowatts from coal mined at DTC's own mine in Leyden. Streetcar operations ceased in 1950, and DTC sold the plant to International Harvester, which used it for warehousing. In 1969, it opened to the public as the Forney Museum of Transportation. After Forney relocated, in 1998 sporting goods cooperative Recreational

Equipment Inc. (REI) bought it to create a 90,000-square-foot flagship store. After extensive renovations, aided by DURA financing, it opened in 2000. The store retained stairs, coal hoppers and a smokestack as reminders of the building's history.

DENVER TROLLEY

1400 Water Street (Highland)
seasonal; ticket required
(303) 458-6255; denvertrolley.org

Board an open-air trolley car behind Denver Tramway Power House (REI) to ride one and a quarter miles on steel rails along the South Platte River Greenway past Downtown Aquarium, Children's Museum and Mile High Stadium, ending at Colfax Avenue. Tickets are available online or at several locations (check the website). Operators narrate the twenty-five-minute ride with area history. The trolley operates daily in summer and in fall on Denver Broncos game days, with shuttle service to Mile High Stadium. This heritage streetcar line has operated since 1989; plans exist to extend it southwest to the Decatur–Federal Boulevard light-rail station. The car is not antique, dating to just 1986, but it replicates a 1903 Brill open streetcar; its frame and steel components come from a 1924 streetcar built for Brisbane, Australia.

DENVER WOMEN'S PRESS CLUB

1325 Logan Street (Capitol Hill); exterior only
(303) 839-1519; dwpconline.org

Shut out from the then all-male Denver Press Club, this club formed in 1898 with seven members. One was Alice Polk Hill, Colorado's first poet laureate; another was Eleanor Lawney, the first woman to graduate from a Colorado medical school. The club grew by allowing non-journalists to join, which continues today. Amusement park operator Mary Elitch was a longtime honorary member. Meeting in members' homes during early decades, in 1924 the club bought its permanent home, the Ernest P. and Lester E. Varian–designed, two-story former home of noted etching artist

George Elbert Burr. Like other Progressive women's groups, the club became involved in social causes, which continues today with annual contests and scholarships. It hosts some programs open to the general public.

EMILY GRIFFITH OPPORTUNITY SCHOOL

1250 Welton Street (Downtown)
DL

Emily Griffith came to Denver in 1895 and began teaching. Witnessing impoverished students dropping school to support their families and observing how ill-equipped for success those families were, she resolved to help. She taught night classes at Longfellow School and then persuaded the school board to create Opportunity School—"For All Who Wish to Learn," per its motto—in the Longfellow building on Welton Street. Griffith recruited instructors for trades that would allow students, many of them working adults with families, to get ahead. From the beginning, Opportunity School instructed immigrants in English and conducted naturalization classes. By her 1933 retirement, the school had graduated more than 400,000 people, and Griffith had won national recognition. The school board honored her by renaming the institution for her; the state honored her with a stained-glass window in the capitol. In 1947 Emily and her sister, Florence, were found murdered in their mountain cabin, likely by an acquaintance.

The school expanded, constructing a four-story Renaissance Revival building next to Longfellow in 1926 and, demolishing Longfellow, expanded further in 1947 and 1956. Across the alley, it built additional facilities, including an auto body shop, where in January 1956 the DPS educational television station KRMA began broadcasting, with Emily Griffith instructors lecturing on air. (The DPS board later spun off KRMA, now Rocky Mountain PBS.) In 2011, the school split into two entities, Emily Griffith Technical College and Emily Griffith High School, dropping "Opportunity," and relocated. To preserve Emily Griffith's legacy, Denver landmarked the school in 2016, and in 2019, a developer announced renovation plans.

FORNEY MUSEUM OF TRANSPORTATION

4303 Brighton Boulevard (River North)
(303) 297-1113; forneymuseum.org; admission fee

J.D. Forney of Fort Collins had a passion for old automobiles, courting his wife, Rachel, in a 1919 Kissel touring car. He built a lucrative business, Forney Industries, after inventing a new type of soldering iron; it manufactured other items, including a personal airplane, the Fornaire Aircoupe. In the 1950s, son Jack Forney bought an antique Kissel and presented it to J.D. A company newsletter photograph of J.D. behind the wheel led to an employee connecting him with a Ford Model T, inspiring him to collect more. In 1961, Forney opened the museum in Fort Collins but ran out of space. In 1968, he moved briefly to Englewood's Cinderella City shopping mall before teaming with another collector, Denver surgeon Dr. James Arneill, to buy the vacant Denver Tramway Company Power House for the growing collection, which now included rail cars and locomotives. The Forney remained there until 1998, when it relocated to its present home; the logistically complex move required temporary rail tracks laid along the riverbank. The new Forney opened in 2001.

Forney owns one of the largest locomotives ever built, a 4884 Alco "Big Boy." Only twenty-five of these articulated steam engines, designed for Union Pacific, were manufactured. A yellow 1923 Kissel Speedster (Gold Bug) once owned by aviator Amelia Earhart is another highlight. Unusual vehicles abound, including an 1817 wooden bicycle, a six-wheel 1923 Hispano Suiza Victoria Town Car once owned by filmmaker D.W. Griffith and a 1963 German-made Amphicar, driven as both automobile and watercraft. In 1981, the Forney bought Denver Wax Museum's assets, and various historical figures, dressed in period attire collected by Rachel Forney, populate the museum today, including Earhart driving her Kissel.

MOUNTAIN STATES TELEPHONE AND TELEGRAPH BUILDING

931 14th Street (Downtown); exterior only
(303) 296-1221 (Telecommunications History Group); telecomhistory.org
NR

The 1929 Mountain States Telephone and Telegraph Building opened, housing its headquarters until 1984. MST&T's history dates to 1879, when

Frederick O. Vaille and partners Henry R. and Edward O. Wolcott established Denver Telephone Dispatch Company under license to American Bell Telephone; they later formed Colorado Telephone Company. Eventually, American Bell, which became American Telephone and Telegraph (AT&T) in 1907, gained control of Colorado Telephone; after consolidating it with companies in nearby states, covering 22 percent of the United State's land area, it established MST&T. With subscriber growth and technological changes, MST&T required more space than its headquarters at 1421 Champa Street (since demolished) could accommodate, and in 1927, it acquired land across the alley, at the Curtis Street corner with 14th. Architect William Norman Bowman carefully followed MST&T's specific technical and engineering requirements, creating something different from typical office buildings.

Despite these limitations, Bowman designed an elegant tower that dominated Denver's skyline for decades. He skirted Denver's twelve-story height limit by setting back upper floors, the only Denver building taking advantage of that zoning clause. Like other Bell "palaces," Bowman utilized American Perpendicular Gothic style, derived from Cass Gilbert's 1913 Woolworth Tower. It may have had an all-steel structure, but its exterior ornamentation, crafted in glazed terra cotta, derives from the medieval. AT&T built other "palaces" in New York and elsewhere during this period, and Denver's was the last completed, opening in September 1929; the October stock market crash ended AT&T's "palace" program. Bowman collaborated with Denver artist Allen Tupper True on the interior, which includes some Gothic elements but is best known for thirteen True murals illustrating the history of communications in Colorado and of the telephone. The public can view four of these at outer lobbies on the 14th Street and Curtis Street sides. Other murals are inside the building, closed to the public. The Telecommunications History Group maintains a small museum; to visit, contact the organization via its website.

MY BROTHER'S BAR

2376 15th Street (Highland)
(303) 455-9991; mybrothersbar.com

Down the block from Denver Tramway Power House, with no identification other than its address, is a bar that Tramway employees undoubtedly patronized after their shifts. It is better remembered, however, for its association with Neal Cassady, the young Denverite who was muse to Jack Kerouac and Allen Ginsberg, inspiring Kerouac's *On the Road* character Dean Moriarty. In a letter sent from Colorado State Reformatory to his former high school teacher Justin W. Brierly, Cassady mentioned, "I frequented the place occasionally & consequently have a small bill run up, I believe I owe them about 3 or 4 dollars. If you happen to be in that vicinity please drop in & pay it, will you?" Today, there is a mini-museum of the bar's Beat associations on the wall between restrooms. The bar has been in business since 1873, when it was the ground floor of the three-story Highland House; upper floors were later demolished. It was known as Paul's Place when Cassady frequented it and at other times as Whitie's and the Platte Bar. Its current name evolved after 1970, when brothers Jim and Angelo Karagas bought it. Operating in what was then a quiet area, business was slow. When creditors looked for payment, one would put them off by saying, "Don't look at me, it's my brother's bar." The next day, the other brother would offer the same story—the name stuck.

STANLEY MARKETPLACE

2501 Dallas Street (Aurora)
(720) 990-6743; stanleymarketplace.com; free
Aurora Landmark

Adjacent to former Stapleton International Airport, Stanley Marketplace repurposes the 140,000-square-foot former Stanley Aviation building, which opened in 1954. Stanley Aviation, led by former U.S. Navy test pilot Robert M. Stanley, the first American to fly a jet aircraft, designed and produced ejection seats for military aircraft, including the B-58 Hustler, which traveled to 70,000 feet and at speeds up to Mach 2. (One Stanley ejection seat is on display at Wings Over the Rockies Air & Space Museum.) Eaton Corporation bought Stanley and closed the plant in 2007. In 2016, it reopened as Stanley Marketplace, two levels housing more than fifty Colorado-owned restaurants, shops and community facilities. Much Stanley history remains evident, as developers were careful to preserve its industrial past.

STAPLETON CONTROL TOWER

3120 Uinta Street (Stapleton)
(720) 500-3788; punchbowlsocial.com/location/stapleton

Repurposed into a restaurant, this fourteen-story tower designed by Paul Reddy and completed in 1962 is all that remains of the world's once fifth-busiest airport. Mayor Ben Stapleton sought to consolidate private airfields scattered around eastern Denver, opening Denver Municipal Airport in October 1929. Initially used by airmail services, Continental and United Airlines began scheduled Denver service in 1937. City council voted to rename it Stapleton Airport in 1944, with Stapleton still mayor. In the 1950s, passenger jets forced new mayors to keep up with growth, even though Denver could not initially handle jets due to too-short runways. In 1967, a new master plan created three concourses connected by a curving terminal. Stapleton grew through the 1970s and 1980s, acquiring land from Rocky Mountain Arsenal and building a freeway-crossing runway and two more concourses, but it could not continue indefinitely, surrounded by neighborhoods and commercial districts that had not existed in 1929. In 1985, Mayor Federico Peña convinced Denver and Adams County voters to approve Denver International Airport (Adams voters had to approve Denver's annexation). DIA opened in 1995, and Stapleton closed. Thanks to this accomplishment, Peña served as President Bill Clinton's secretary of transportation.

Subsequently, following the "Green Book" created by city planners, a redevelopment foundation and a citizens' board, a master developer has transformed Stapleton's 4,700 acres into communities inspired by Denver's adjacent historic neighborhoods, along with commercial projects. Initially, some hoped to convert the airport terminal into retail and community uses, but it was demolished, except for this tower. Around Stapleton, a few other vestiges of aviation history remain. Most prominent is United Airlines' training facility at 7500 East 35th Avenue. United has trained pilots in Denver since 1943, and this center opened in 1968, followed by several expansions. Hangar 61 (8695 Montview Boulevard; DL), a soaring Modern thin-shell concrete structure designed in 1958 by Fisher, Fisher and Hubbell for Claude Boettcher's airplane, now houses a church.

In recent years, Denverites have reawakened to Mayor Stapleton's Ku Klux Klan connections. During the KKK's 1920s revival across the United States, he was a member, as was Colorado governor Clarence Morley, and

Stapleton International Airport control tower, now a restaurant. *Photograph by Ryan Dravitz.*

in 1924, Stapleton pledged, "I will work with the Klan and for the Klan… heart and soul." He later disavowed the KKK. Whether activists will be successful in removing his name from this section of Denver remains to be seen. Some community groups have deleted Stapleton from their names, while others have not.

UNION STATION

1701 Wynkoop Street (Lower Downtown)
(303) 592-6712; unionstationdenver.com
DL, NR

When it reopened in 2014 after a two-year renovation, Union Station suddenly became again the most interesting place to pass through in downtown Denver. Like most American train stations, its heyday came during the twentieth century's first half. Train travel declined after World War II, and fewer people passed through. By the turn of the twenty-first century, it was mausoleum-quiet, with Amtrak's California Zephyr's daily arrival and departure providing the only diversion. In 2004, voters in the

Regional Transportation District (RTD, encompassing Denver and several suburban counties) approved sales tax–funded FasTracks, encompassing light and commuter rail lines, a new bus terminal and Union Station's renovation into a multimodal transportation hub. RTD partnered with private consortium Union Station Alliance to renovate and repurpose the depot to not only serve transportation needs but also re-create its former bustling character. The alliance included Dana Crawford, who envisioned the Great Hall as "Denver's Living Room." It certainly functions as that: part lobby for the Crawford Hotel upstairs, part Amtrak waiting area, part dining and shopping destination, as well as a people-watching place *par excellence*. In front, parking lots became intimate plazas, one featuring dancing fountains and the other programed for events and farmers' markets. Rear doors open to platforms for Amtrak and RTD's commuter rail lines to DIA, Arvada, Westminster and Thornton. Belowground, a twenty-two-bay bus terminal connects Union Station to RTD's light-rail station for lines to Aurora, Golden, Littleton and Lone Tree.

Union Station opened in 1881, replacing scattered depots. Railroad baron Jay Gould, who had just merged Kansas Pacific with his Union Pacific, worked with Walter Scott Cheesman assembling land, and several Colorado railroads joined UP as partners. Kansas City architect William E. Taylor's Italianate design consisted of two long wings flanking a tower-topped waiting room. The wings, which remain today, are of Colorado materials: Castle Rock rhyolite and Morrison sandstone trim. An 1894 fire destroyed the waiting room and tower, and Kansas City firm Van Brunt & Howe designed replacements in Second Empire style. By 1912, Denver's population increase and consequent passenger traffic growth necessitated something larger.

That year, a new partnership of Union Pacific and several new railroads took over. They replaced the waiting area with the current granite-clad Great Hall, designed by Aaron Gove and Thomas Walsh in Beaux-Arts style. Possibly influenced by Warren and Wetmore's 1913 Grand Central Terminal in New York, their 1914 design similarly features multi-story arched windows on opposite sides, albeit on a smaller scale. Its Neoclassical design reflects contemporaneous efforts at creating the City Beautiful. One element, however, is gone. In 1906, Robert Speer's administration sponsored a contest for a gateway arch in front, won by East High School student Mary Woodsen. Sixty-five feet high, built of iron and adorned with 1,600 lightbulbs and the city seal, the Welcome Arch bore the word *Welcome* on the station-facing side and *Mizpah*, a Hebrew word meaning "the Lord watch between me and thee, when we are absent from one another," on the city-facing side. In 1931, Mayor George Begole declared it a traffic hazard and ordered it removed; maintenance costs also influenced his decision.

Celebrities, politicians and presidents passed through Union Station. Dwight Eisenhower came through Denver often during his army career and as president. Conventioneers (including 1908 Democratic National Convention delegates), Elks and Knights Templar, along with ordinary tourists, first saw Denver from Union Station's front doors. During two world wars, newly minted armed service members boarded troop trains here. In 1958, with passenger traffic slipping below that of Stapleton Airport, managers added bold, red neon signs to front and rear façades, reading "Union Station—Travel by Train," reminding people that railroads, while not as glamorous as airplanes, were still ready to serve. Those signs remain illuminated today, and if train travel's golden era never returns, at least Union Station bustles again.

BIG CITY DREAMS

Relatively young, Denver has always aspired to be perceived as larger, more sophisticated and greater than it might seem at first glance. This is as true in the twenty-first century as it was in the nineteenth—peruse *5280* magazine or read Downtown Denver Partnership's annual report to find evidence of modern boosters, perhaps more subtle than William Byers, who loudly trumpeted Denver's qualities in early *Rocky Mountain News* editions, but not different in intent to highlight Denver's best qualities. As this chapter demonstrates, bragging is unnecessary: from the 1880s on, Denver has always possessed "big city" attributes. This is evident from that era's newspapers, with stories of impressive new buildings alongside advertisements for as sophisticated a lineup of department stores and smart specialty shops as could be found in eastern cities. That boom era was fueled by easy money coming from silver mines, and it all came crashing down in the Panic of 1893. Yet booms came again and again, with each subsequent downturn followed by a new version of Denver. This chapter could be called simply "Downtown," as every site described is within the central business district, but downtown Denver is a dreamscape as much as a geographical designation. The sites described here make manifest the fondest hopes of Denver's earlier generations of fortune seekers who believed that they were building a great city.

BAUR'S CONFECTIONERY COMPANY

1512–14 Curtis Street
DL

Three red brick stories tall, this 1881 Italianate building survives as the lone remnant of Denver's onetime entertainment district, Curtis Street between 15th and 18th. Beginning with Tabor Grand Opera House (1881) at 16th, Curtis came to be lined with about fifteen theaters, originally vaudeville and later showing movies, most illuminated with thousands of lightbulbs. Other night-on-the-town businesses joined them, including restaurants, billiard halls and Baur's Confectionery. Founded by German immigrant Otto Paul Baur at 16th and Lawrence Streets in 1871, Baur's specialty was the ice cream soda, a concoction of ice cream, fruit juice and seltzer that Baur claimed to have invented. Baur moved to Curtis Street in 1890, installing a marble soda fountain, crystal chandeliers and white and gold display counters for pastries and candies. Otto's nephew John Joseph Jacobs later took over, adding a restaurant famous for deviled crab and Mija pie, a chocolate pie topped with ground toffee. Baur's made a point of serving everyone, advertising in the African American newspaper *Colorado Statesman* and hosting contralto Marian Anderson when she visited Denver. Jacobs branched out, opening Baur's Uptown at 16th Street and Glenarm Place, catering to shoppers and Paramount and Denver Theater patrons, as well as a branch inside the May Company department store. After World War II, Baur's opened elegant dining rooms at Cherry Creek Shopping Center and in Lakewood. Baur's closed in 1970, and the building has since housed a succession of restaurants. One of these adopted the Baur's name, replicating its early twentieth-century blade sign "Baur's," outlined in lightbulbs.

DENVER ATHLETIC CLUB

1325 Glenarm Place; private club
(303) 534-1211; denverathleticclub.cc
DL, NR

One of the nation's oldest downtown athletic clubs, Denver Athletic Club was formed in 1884 when commission merchant William D. Rathvon gathered together several men who wanted an exercise gymnasium. Initially occupying a former Baptist church, DAC hired Ernest Varian and Frederick J. Sterner for its Richardsonian Romanesque–style building. It opened in 1890, and the architects designed a matching addition in 1892. DAC attracted Denver's wealthier men, who swam, fenced, boxed and enjoyed other pursuits. In 1890, its football team played University of Colorado's team at DAC's offsite field opposite City Park; this was Denver's first organized football game, and DAC soundly defeated the Boulder boys, not yet called Buffaloes. The club introduced indoor bowling and squash to Denver. DAC has always served as setting for social events, wives included, with the gymnasium converted into a ballroom. In 1931, DAC allowed unmarried women to join. It suffered a devastating fire in 1951, killing four, and that year it added another wing, converting the gym permanently into a ballroom. Further additions came in 1973, 1984 and 1996.

17TH STREET

Long dubbed "Wall Street of the Rockies," 17th Street evolved into Denver's financial center organically from the 1890s through the 1920s, just as nearby 16th had evolved earlier into its retail spine. Businessmen recognized this even before the Panic of 1893 wiped out so many; an 1892 booklet promoting the Equitable Building accurately foretold that 17th would become the "Wall Street of Denver." It grew into something larger, a financial center for the inland western United States. Union Station's 1881 construction at 17th and Wynkoop Streets undoubtedly aided its rise to prominence—business people (exclusively business*men* then) need easy access to transportation. The Brown Palace, Denver's finest hotel, opened in 1892, anchoring 17th Street's Broadway terminus. An exclusive men's organization, the Denver Club, occupied a grand clubhouse, now demolished, at 17th and Glenarm Place. Important office buildings arose prior to 1893, and while the Boston and Equitable remain, others of that era have been lost. Once Denver recovered from the Panic, 17th Street slowly regained momentum, and by the 1920s it was lined from Larimer to Broadway almost entirely with multistory buildings boasting modern conveniences and tenanted by leading banks, financial firms and attorneys. While other downtown streets, particularly 15th and 16th, boasted some notable office structures, only 17th felt architecturally complete, its buildings comprising Denver's most big city–like street. Several high-rise towers arose in the 1950s, some erected by Texas or New York developers, and the late 1970s and early 1980s oil boom saw another wave

"Wall Street of the Rockies." Colorado National Bank Building, now a hotel, on the right. Farther up the street: the Boston Building, the First National Bank Building and the Equitable Building. *Photograph by Ryan Dravitz.*

of change, with shining new towers that spoke to Denver's short-lived status as "Houston of the North." Today, locally owned banks and brokerages that were 17th Street's financial lifeblood are gone, swallowed up by national firms, but their legacy, particularly at 17th's intersections with Stout and Champa Streets, remains somewhat intact.

Boston Building

828 17th Street
Businesses open to the public
DL, NR

When Episcopal girls' school Wolfe Hall opened on this 17th and Champa Street site in 1867, it was on the edge of town, but just twenty-one years later, when Henry Wolcott bought it, Denver's financial district had grown up around it. Boston investors—hence the building's name—financed construction of this nine-story structure, one of Denver's last all-masonry office towers when it opened in 1890. Wolcott chose Boston firm Andrews, Jacques and Rantoul to design it in Richardsonian Romanesque style, with a heavily rusticated base and wide arched window openings on three floors. Unfortunately, the material chosen, Manitou sandstone, is soft, and much original ornamentation, as well as rustication on lower floors, had to be shaved off later for safety. For nearly sixty years, this was headquarters to Denver's leading blue-chip investment firm, Boettcher & Company (originally Boettcher, Newton & Company). Boettcher, the first Denver firm to acquire a seat on the New York Stock Exchange, financed many Colorado projects, including the Moffat Tunnel, Boulder Turnpike, Vail ski resort, college buildings and hospitals. In 1998, the building, combined with the adjacent Kistler Stationery Company Building, became apartment lofts.

Brown Palace Hotel

321 17th Street
(303) 297-1111; brownpalace.com/our-hotel/history/hotel-tour
DL, NR

Called by historian Richard Brettell "one of the greatest nineteenth-century commercial structures in America," the eight-story Brown Palace has been Denver's finest hotel since it opened. Henry Cordes Brown, an 1860 pioneer, had made his fortune through real estate, developing "Brown's Bluff" into Capitol Hill. In 1888, Maxcy Tabor and William H. Bush, both previously associated with the Windsor Hotel on Larimer Street, optioned from Brown the triangular block bounded by 17th Street, Broadway and Tremont Street and began building. Their funding ran out, so Brown took over, eventually spending $2 million. He envisioned a first-class hotel, hiring Frank Edbrooke to design it. Edbrooke gave Brown's Palace (as it was originally called) a Richardsonian Romanesque façade, rendered in Pikes Peak granite and brown Arizona sandstone. His design has no backside; all three façades originally had central doors leading to the lobby; the Broadway entrance is now closed. He masterfully curved the façade around each corner, anticipating, as many have noted, Daniel Burnham's 1902 Flatiron Building in New York. Sculptor James Whitehouse carved twenty-six circular medallions above the seventh floor, each representing Colorado animals.

The hotel opened on August 12, 1892. Visitors entered and looked up, as first-timers still do, marveling at the hotel's chief wonder, its eight-story atrium lit by a stained-glass ceiling. One of the first atrium hotels built, the Brown's Italian Renaissance–style interior includes 12,400 square feet of golden onyx on walls and ornate cast-iron panels (two of which are upside down) lining open balcony corridors. The Brown was famous even before opening, as *Scientific American* had featured its unusual design and construction technology in its May 21, 1892 issue. The hotel is built of steel and cast iron, with white terra-cotta blocks wrapping structural elements, including floors and walls, rendering it fireproof. Brown spared no expense, filling guestrooms and public spaces with fine furnishings and serving meals on fine china. The Brown's artesian well provided water.

The rich and famous have always signed Brown Palace's guestbook. Augusta Tabor, divorced wife of Horace Tabor and mother of Maxcy, moved from her house across Broadway into the Brown. Other early guests included William Cody, John Philip Sousa, Sarah Bernhardt, Queen Marie of Romania, the Prince of Wales (later King George V) and Sun Yat-sen. After Margaret Brown split from husband J.J., she stayed at the hotel when visiting Denver. When Colorado mining heiress Evalyn Walsh McLean stayed, she likely stored her Hope Diamond in the Brown's safe. During Helen Keller's 1921 stay, violinist Jascha Heifetz played for her; Keller "heard" music by touching his violin. In 1964, the Beatles occupied an eighth-floor suite before and after their Red Rocks concert; folksinger Joan Baez stayed simultaneously, playing Red Rocks two nights later. Also that year, the Brown hosted Debbie Reynolds, in Denver to world-premiere her movie musical *The Unsinkable Molly Brown*. Presidential guests have included William Howard Taft, Warren Harding, Harry Truman, Dwight Eisenhower, Ronald Reagan and Bill Clinton. Hillary Clinton stayed at the Brown again during 2008's Democratic National Convention.

Locals have made the Brown central to their lives, at least once with deadly consequences. In 1911, Isabel Patterson "Sassy" Springer, young wife of wealthy rancher John Wallace Springer, checked in. She had been conducting affairs with two men: Sylvester von Phul and an associate of her husband's, Frank Henwood. The two men (but not the husband) knew of the other's attentions to Isabel and were exceedingly jealous. After all three attended a Broadway Theater performance across the street, the men encountered each other in the Marble Bar (no longer extant), adjacent to the Broadway entrance. After a verbal altercation, Henwood fired gunshots, mortally wounding von Phul and killing a bystander. Newspapers covered the scandal avidly.

The Brown has served as venue for countless debutante balls and social events. Since 1987, it has kicked off the holidays with the Champagne Cascade. A master swordsman wielding a Napoleonic saber severs necks of Champagne bottles. A VIP then pours bubbly into the top glass of a two-story-high, Christmas tree–shaped pyramid built of six thousand glasses. Champagne flows from the top glass to the tier below, then the third and so on, providing a show for hundreds lining balconies (tickets required, with proceeds to charity). Simultaneously, the hotel illuminates its holiday decorations, which remain in place for the National Western Stock Show. Although that event takes place elsewhere, the Grand Champion Steer and Reserve Champion from its Junior Market Steer Championship have made visits to the Brown's lobby since 1945. The animals stay for two hours before returning to the Stock Show, where they sell at auction.

The atrium hosts English-style afternoon high tea. The Brown boasts two historic dining rooms, Palace Arms and Ship Tavern. The latter, designed by Alan Fisher, opened in 1934 celebrating Prohibition's end. The Boettcher family owned the hotel then, and Claude Boettcher had recently vacationed on Cape Cod, where he acquired a dozen models of famous sailing ships. His wife did not relish decorating their home with them and suggested a seafaring theme for the bar. Claude wisely agreed, and his models grace the room today. The Palace Arms displays items from Boettcher's European military paraphernalia collection. In 1937, the Brown commissioned Allen True for two murals in the Tremont lobby, *Stage Coach* and *Airplane Travel*. In 1959, the hotel opened Brown Palace West, a modern tower across Tremont, linked to the original via a second-floor sky bridge. Although it shares ownership (which has changed several times), today the tower operates separately. Since 1977, Brown Palace has employed an official hotel historian. Tours are available, free to hotel guests and for a fee to the public.

Colorado National Bank Building

918 17th Street
(303) 867-8100; rendendowntown.com
NR

"The bank that looks like a bank" was Colorado National's motto after it moved into this 1915 Greek pure white Colorado Yule marble temple designed by William and Arthur Fisher. With its row of Ionic columns and massive bronze doors and window grills, it conveyed CNB's history of conservative financial management. In 1926, CNB expanded along Champa, in the same Greek style. In 1964, CNB removed the top floor, replacing it with several new floors in Modern style but still utilizing Colorado Yule marble. In 2007, the bank moved next door to the former Colorado National Bank Tower (1972, Minoru Yamasaki). The original building sat empty, with preservationists fearing demolition. Instead, a historically minded developer partnered with a national hotel operator, transforming it into an elegant hotel in 2014. The two-story-high banking hall serves as hotel lobby, where visitors admire the fully restored *Indian Memories*, sixteen Allen True murals painted in 1925 illustrating lives of Native Americans prior to arrival of white men. Renovation preserved three vaults, complete with thirty-three-inch-thick doors.

CNB was one of Denver's earliest banks, founded as Kountze Brothers Bank in 1862 by Luther Kountze, buying gold dust and performing traditional banking functions. Luther was one of four banking brothers, and in 1866, the youngest, Charles B. Kountze, came to Denver as president, with Luther relocating to New York. At this time the bank, then at 15th and Market Streets, became Colorado National, the name it bore until its 1992 takeover by U.S. Bank. Although CNB was known for safety, it also innovated. In the 1960s, newly hired executive D. Dale Browning partnered with San Francisco–based Bank of America, forming a national credit card issuer, later known as Visa Inc. Browning collaborated with IBM in developing the automated teller machine, and CNB installed the first six that IBM manufactured at this bank. Later, Browning founded Plus Systems, now owned by Visa, networking ATMs for cash access anywhere.

Equitable Building

730 17th Street
Businesses open to the public
DL, NR

Henry Wolcott, after constructing the Boston Building, bought another 17th Street corner, at Stout Street, for another first-class office block. With financing from New York's Equitable Life Assurance Society, Wolcott again engaged Andrews, Jacques and Rantoul, resulting in Denver's finest office building. Designed in Italian Renaissance style, the nine-story composition features granite on lower floors with light pressed brick above, as well as copious ornamentation. In plan it resembles two capital *E*s placed back to back, giving tenants access to light and air. The first-floor lobby features Vermont yellow marble wainscoting, red marble floors and a groin-vault ceiling covered in marble tesserae. An open stairway, with bronze railings, connects the first floor with the second and basement. Above the landing, a Tiffany stained-glass window, *The Genius of Insurance*, portrays the goddess Minerva protecting a widow and an orphan.

The building's 1892 opening marked the apex of Colorado's silver boom. City boosters felt that with the Equitable, Denver could show eastern capitalists that it had come of age and would be safe for investments. A-list tenants immediately filled it, including Equitable Life's western regional office, First National Bank of Denver, Wolcott's brother, Senator Edward Wolcott and, in 1893 and 1894 prior to the capitol's completion, the executive office of Governor Davis H. Waite. This was ironic, as he had run on the Populist Party ticket and now rode elevators with wealthy plutocrats. The fifth floor housed the region's largest law library, and undoubtedly one tenant, attorney Mary Lathrop, one of the first women admitted to the American Bar Association, used it. The Equitable was Denver's tallest building when it opened, remaining so until 1911. In the 1920s, it had its

The Equitable Building. *Photograph by Ryan Dravitz.*

own ticker tape machine, attracting stockbrokers from up and down 17th Street. The Equitable has changed hands many times; its 1980 owner spent significant sums to restore it to its 1893 condition, and in 2000, another owner spent even more to "polish" it.

First National Bank Building

818 17th Street
(303) 607-9000; magnoliahotels.com/denver
NR

This building's chief historical interest has to do with its original occupant, First National Bank of Denver. Clark & Company, previously Clark, Gruber & Company, had been founded in 1860 as bank, assay office and mint. The federal government acquired the mint in 1862, and in 1865, the Clark brothers joined with Jerome Bunty Chaffee and others to form the bank, with Chaffee, later one of Colorado's first senators, as president. The list of bank stockholders during its early years reads like a Colorado *Who's Who*, including Horace Tabor, Walter Cheesman, George Washington Clayton and Henry Wolcott. Its name was not merely decorative; it was the *first* national bank chartered in Colorado under National Banking Acts of 1863, 1864 and 1865. Occupying a succession of spaces in early decades, First National moved into the Equitable Building in 1896, the first Denver bank to open its doors on 17th. It had grown into the twenty-first-largest bank in the United States and the largest west of the Mississippi. In 1911, First National moved across Stout to this new steel-framed building, designed by Harry W.J. Edbrooke under his uncle Frank's supervision. He designed it in Chicago style, with base, shaft and capital, the shaft being a grid of large, regularly spaced windows. Its height proved controversial. The building's Seattle-based developer proposed fourteen stories, which would exceed a recently enacted nine-story limit; Mayor Speer negotiated a compromise, and city council enacted a twelve-story limit that remained in place until 1953.

In 1958, First National relocated to a new tower at 17th and Welton, and American National Bank moved in after giving the building a Modernist makeover. American National was historic as well, having formed in 1905 as German-American Trust Company, dropping the "German" in 1917 and becoming a national bank in 1924. American occupied the building from

1962 until 1984, and after it sat empty for ten years, a developer transformed it into a hotel. The renovation amazed younger Denverites, unaware that beneath the Modernist façade lurked a historic building. While upper floors are original, the first two, corner clock and cornice are re-creations based on Edbrooke's designs.

Ideal Building

821 17ᵗʰ Street
DL, NR

Ancient Romans used concrete as a building material, but in the early twentieth century, most architects were captivated by structural steel. Charles Boettcher—who in 1901 had formed Colorado Portland Cement Company with Pueblo's Charles and John Thatcher and mining magnate John F. Campion—decided to demonstrate concrete's fireproof quality and strength. Boettcher had become interested in Portland cement at about the time he had begun investigating sugar beets (see the first chapter), and he knew that importing it was expensive and that Colorado had plenty of lime, silica and alumina, its components. Requiring a headquarters for his growing concern, now Ideal Cement, in 1907 he commissioned Montana Fallis and John Stein for an eight-story Neoclassical edifice in steel-reinforced concrete. Once the concrete had set, Boettcher ordered wooden supports set ablaze, while city building inspector Robert O.

The Ideal Building, later Denver National Bank. *Photograph by Ryan Dravitz.*

Willison watched. Temperatures reached 1,800 degrees Fahrenheit, yet the structure was undamaged, giving Boettcher priceless publicity. This was the first reinforced concrete high-rise west of the Mississippi, and Boettcher moved into a fifth-floor corner office, where he continued working for forty more years, into his nineties.

In 1927, Denver National Bank, founded in 1884, leased the first two floors and basement. It hired the Fisher brothers to remodel and add to the building along Champa Street, doubling its size. They created a Romanesque Revival two-story banking lobby and commissioned local artists to sculpt exterior elements, including corner griffins and stylized Colorado flora and fauna around the entry. Most spectacular are bronze entry doors depicting Native American dancers. Denver National remained here until 1959, and other banks have called it home since. For more than forty-five years until it closed in 2017, the Broker Restaurant, occupying the basement, filled Denver stomachs with expensive steak and complimentary shrimp.

SIXTEENTH STREET MALL

Stretching from Broadway to the Millennium Bridge, the Sixteenth Street Transitway Mall is one of the few truly successful pedestrian malls built in the era when such projects were fashionable. It thrives because, unlike many pedestrian malls, it was designed not as a shopping destination, a role 16th Street had played since the 1880s, but as a transportation project. By the mid-1970s, RTD, chartered in 1969, was increasingly struggling to run buses through congested downtown streets. This mall, with bus terminals at each end connected by free, frequent-service shuttle buses, solved the problem. The constant presence of shuttles, which have always been low- or nonpolluting and easy to board, has kept the mall activated since its 1982 completion. Henry N. Cobb, associated with I.M. Pei in Pei Cobb Freed & Partners, designed it, basing its distinctive pavement pattern, most apparent when its light-gray, dark-gray and rose-colored granite pavers are wet, on rattlesnake skin. In recent years, RTD and Downtown Denver Partnership have proposed fixes for chronic problems, particularly granite pavers in bus lanes, which require frequent re-setting, but as of this writing the mall's original design is largely intact.

Originally "G Street" on early maps, 16th has been Denver's "Main Street" for more than a century, usurping that role from Larimer in the

1880s thanks to streetcar lines and the general trend of wealthier residents migrating southeastward from the original settlement. This was where people not only shopped in big department stores or smaller boutiques but also mailed letters at the main post office or served on juries in the Arapahoe County (later Denver County) Courthouse. They had their teeth cleaned at the Republic Building (demolished). Young lovers shared ice cream sodas at Baur's Uptown before taking in movies at the Paramount or Denver Theatres, while their fathers attended lodge meetings at the Masonic Building. People requiring lawyers could find one in the Majestic or Metropolitan Buildings. On special occasions, 16th Street always served as the natural parade route, often for visiting luminaries like Presidents Theodore Roosevelt and Woodrow Wilson or aviator Charles Lindbergh. Today, while the department stores, doctors' offices, post office and courthouse are gone 16th Street still attracts crowds.

Of particular historic interest is the southwest side of 16th between Welton and Curtis Streets. Beginning with the Sage Building at Welton and ending with the Tritch Block at Curtis, this rare stretch of historic edifices is uninterrupted by newer construction; visitors can gaze on this four-block array of eight buildings and imagine what Denver's "Main Street" might have looked like a century ago.

Colorado Building

1615 California Street

A Victorian/Art Deco hybrid, this is the work of three architects across four decades. In 1891, John Roberts designed the original five-story block, dubbed the Hayden, Dickinson and Feldhauser Building, and leased to Colorado Dry Goods Company, which closed in 1902. The ground floor was then subdivided, with one space leased to the first Denver F.W. Woolworth store. In 1909 new owner Charles Boettcher commissioned Frank Edbrooke for two more floors but specified lower ceiling heights, clearly evident from outside. Boettcher also renamed it for the state that had been the source of his wealth. Finally in 1935, his son Claude hired J.J.B. Benedict for a facelift. Benedict, better known for his Neo-Renaissance domestic work, transformed the fusty Victorian office block into an Art Deco landmark, with a stylized, Colorado-inspired frieze above first floor shops and dramatic, spiky piers rendered in glazed terra cotta running

The Colorado Building. *Photograph by Ryan Dravitz.*

to the roof and beyond, giving it a distinctive crown-like skyline. He left alone the cast-iron spandrels between piers, so its nineteenth-century roots are still apparent in the twenty-first. Today, the fifth floor houses the Dikeou Collection, a private contemporary art collection open to the public (dikoucollection.org).

Daniels and Fisher Tower

1601 Arapahoe Street
closed to the public
DL, NR

A 330-foot tower (375 with flagpole) patterned after Venice's Campanile di San Marco is all that remains of department store Daniels and Fisher. A 1911 monument surrounded by 1970s and 1980s office buildings and hotels, the tower survived, even as DURA demolished nearly every building across seventeen blocks, including the store attached to the tower. Built by William Cooke Daniels, son of the store's founder, it was Denver's tallest building for forty-six years, visible for miles. It

The Daniels and Fisher Tower. *Photograph by Ryan Dravitz.*

symbolized the store and reflected Denver's aspirations of becoming a major city. Developer David French renovated it, reopening it in 1982 as office condominiums, each floor owned separately. Architect Gensler & Associates utilized contrasting brown brick on sides where the store had been attached, a reminder of its history. The revolving door, installed in the 1990s, came from the former Ford Motor Company headquarters in Dearborn, Michigan. Although upper floors are inaccessible, the ornate lobby, with an exhibit of Daniels and Fisher historical artifacts, is open. The Denver Architecture Foundation's annual Doors Open Denver event usually features tower tours (fee), and Historic Denver's walking tours often include the tower (fee).

The Denver Dry Goods Company Building

702 16th Street
DL, NR

This six-story building stretching along California Street from 16th to 15th was Denver's largest department store for nearly a century. Its roots date to 1877, when dry goods shop Drew & McNamara, later McNamara Dry Goods Company, opened at 15th and Larimer. In 1889, Michael J. McNamara moved to a three-story red brick structure at 16th and California, designed by Frank Edbrooke. It was the farthest uptown of Denver's major stores, and some nearby lots still had houses on them. McNamara lost his store during the Panic of 1893, and two Colorado National Bank executives, Dennis Sheedy and Charles B. Kountze, acquired it at auction. In May 1894, Sheedy renamed it The Denver Dry Goods Company, and as business improved, they added a fourth floor in 1898 and a six-story wing on the 15th Street corner in 1906–7. The Denver bragged of Denver's first escalator and the "longest department store aisle in the world" (surely a hyperbolic claim). The building reached its final form in 1924, when new owners added two more floors to the 16th Street side, one devoted to a tearoom. Older Denverites still fondly remember the Tea Room and its signature dish, Chicken à la King. At one end, a men's only "Grill Room," with two immense round tables, served 17th Street businessmen and lawyers. The "Stockmen's Store" featured full lines of clothing and equipment for professional working cowboys; it even manufactured its own saddles. Always well maintained by its owners (Associated Dry Goods after 1964), The Denver's business declined in the 1960s and after. May Department Stores of St. Louis, itself a Colorado legacy having been founded in Leadville by David May in 1877, acquired Associated in 1986 and in 1987 shuttered The Denver and its branches. Fearful that a historically important building would be demolished, DURA, led by Susan Powers, bought it and, working with partners, reopened it in 1993 with retail and office space, income-qualified and market rate apartments and loft condominiums.

Joslin Dry Goods Building

934 16ᵗʰ Street
NR

Originally named Tritch Block for its builder, hardware merchant and banker George Tritch, this 1887 Frank Edbrooke–designed red brick structure housed department store Joslin Dry Goods, better known as Joslin's (no apostrophe after 1964). John Jay Joslin of Poultney, Vermont, came west in 1872 to visit his brother Jervis, liking Denver's prospects so well that he came back permanently in 1873. He bought the New York Store at 15ᵗʰ and Larimer Streets, renamed it for himself and became a leading citizen, cofounding the chamber of commerce and indulging in his passion, choral singing. Moving from Larimer, he occupied a Lawrence Street building before leasing most of the Tritch Block in 1888. He eventually occupied the whole, and for six months in 1897, he employed a young go-getter named James Cash Penney, who would found his own department store. Joslin continued managing his store until 1926, passing away at ninety-six. Denver newspapers and even rival merchants all mourned the loss of Denver's "Grand Old Man." Joslin's, part of Mercantile Stores Company, added a fifth floor in 1927. It began opening branches in 1944 but kept the flagship going until 1995, when it was the last of downtown's department stores to shutter; developers renovated it into a hotel in 1997. The Joslin name disappeared in 1998 when Dillard's bought Mercantile.

Kittredge Building

511 16th Street
NR

A. Morris Stuckert designed this 1891 Richardsonian Romanesque building for Charles Marble Kittredge, who hoped to lure a department store tenant. It was too far uptown for that, so instead he opened an office building with ground floor shops; the Casino Rooftop Garden was a popular nightspot. Legend says that the first basketball game west of the Mississippi was played on the second floor. Constructed with a frame of iron and steel, some locals unfamiliar with the technology feared its collapse, but Stuckert and Kittredge promised that it would stand. Kittredge later helped develop Montclair, and the foothills town that bears his name. From 1930 to 1984, the two left-most bays on the 16th Street side served as the Paramount Theatre's main lobby entrance. After World War II, New York builder William Zeckendorf bought it as a potential development site but, fortunately, never pursued it. The building saw renovations in

The Kittredge Building. *Photograph by Ryan Dravitz.*

1981 and 1992, restoring rusticated granite and rhyolite façades to their 1890s glory. Elaborately carved stone elements include the cornice with its corner gargoyles and Romanesque foliage above the main entrance.

A. T. Lewis & Son Building

800 16ᵗʰ Street

One of Denver's least-remembered department stores, A.T. Lewis & Son began as a ladies' dry goods shop in 1890. Aaron Dennison Lewis, the son, had worked for Daniels and Fisher and had subsequently co-owned a Breckenridge general store; his father, Aaron Thompson Lewis, invested in his vision. Growing rapidly, in 1895 it moved to this 1891 structure built for Salomon's Bazaar, which had closed after the Panic of 1893. Initially, the Robert Sawers Roeschlaub–designed building was a mid-block structure abutting the alley; in 1901, Lewis hired Roeschlaub to extend it to the corner. Lewis continued expanding into the new century, in 1916 engaging Harry Edbrooke for a six-story addition. This building, at 1531 Stout, shows fine use of white glazed terra cotta, its ornamentation likely inspired by Louis Sullivan's *art nouveau* work in Chicago and elsewhere. A.T. Lewis & Son catered to Denver's better-heeled shoppers, and when the Great Depression hit, Lewis was saddled with a large store that saw fewer shoppers each month; he closed in January 1933. The original building filled in with smaller tenants, and in 1942, Denver and Rio Grande Western Railroad bought the Stout wing for its headquarters and ticket office. In 1995, both were renovated into apartment lofts, with nearly half reserved for people making no more than 60 percent of Denver's median income.

Neusteter Company Building

720 16ᵗʰ Street
DL, NR

The Neusteter Building was saved from demolition in the 1980s by developers who appreciated its fine architecture and importance to Denver's retail history. Founded in 1911 by brothers Max, Meyer and Edward Neusteter, the Neusteter Company initially occupied one floor of a three-story building abutting the alley. Catering to discerning tastes, they leased upper floors and, in 1924, commissioned the Fisher brothers for this five-story Neoclassical emporium clad in limestone with large windows to illuminate the fashions within; the original three-story building was incorporated into it, refaced to match. Neusteters (no apostrophe after 1951) thrived after World War II, opening branches and catering to shoppers seeking high fashion and superior quality and willing to pay for them. Overexpansion coupled with economic downturn resulted in Neusteters' 1986 closure. Today, the building houses loft condominiums with ground-floor retail.

Sage Building

600 16th Street
DL

Steel's was a Buffalo, New York–based popular-price department store chain that in 1922 commissioned Merrill Hoyt for this four-story Denver branch. Hoyt's glazed terra-cotta façade shows classical Greek influence, particularly its ornate cornice. Steel's opened with great fanfare in December 1922; shoppers lined up around the block. The third-floor home department featured a six-room, fully furnished bungalow, and patrons refreshed themselves at a soda fountain or in the five-hundred-seat Persian Gardens basement cafeteria. Its glory was brief: financially stretched founder Leonard Steel died of a brain aneurism in March 1923, and Steel's was liquidated. The cafeteria continued operating for years under the name Hoff-Schroeder. The street floor was divided into small shops, with upper floors leased as offices. By the late 1980s, it was vacant and sat empty for two decades before Evan Makovsky bought it. His multimillion-dollar renovation included painstaking renovation of Hoyt's exterior ornamentation, and the building reopened, named for office tenant Sage Hospitality, in 2008.

Symes Building

820 16th Street

Designed by New York's Joseph Howland Hunt and Richard Howland Hunt in Chicago style, with an all-steel frame (Denver's first), large windows and simple Neoclassical lines, this 1906 eight-story office building opened as one of Denver's most prestigious. Original tenants included lawyers, insurance companies, mining companies and American Smelting and Refining Company. The ground floor initially housed several shops, including shoe retailer John J. Fontius, but by the mid-1920s, national five-and-dime chain F.W. Woolworth had leased all of it. After World War II, Woolworth obtained abutting properties running to 15th Street and enlarged the store twice, occupying 175,000 square feet by 1963 and calling itself the "World's Largest Woolworth." It closed in 1994, and its Symes Building space once again houses several small retailers. This building replaced an earlier, three-story Symes Building erected by Judge George G. Symes in 1883 after tearing down his own 1870s residence. The earlier Symes Building, which burned in 1905, housed Edward T. Monash's department store, The Fair, which closed in 1901.

University Building

912 16th Street
NR

This steel-framed twelve-story tower, built by banker Alexis C. Foster and originally named for him, was one of Denver's tallest when it opened in 1911; his partners were James Causey and later Colorado governor William Sweet. The Fisher brothers designed it along classical lines, with base, shaft and crown, the latter embellished with distinctive green and white pinstripes. In 1924, Causey donated it to the University of Denver, which renamed it and gave it a new Art Deco entrance. Although it was not planned as Denver's "diamond district," it evolved into one, with jewelers occupying street-level space and upstairs suites. In the early 1980s, new owners restored the first two floors' exterior, which had been stripped away through insensitive 1950s "modernization." As this book went to press, a developer proposed transforming the building into a hotel.

INSTITUTIONAL DENVER

A s much as Denver has always been a city driven by (some might say "ruled by") its businesses, from early days city leaders have recognized the importance of establishing the accoutrements of civilization—without those there is no real city. Jerome Smiley, in his 1901 *History of Denver*, devoted considerable attention to early efforts at establishing culture, from the first Masonic meetings and church services to schools and institutions of higher learning. Some of the earliest Denver institutions, founded in the 1850s or 1860s, are thriving today. This chapter explores several of the longest-lived ones.

CATHEDRAL BASILICA OF THE IMMACULATE CONCEPTION

401 East Colfax Avenue (Uptown)
(303) 831-9514; archden.org/parish/cathedral-basilica-of-the-immaculate-conception
DL, NR

The Archdiocese of Denver's mother church, Immaculate Conception, replaced an earlier Cathedral of St. Mary at 15th and Stout Streets. Cathedral Parish dates to 1860, when Bishop J.B. Miege arrived from Leavenworth, Kansas, to form Denver's first Roman Catholic congregation. Construction on Immaculate Conception began in 1906, and the first mass was celebrated on October 27, 1912. In 1979, Pope John Paul II designated it a minor basilica, and in 1993, he celebrated mass here during his World Youth Day. For that visit, and again more recently, the archdiocese has funded cleanings and restorations, undoing unsympathetic 1970s modifications.

Detroit architect Leon Coquard based the outstanding French Gothic design on the thirteenth-century St. Nicholas Collegiate Church of Munster, France, birthplace of Bishop Nicolas Matz, overseer of the cathedral's construction; after Coquard withdrew due to poor health, Aaron Gove and Thomas Walsh saw the building to completion. The exterior features twin 210-foot spires facing south; these have been struck by lightning twice, in 1912 and 1997, necessitating repairs. Exterior walls are faced in Indiana limestone above a Gunnison, Colorado granite foundation. Sides feature flying buttresses characteristic of the French style. Interior walls are of white Colorado Yule marble, and altars, pedestals, pulpit, bishop's throne and communion rail are of white Carrara marble. While the sixty-eight-foot-high nave is not as lofty as some French ones, the effect is similar, drawing eyes upward toward seventy-five stained-glass windows. F.X. Zettler, a chemist renowned for colors and dyes, created these at Munich's Royal Bavarian Art Institute. His secrets were lost when the Allies bombed Munich during World War II; re-creating these today would be impossible.

CENTRAL PRESBYTERIAN CHURCH

1660 Sherman Street (Uptown)
(303) 839-5500; centraldenver.com
NR

When Reverend A.T. Rankin arrived in Denver in 1860, William Larimer showed him around. They called at the *Rocky Mountain News*, where they found editor/publisher William Byers in danger of being shot by a disgruntled citizen—a not infrequent occurrence—and calmed down the hothead. Rankin had come to organize a Presbyterian congregation; Larimer would become a church trustee. Early Denver churches sought quarters wherever they could, and for a time Presbyterians conducted services on Apollo Hall's second floor, decamping for safer quarters after gunfire from the downstairs bar halted a Sunday sermon. Known initially as First Presbyterian, it became Central Presbyterian in 1882 after Presbyterians divided into "old school" and "new school" factions, with Denver's "new school" devotees adopting Central. In 1878, it built its first permanent home at 18th and Champa

Streets. Jokers called it the "Church of the Seven Spot Diamonds," for black and red slate roof tiles that formed diamond shapes, resembling a playing card—and, appropriately, largely paid for by donations from saloonkeepers and gamblers. As members moved to Capitol Hill, Central Presbyterian followed, buying lots at 17th Avenue and Sherman Street. Having sold the old church, they met for two years at the Broadway Theatre (demolished), designed by their church architect, Frank Edbrooke. Central Presbyterian, completed in 1892, is considered one of his finest works. Built in red Colorado sandstone in Richardsonian Romanesque style, it feels enormous inside and out. His cruciform plan gives it solidity and grandeur, and his tall corner tower with narrow lantern openings competes boldly with the capitol as a standout Capitol Hill landmark.

Central Presbyterian has long associated itself with outreach and charitable causes. It cofounded Presbyterian Hospital (now Presbyterian–St. Luke's), and until 1928, it operated a Railroad Union Mission near Union Station to minister to railroad workers. It also ran the Chinese School in Denver from 1877 to 1919, aiding Chinese immigrants educationally and spiritually.

LORETTO HEIGHTS CAMPUS

3001 South Federal Boulevard (Harvey Park South)

With its 1891 Frank Edbrooke–designed, red sandstone administration building's 160-foot tower dominating southwest Denver's skyline and its collection of Mid-Century Modern structures, the former Loretto Heights College campus is southwest Denver's most important architectural asset. The school dated to 1864, when Father Joseph P. Machebeuf arrived in Denver with three Sisters of Loretto. They opened St. Mary's Academy for girls at 15th and California Streets, then on Denver's edge. As Denver grew up around it, Mother Pancratia Bonfils, worried about the city's corrupting influence, urged establishment of a new school, obtaining forty acres seven miles southwest of town, high on a hill, in 1888. "The view was uninterrupted by any habitation of man," save for Denver's far-distant church steeples and Fort Logan two miles south.

The six-story Loretto Academy included classrooms and dormitories. The school nearly failed during the Panic of 1893. During World War I, it provided military training for women, and in 1918, the Sisters established

Right: Central Presbyterian Church. *Photograph by Ryan Dravitz.*

Below: The Loretto Heights College Administration Building. *Photograph by author.*

Loretto Heights College within the building. The 1920s saw accreditation for the college and construction of a separate dormitory, Pancratia Hall. The academy closed in 1941, and in 1948, the college established a nursing school. In the 1960s and 1970s, it continued innovating, with a Women's Studies Research Center and a University without Walls program; men were accepted beginning in 1970. Enrollment declined, however, and in 1988 the college closed, with Regis College taking over some programs, including nursing. Tokyo-based Teikyo University, building a chain of overseas satellites, bought the campus in 1988 and opened Teikyo Loretto Heights University; renamed in 2009 Colorado Heights University, it closed in 2017. As Teikyo it served international students, bringing a cosmopolitan flavor to campus. As of this writing, Loretto Heights is in transition. A developer is working with neighborhood residents and city planners. Preservationists hope to save important elements, including Edbrooke's Administration Building, his 1911 chapel, Harry Edbrooke's Pancratia Hall, John K. Monroe's Machebeuf Building (student union and cafeteria), G. Meredith Musick's May Bonfils Stanton Theatre, the swimming pool and the cemetery, consecrated in 1912 and hosting the graves of sixty-two Sisters of Loretto.

MASONIC TEMPLE BUILDING

1614 Welton Street (Downtown)
(303) 534-0939; denver5.org
DL, NR

The Order of Ancient, Free and Accepted Masons has been established in Denver longer than any other fraternal group, with its first informal meeting held on November 3, 1858. The first Lodge organized two months later, the first of several. Members came from all social ranks. Jerome Smiley claimed that "secret orders and societies, and fraternal benevolent associations, flourish in Denver to an extent certainly not surpassed…by…any other city of the same size." The reason, he claimed, was that membership "was desirable, if not essential, to…thousands of isolated men seeking to establish themselves in a new, distant and hurrying community" and was "important as a means of forming acquaintances and friendships, of giving or receiving needed aid and comfort in misfortune and distress." Masons knit early Denver together, even working to ensure law and order.

The Masonic Building. *Photograph by Ryan Dravitz.*

As membership grew, Masons formed Masonic Temple Association of Denver to erect a facility that could house several lodges. They engaged 33rd-degree Mason Frank Edbrooke to design a multipurpose structure. Three floors would be leased as shops and offices, with the revenue sustaining upper floors devoted to Masonic ceremonial activities. The Grand Lodge of Colorado A.F. & A.M. laid the cornerstone in 1889, and the temple opened in 1890. A 16th Street entrance led to offices on second and third floors, while Masons entered on Welton through a fifteen-foot-wide, richly carved archway. Ceremonial floors originally featured elaborate leaded and stained-glass windows, but Masons later removed them and filled openings with concrete blocks. These obstructions proved disastrous on March 2, 1984, when a four-alarm arson fire gutted the building and firefighters could not direct water effectively. The Masons had recently sold the building to a developer, who planned renovation. The ceremonial rooms, still in their original, ornate condition, were lost, along with Masonic artifacts. Firefighters saved outer walls, which the construction company supported with trusses until it could clear debris and build a new, steel-supported structure inside.

MOSQUE OF THE EL JEBEL SHRINE

1770 Sherman Street (Uptown)
DL, NR

Shriners, more formally the Ancient Arabic Order of the Nobles of the Mystic Shrine, are 33rd-degree Masons. Denver's chapter, El Jebel ("the Mountain" in Arabic) Shrine, the thirty-ninth established, dates to 1887, and it grew large and wealthy in the late nineteenth and early twentieth centuries. El Jebel commissioned Harold and Viggio Baerresen to design their Shrine and dedicated it in 1907. "Marvelously tasteless," per historian Richard Brettell, the eclectic, Moorish-style building stands as the Baerresens' finest work. The exterior combines elements derived from Islamic architecture—onion domes, a minaret, Venetian arcades—affixed onto a five-story red brick box. The interior is even more eclectic, with each room in a different style, with elements drawn from ancient Egypt, medieval Byzantium, Spain's Alhambra, Japan and other places. The ballroom features painted calligraphy with the architects' names worked into it.

Despite its status as the largest Shrine temple in the country in 1907, by 1924 it was too small for its 5,500 Nobles. El Jebel took over a defunct

Mosque of the El Jebel Shrine, later Rocky Mountain Consistory No. 2. *Photograph by Ryan Dravitz.*

northwest Denver country club, selling the Sherman Street building to another Masonic entity, Rocky Mountain Consistory No. 2. In 1992, this group merged with another and sold the building to the Eulipions, an African American theatrical group, which planned to open a theater and nightclub, with rooftop cabaret. They were undercapitalized and sold it to another group that operated an events center for several years. In 2003, the parking lot was rezoned to allow a 650-foot skyscraper (never built), which would have included renovating the Shrine. In 2006, Donald Trump announced "Trump Tower Denver," which would have been even taller, but nothing came of it. A historic easement owned by Historic Denver Inc. protects the building. Neither the exterior nor the interior, which remains largely as built in 1907, can be changed, regardless of whatever might be built on its parking lot.

REGIS UNIVERSITY

3333 Regis Boulevard (Regis)
(303) 458-4126; regis.edu

In 1877, Italian Jesuit priests founded Las Vegas College in New Mexico. Some years later, Colorado's Bishop Joseph Machebeuf invited the Jesuits to open a school in Colorado, and in 1887, they established Sacred Heart College in Morrison. That town proved too isolated, and neither school was on sound footing. When John Brisben Walker, who was developing Berkeley northwest of Denver, offered the Jesuits fifty acres if they would move their school from Morrison, they accepted, merging Las Vegas College with it. Walker hoped it would attract high-class buyers for his home sites, and to ensure that it appeared substantial, he stipulated that it must be at least 297 feet long, 60 feet high and built of stone. Father Dominic Pantanella, novice Edward Barry and architects Henry Dozier and Alexander Cazin came up with a Second Empire design, specifying rhyolite and sandstone as primary materials; students nicknamed it "the Pink Palace" for its color. From early years, it conducted a combined high school and college; in 1990, the former left the campus for Aurora. The school changed its name in 1921 to Regis College, honoring John Francis Regis, a seventeenth-century Jesuit saint. Regis received accreditation as a four-year college in 1952; it became Regis University in 1991. Initially all male, women began enrolling in 1968. Pope John Paul II visited on

Main Hall, Regis University. *Photograph by author.*

August 12, 1993. President Bill Clinton flew out to meet him, and the two spent an hour together on campus. The school's most famous alum, actor Bill Murray, attended briefly but did not graduate; television journalist Campbell Brown received her BA from Regis.

ST. JOHN'S CATHEDRAL

1313 Clarkson Street (Capitol Hill)
(303) 831-7115; sjcathedral.org
DL, NR

Completed in 1911, this Episcopal cathedral houses another of Denver's oldest congregations. Father John Kehler arrived from Maryland in 1860, establishing St. John's Church in the Wilderness, its name reflecting Denver's isolation. Meeting initially in temporary quarters, the Civil War's outbreak allowed St. John's to take over the abandoned Southern Methodist church at 14th and Arapahoe Streets. In 1879, John Franklin Spalding, missionary bishop of Colorado and Wyoming, established a Cathedral system for Colorado, renaming the church Cathedral of St. John the Evangelist. St. John's naming as the third Episcopal cathedral in the country attested to Denver's new city status. The congregation built a cathedral at 20th and Welton Streets, holding its first services there in November 1881. The dean, H. Martyn Hart, crusader against remnants of Denver's wild and wooly frontier past, worked ecumenically with other spiritual leaders. In 1887, he joined Monsignor William O'Ryan of St. Leo's Roman Catholic, Reverend Myron W. Reed of First Congregational, Rabbi William S. Friedman of Temple Emanuel and Frances Wisebart Jacobs to found Denver Charity Organization, America's first community charity solicitation fund and ancestor of today's United Way, the world's largest privately funded nonprofit charitable organization.

In 1903, an arsonist destroyed the cathedral. Rabbi Friedman allowed St. John's to use Temple Emanuel for Sunday services until St. John's could build its new home. It launched a national architectural competition for its new site at 14th Avenue and Washington Street. New York's Gordon, Tracy and Swartwout won with an English Gothic design, but despite a rather large budget, it could not be fully built with available funds. There was enough money for the nave, which is 185 feet long, 52 feet wide and 65 feet high, and a "temporary" brick chancel. The original central tower, choir and transepts remain unrealized. The cornerstone was laid in 1909, with the first service held in November 1911. Clad in Indiana limestone, two square towers, housing a fifteen-bell carillon, dominate the northern façade. Fifty-one stained-glass windows, including some from the Edward Frampton (London) and Charles J. Connick (Boston) studios, inspire churchgoers. One window, depicting Eve in the Garden of Eden, had to be modified— artists added a decorous rosebush to replace fig leaves that left little to the imagination. Dean Hart, while directing firefighting efforts at the old cathedral, managed to save its carved oak altar, altar screen and reredos, and they grace St. John's today. These came from Oberammergau, Germany, carved by Joseph Mayr. St. John's has always included prominent Denver Episcopalians in its congregation, but despite its reputation as a "society church," it has consistently aided the needy, most recently leasing land across 14th Avenue for one dollar per year to St. Francis Center, which has built St. Francis Apartments at Cathedral Square, providing supportive housing for fifty formerly homeless people. East of the Cathedral, All Souls Walk is the final resting place of U.S. Supreme Court justice Byron White.

TRINITY UNITED METHODIST CHURCH

1820 Broadway (Downtown)
(303) 839-1493; trinityumc.org
DL, NR

In 1859, William Goode and Jacob Adriance established Denver's first organized church, initially called Auraria and Denver City Methodist Episcopal Mission. It conducted services in several spaces, including Henry Brown's store, washed away in 1864's Cherry Creek flood. By 1865, the congregation occupied a red brick Gothic Revival church at 14th and Lawrence Streets, diagonally opposite the residence of prominent congregant John Evans. As the business district expanded and church members moved away, the Lawrence Street Church, as it was called, followed. Buying land at 18th Avenue and Broadway, it hired architect Robert Roeschlaub. The cornerstone was laid in 1887, with the building being completed in 1888. The church, then led by Reverend Henry Augustus Buchtel (later University of Denver chancellor and seventeenth Colorado governor), spared no expense, and the congregation's passion inspired Roeschlaub to create his life's masterpiece in Trinity Methodist Episcopal Church.

Influenced by the Arts and Crafts movement, which rejected machine production for the handmade and natural, Roeschlaub chose Castle Rock rhyolite as the primary material. Rhyolite varies in color, and he carefully specified different rose or blue shades for various design elements; he rusticated the stone, giving the church a handmade appearance. The overall style is Modern or Reformed Gothic, as opposed to earlier nineteenth-century Gothic Revival. Roeschlaub took advantage of the corner site, where two street grids meet, designing a 183-foot, seven-and-a-half-inch-tall spire visible from Tremont Street, 18th Street, Broadway and 18th Avenue. Trinity symbolism is everywhere, even in the octagonal steeple, divided by limestone into three sections. Congregants enter through three Gothic arches, windows are in sets of three and pews feature carved sets of three interlocking rings. Other numerical symbols include twelve spokes of the two rose windows symbolizing Twelve Apostles and Twelve Tribes of Israel, and sixty-six lightbulbs above the organ represent sixty-six books of the Bible. Roeshlaub's Arts and Crafts aesthetic carries over to Trinity's stained-glass windows. Rather than painted glass, their creators, Chicago's George Lewis Healy and Louis J. Millet, utilized colored and textured opalescent

Trinity United Methodist Church. *Photograph by Ryan Dravitz.*

glass for most, giving them a medieval quality. However, the standout work, the west façade's three-panel Resurrection window depicting a welcoming angel, uses painted glass.

Music is important in Methodist services, and this building can serve as a concert hall. Trinity commissioned its organ from Roosevelt Organ Works of New York. Founded by Hilbourne Roosevelt, the firm was then led by his brother Frank (both cousins to Theodore Roosevelt). He produced what was then the largest organ west of the Mississippi and the fourth largest in the United States, its 4,275 pipes occupying a space sixteen feet deep by forty-six feet wide and standing thirty-six feet tall. Its construction took eighteen months, plus five more to ship and install. Sir George Ashdown Audsley of London designed the carved ash wood casing. Trinity's organ is one of only twelve known Roosevelt pipe organs remaining and is the largest nineteenth-century American-built organ still in use. Visitors may take self-guided tours on weekdays during church business hours (check in with the front office), and guided tours are available.

UNIVERSITY OF DENVER

2199 South University Boulevard (University Park)
(303) 871-2000; du.edu

Territorial Governor John Evans founded Colorado Seminary, a Methodist institution, in 1864. It was undercapitalized, closing in 1867. The charter remained active, however, and in 1880 it reopened as University of Denver (DU), a four-year institution; in 1891, it added postgraduate studies. Initially located near 14th and Arapahoe Streets, in the late 1880s the College of Liberal Arts' dean agitated to move away from sinful surroundings. South Denver farmer Rufus "Potato King" Clark donated land and organized neighbors to give also, and the University Park campus was born. Law, medicine, business and library science programs remained downtown; for most of its history, until recently, DU has conducted classes across Denver. The new campus, seven miles from downtown, opened in 1892, with one building, today's University Hall, on 125 acres. DU was nicknamed "Tramway Tech" because male students, who lived downtown due to lack of campus dormitories, commuted to class on streetcars. The Panic of 1893 was not kind to DU, and when Henry Buchtel became chancellor in 1900, it was in danger of shutting down. A talented fundraiser, he soon had DU's finances in healthy shape, with all debts paid by 1906. DU grew significantly after World War II when the GI Bill swelled enrollment to its largest-ever size, nearly thirteen thousand; army surplus Quonset huts erected to ease a space crunch continued in use until the 1970s. In 1970, DU experienced unrest, culminating in May, when after Ohio's Kent State massacre about two thousand students founded "Woodstock West," an encampment protesting the slayings and the Vietnam War. In 1982, DU purchased the Colorado Women's College campus in Park Hill, moving several programs to it; this put DU in financial difficulty again, and all programs have since relocated to University Park.

Daniel L. Richie became chancellor in 1989, serving until 2005. As central as Buchtel was to DU's earlier history, future historians may regard Richie as equally important, transforming DU from a sleepy regional institution to a more academically prominent one. A master fundraiser, he paid off the Colorado Women's College debt and then transformed the campus. He established the Chester M. Alter Arboretum, named for an earlier chancellor, with about 2,100 trees and other plants representing more than four hundred species. He worked with architect Guion Cabell "Cab"

Mary Reed Hall at the University of Denver. *Photograph by author.*

Childress and his successor, Mark Rodgers, to spend $450 million on major new buildings, establishing a new, "uniquely DU" architectural legacy that has enhanced its attractiveness to students. Today, DU enrolls about 5,600 undergraduates and 6,100 postgraduate students.

Topping DU's list of distinguished alumni are journalist Lowell Thomas, best remembered for publicizing T.E. Lawrence ("of Arabia"), and Condoleezza Rice, who served as secretary of state under President George W. Bush. Rice's father was assistant dean at DU when she received her undergraduate degree in 1971, and she earned her PhD in 1981 at DU's Josef Korbel School of International Studies. Rice has described Korbel, the father of Secretary of State Madeline Albright, as a significant figure.

Today's DU leadership is well aware of Evans's legacy of authorizing the 1864 Sand Creek Massacre. John Evans was not only territorial governor but also superintendent of Indian affairs for Colorado Territory. Additionally, the Colorado Third Cavalry's commander, Colonel John Chivington, was a Colorado Seminary trustee. Efforts by DU to engage with descendants of massacre victims continue. In a 2014 report by a John Evans Study Committee, the university concluded that "John Evans's pattern of neglect of his treaty-negotiating duties, his leadership failures, and his reckless decision-making in 1864 combine to clearly demonstrate a significant level of culpability for the Sand Creek Massacre."

Chamberlin Observatory

2930 East Warren Avenue (University Park)
denverastro.org/?page_id=64; admission fee
DL, NR

Technically not on campus but near it in Observatory Park, this 1890 domed observatory was the gift of real estate baron Humphrey B. Chamberlin, an amateur astronomer. Robert Roeschlaub produced a solid, Earth-anchored Richardsonian Romanesque design, in rusticated red sandstone. Astronomy professor and later DU chancellor Herbert A. Howe commissioned the twenty-eight-foot-long Alvan Clark-Saegmuller refracting telescope with twenty-inch aperture and three-hundred-inch focal length, traveling with it from the factory. Although still used by students, it is open to the public on Tuesday and Thursday evenings, when Denver Astronomical Society lecturers give multimedia presentations. Visitors may view the heavens through the telescope, weather permitting.

Evans Chapel

Harper Humanities Gardens between East Evans and East Iliff Avenues
DL, NR

The campus's oldest building, this Gothic Revival chapel was John Evans's memorial to daughter Josephine Evans Elbert, who had died young in 1868. It originally stood on 13th Avenue across from his home (Byers-Evans House) behind Grace Methodist Church. In 1959, DU's law school, then nearby, wanted the land for parking. The chapel was dismantled, its stones numbered, and then reassembled on campus in 1960, on an axis connecting Mary Reed Library with Mount Evans. It may be rented for weddings and other events.

Iliff School of Theology

2323 East Iliff Avenue (University Park)
(800) 678-3360; iliff.edu

The Iliff School of Theology was founded by DU in 1889 to revivify Colorado Seminary's mission but has been independent since 1902; although its campus adjoins DU's, it is not part of it. Formally affiliated with the United Methodist Church, this progressive school also serves other denominations, emphasizing peace, justice and ethics. It is named for Colorado cattle king John Wesley Iliff, who had amassed Colorado's largest-ever ranch. After his death, his widow, Elizabeth, married Bishop Henry White Warren. He founded Iliff School with a bequest provided by Elizabeth. Iliff Hall (NR), its main building, stands opposite DU's University Hall. New York architects Albert W. Fuller and William A. Wheeler designed it in Richardsonian Romanesque style with Gothic elements, utilizing Colorado red sandstone.

Mary Reed Hall

University Boulevard between East Evans and East Iliff Avenues

Harry James Manning designed this 1932 former library in Collegiate Gothic style, replete with patterned red brick, Gothic arches, wrought iron, carved stone details and a 126-foot-high central tower. It replaced an earlier library built with Andrew Carnegie funding. DU converted it to an administration building in 1972 when Penrose Library (now Anderson Academic Commons) opened. Its namesake, Mary Reed, was widow to Verner Zevola Reed, whose fortune had come from Cripple Creek gold mining, oil, ranching and banking.

University Hall

University Boulevard between East Evans and East Iliff Avenues

University Hall opened in 1890. Robert Roeschlaub gave it Richardsonian Romanesque lines rendered in pink Castle Rock rhyolite, not unlike his recently completed Trinity Methodist Church. Initially, it served all campus functions, including a gymnasium, but today it houses student service departments and classrooms.

CITY BEAUTIFUL

In the early 1900s, Denver looked at itself with a critical eye and found things wanting. Streets, lined with telephone, telegraph and streetcar poles, went unpaved, and there was little municipal lighting. Parks were few and lacked playgrounds. Robert Speer decided to change all that. As mayor, he appointed Englishman Henry Read to chair the Art Commission. Read recommended a "civic center," a central green space adjacent to the capitol lined with stately buildings. Civic Center was one of three elements in Speer's City Beautiful program. The second was a parkway system linking existing and new parks. The third was the Mountain Parks System, foothills natural areas linked by new roads. This last element cannot be ascribed entirely to Speer, as the chamber of commerce had been promoting the concept as early as 1901, but Speer actively campaigned for the city charter amendment authorizing mountain parks.

Speer's City Beautiful vision encompassed smaller projects too, including a Municipal Auditorium, a public bathhouse and playgrounds. Denver needed shade; he established a city forester position and staged annual tree giveaways. He grew parkland from 573 acres in 1904 to 1,183 in 1918 and eliminated "Keep Off the Grass" signs. He paved more than three hundred miles of streets and illuminated them with attractive new light standards. His public works department walled-in the flood-prone Cherry Creek, lining it with landscaped automobile drives, which were named for him by a 1910 city council vote. Irked by newspapers' criticisms, Speer founded *Municipal Facts* magazine to promote the benefits of living in his town.

After Speer died, other city leaders built on his legacy. Benjamin Stapleton pushed for the City and County Building and added more parks and mountain parks, including Red Rocks. His postwar successor, Quigg Newton, built a new library and oversaw Denver Art Museum's move to Civic Center. Although the 1960s and 1970s saw Denver turn away from Speer's legacy, Federico Peña's 1983 election represented a return, as Peña, asking voters to "Imagine a Great City," proceeded on multiple fronts, including a new convention center, library and airport; like Speer, he faced criticism. He added to parks and trails and opened up a vast tract along the South Platte for development and beautification by demolishing aging railyard-spanning viaducts. His successor, Wellington Webb, prioritized parkland in his three terms.

CHEESMAN PARK

1599 East 8th Avenue (Cheesman Park)
denvergov.org/content/denvergov/en/denver-parks-and-recreation/parks/find-a-park
DLD, NRD

Today lawns and greenery surrounded by mansions, towers and Denver Botanic Gardens, Cheesman originated as a cemetery, and occasionally workers still discover evidence of it. William Larimer claimed a 160-acre plot two miles southeast of town, on a rise with magnificent mountain views. With partner William Clancey, he founded Mount Prospect Cemetery, Denver's first. Larimer and Clancey claimed the land, but undertaker John Walley, who performed many burials, disputed their claim. In 1865, Walley sold 40 acres to the Catholic diocese, which named its cemetery Mount Calvary. In 1866, Walley sold land east of Mount Calvary to the Hebrew Cemetery. The remaining 80-acre Protestant burial ground forms today's Cheesman Park; Denver Botanic Gardens occupies much of Mount Calvary, and Congress Park occupies the former Jewish section.

The U.S. Land Office decided in 1870 that neither Denver nor Walley owned the land because it had been originally granted to the Arapahos and was then federal property. In 1872, Congress passed a bill selling the acreage to Denver, stipulating it must always be used for burials; Catholics and Jews then obtained their sections from the city. By the 1890s, however, Denver had expanded southeastward, and surrounding land had become valuable. Lacking water, landscaping withered. After Riverside Cemetery opened

The Cheesman Memorial at Cheesman Park. *Photograph by author.*

in 1876, those with means moved deceased relatives to it and bought their own plots; Mount Prospect (now City Cemetery) grew increasingly dreary. Nearby landowners agitated to convert the cemeteries to parks, but Congress had to reverse its earlier law. In 1890, Senator Henry M. Teller spearheaded that successful effort. In gratitude, the city named the land Congress Park.

Naming was easy. Removing five thousand bodies and landscaping a park proved problematic. In 1893, Denver hired Edward McGovern to transport bodies to other cemeteries for reburial, but McGovern performed so poorly that the city fired him. Many corpses remained in place. After the Panic of 1893, the city could not afford further work and mothballed the project. In 1898, Denver hired German-born Reinhard Schuetze as designer. His plan featured curving carriageways, a lily pond and parallel rows of linden trees flanking a Franklin Street parkway. At its highest spot, he proposed a pavilion. Workers soon transformed the former cemetery, and Denverites enjoyed its mountain views. Yet there were no funds for the pavilion. After Speer became mayor, he decided that it could only be built by offering naming rights. There were no takers until 1907, when Walter Cheesman died. An 1861 pioneer, he had grown wealthy through railroads, water and real estate. His family donated $100,000, and Cheesman Park was born. Willis A. Marean and Albert J. Norton designed the Colorado Yule marble Neoclassical pavilion, completed in 1910.

An urban park, Cheesman has seen many uses, and opinions have clashed over its future. The Franklin Street parkway proved too popular with early motorists, and Denver closed it to vehicles. Other park roads became popular drives and remained so for decades. In the 1990s, the city removed the 11th Avenue connecting link between eastern and western roads, hoping to reduce traffic. In 1934, the *Denver Post*, led by Helen Bonfils, began sponsoring summer entertainment, with plays, Broadway musicals and light operas, continuing until 1972. In the 1960s, Cheesman became popular with flower children, and in the 1970s, gay men, many living in Capitol Hill, adopted it for socializing and meeting. This did not sit well with some neighbors or the police department, but since then, relations have improved. Cheesman Park serves today as a starting point for Denver's annual PrideFest Parade and AIDS Walk Colorado. Art historian Vincent Scully considered Cheesman "one of the finest urban spaces in America."

CITY AND COUNTY BUILDING

1437 Bannock Street (Civic Center)
(720) 865-7800; denvergov.org

Facing the capitol across three blocks of lawns and monuments, the City and County Building embodies "combined government," but it took three decades after the legislature authorized consolidation for it to open. Until it did, the old, cramped city hall at 14th and Larimer Streets had to suffice, along with the equally inadequate Denver (formerly Arapahoe) County Courthouse at 16th Street and Court Place. The site was first proposed in the 1907 Frederick MacMonnies Civic Center plan. It took Denver voters until 1923 to authorize land purchase and until 1925 to issue bonds. Groundbreaking occurred in 1929; the building, with quarters for city council, the mayor, courtrooms and city offices, opened on August 1, 1932.

The building proved politically fractious during design and construction. Mayor Benjamin Stapleton was first elected in 1923 and worked at getting it built through his first two terms. Rather than mount an architectural competition, he favored the American Institute of Architects' Colorado chapter's proposal to form Allied Architects, comprising fifteen (later thirty-nine) AIA members. Led by Robert K. Fuller, Allied's Neoclassical design, with Doric-columned wings and central Corinthian-columned temple, surmounted by a slender tower, embraces Civic Center. Architect J.B.B.

Benedict despised the design, opining that it "will stand as a monument to stupidity." The *Denver Post* also disparaged it; publisher Frederick Bonfils was implacably against whatever Stapleton was for, and front-page editorials railed against waste. Mayor George Begole cut the ribbon. He ousted Stapleton in 1931, and even though he was no fan of the project, he felt obligated to see it through. He cut costs wherever he could; statue niches remain empty today, as does the pediment, intended for sculptures depicting city pioneers. Stapleton won again in 1935, serving as mayor until 1947, Denver's longest serving. Begole may have had the last laugh, however: some believe he haunts the building, turning off lights randomly to save money.

Regardless of Benedict's disdain and Begole's penny-pinching, the City and County Building remains Denver's greatest civic ornament. With its Colorado Cotopaxi granite façade and a dozen varieties of stone inside, it celebrates the stonemason's art. The stone was itself political, as specifications called for types quarried elsewhere, contravening a law mandating Colorado materials for government buildings. The city prevailed in court, so the interior features not only Colorado Yule marble but also stone from Tennessee, Vermont and Italy. The nineteen-foot-high main lobby columns were cut from single blocks and are purportedly the world's largest travertine monoliths. The lobby also features Allen True's mural *The Miners' Court* and Gladys Caldwell Fisher's sculpture *Montezuma and the Animals*. The tower, designed by George Koyl of New York's McKim, Mead and White, houses the Speer Memorial Chimes, a carillon donated by Speer's widow, Kate. In 2017, Denver's art program commissioned Kevin T. Padworski to compose an air, which he named "Ascent," to be played on "significant and special days." The city has long celebrated Christmas by illuminating the building with seasonal colors and decorating it festively. Formerly incandescent, the lighting is now LED, allowing different colors throughout the year.

CITY PARK

1700 York Street (City Park)
denvergov.org/content/denvergov/en/denver-parks-and-recreation/parks/find-a-park
DLD, NRD

Today, people associate City Park with its two busy attractions, Denver Zoo and Denver Museum of Nature and Science, but from its 1881 beginning, park planners always intended it to soothe the soul. Denver's largest urban park at 317 acres, City Park's importance to Denverites' health and wellbeing has only grown over time. Former mayor Richard Sopris, "Father of City Park," after becoming Denver's first parks commissioner bought 320 acres of school land, acreage granted by the federal government to provide financial resources for schools; a Colorado law sponsored by Henry Lee enabled the purchase. The waterless site, one mile deep by a half mile wide, was not immediately promising. Sopris engaged civil engineers Henry F. Meryweather and Walter Graves to survey and plan. Familiar with Frederick Law Olmsted and Calvert Vaux's park designs, Meryweather envisioned romantic, curving carriageways and impressive vistas, capitalizing on the eastern end's higher elevation. He converted a natural swamp into today's Duck Lake and had roads and paths graded. Schoolchildren planted trees every Arbor Day, and in 1884, City Ditch began providing irrigation. After Denver hired Reinhard Schuetze, City took on its present form. Schuetze reconceived it into distinct zones, centered on "Big Lake." The active north end featured a zoo and horseracing course. Schuetze reserved a museum site, added lily ponds, planted gardens and placed a circle near the southwest corner, with drives connecting to city streets. Upon Schuetze's 1910 death, Denver hired Frederick Law Olmsted Jr. to refine the plan. Mayor Speer later appointed Saco Rienk DeBoer as Denver's official landscape architect; both recognized Schuetze's genius and did nothing to ruin his work.

City Park is dotted with memorials, statues, buildings and impressive gateways. The 17th Avenue and Fillmore Street Richard Sopris Gateway honors the parks commissioner, Joshua Monti Gateway at Colorado and Montview Boulevards honors a mining millionaire and William McLellan Gateway at York Street and 21st Avenue honors the city councilman who wrote parks legislation. The McLellan originally stood at 18th Avenue but was moved in 1957, when traffic engineers lopped off the park's southwestern corner. Big Lake was renamed for Colorado poet laureate Thomas Hornsby Ferril in 1996; he had once written a poem, "This Lake Is Mine," about it. In 1908, Speer installed an electric fountain designed by Frederic W. Darlington, complete with spectacular lighting, in time for the Democratic National Convention; the fountain and lights, now LED, were replicated in 2008. The twin-towered Pavilion, originally built in 1896 and remodeled in 1929, commands the western shore; it once housed a restaurant and a jail cell for unruly park visitors. Nearby, the floating bandstand (1896) hosted Denver Municipal Band concerts. Near the Pavilion stands a statue of Scottish poet Robert Burns, donated by the Colorado Caledonian Club; three Civil War cannons, placed by the Grand Army of the Republic, guard

The Joseph Addison Thatcher Memorial Fountain in City Park. *Photograph by author.*

the bard. Southwest of Burns, a 2002 memorial honors Martin Luther King Jr. Farther southwest, the 1918 Joseph Addison Thatcher Memorial Fountain, honoring a banker, features an eighteen-foot female *Colorado* surrounded by *Loyalty*, *Learning* and *Love*; Lorado Taft sculpted them. This terminates the two-block Esplanade, envisioned by Schuetze as City Park's primary entrance, completed in 1907. In 1917, Chicago's Edward H. Bennett designed a Dolphin Fountain and Dennis Sullivan Gateway, two forty-foot columns topped by the twelve-foot sculptures by Leo Lentilli, *Mining* and *Agriculture*, for the Colfax Avenue terminus.

North of 23rd Avenue, City Park Golf Course runs to 26th. Opened in 1913, it was Denver's first municipal course and helped popularize golf. The East Denver Golf Club, an African American organization, formed in 1942 and played City Park through the mid-1970s. The course's historic design was reconfigured in 2018–20 to provide a flood-control basin.

CIVIC CENTER

101 West 14th Avenue (Civic Center)
denvergov.org/content/denvergov/en/denver-parks-and-recreation/parks/find-a-park
DLD, NRD

Civic Center covers two city blocks, plus portions of others. It is end point for parades and the setting for public festivals, including Cinco de Mayo, Denver PrideFest, A Taste of Colorado and others. After Municipal Art Commission chair Henry Read suggested a civic center, Denver commissioned urban planner Charles Mulford Robinson to design it. To reconcile downtown's clashing street grids, he proposed a landscaped mall connecting the capitol to Denver County Courthouse at 16th Street and Court Place, with small parks along Colfax Avenue to bring the planned Denver Public Library and U.S. Mint into the composition, which also included a municipal auditorium. Voters rejected this expensive plan, so in 1907 Speer turned to sculptor Frederick MacMonnies. He decided that an east–west axis was best, proposing to level two blocks between Broadway and Bannock Street, from Colfax to 14th Avenues, and reconcile with downtown's grid by adding a triangular block north of Colfax, running to Cleveland Place. To balance this on the south, he would lop corners from two other blocks. From the capitol dome, viewers' eyes would rest on a stately municipal building before rising toward the mountains.

Voters approved funding this time. In 1911, Denver began buying and demolishing buildings. After Speer left office in 1912, the city commissioned Frederick Law Olmsted Jr. to re-plan Civic Center. When Speer returned in 1916, some of Olmsted's elements were already built. He commissioned Edward Bennett for yet another design. Returning to MacMonnies's ideas, Bennett established a secondary, north–south axis aligned with Acoma Street, with major features at each end and a large central fountain where the two axes met; much of his design (*sans* fountain) was realized. Various stakeholders have developed plans to "improve" Civic Center in recent years.

Greek Theater and Colonnade of Civic Benefactors

South end of Civic Center

The Olmsted plan included a concert grove for the central promenade's southern end, within the curve of 14th Avenue, and Bennett's subsequent design placed a theater at the same spot. Speer also envisioned a memorial to donors to Civic Center's construction and other projects; such a monument would inspire others to "Give While You Live," he believed. Both theater and colonnade, built of Turkey Creek sandstone and completed in 1919, are by Willis Marean and Albert Norton. The theater's elevated stage is open in the rear; a retracting glass screen was used to protect performers. Curving colonnades project on either side, wrapping around a sunken oval. Two Allen True murals, depicting a trapper and a prospector, grace the stage's flanking walls. On the theater's two sides, walls feature names of civic benefactors, with space for future names.

McNichols Civic Center Building

144 West Colfax Avenue (Civic Center)
(720) 865-4220; mcnicholsbuilding.com

Civic Center's only enclosed building opened in 1910 as the Denver Public Library; Andrew Carnegie donated about 45 percent of the cost. Designed by New Yorker Albert Randolph Ross in Greek Revival style, fourteen Corinthian columns of Turkey Creek sandstone march across the north façade. It has three floors; the seven-floor south wing housed the library's then-novel open stacks. Marble steps once led to the Colfax-facing main entrance, but after the library relocated in 1955, the city removed them in favor of a sunken entrance at basement level. Remodeling also destroyed many original interior features. The building housed the water board for years; later, as "Annex 3," it accommodated city departments. In the 2000s, Denver's Arts and Venues division rechristened it for former Denver auditor William H. McNichols Sr. and his sons, Stephen McNichols (Colorado governor, 1957–61) and William H. McNichols Jr. (Denver mayor, 1969–83). Today, it functions as cultural center and venue for art and performances.

The MacMonnies, Olmsted and Bennett plans envisioned a twin, ideally an art museum, to balance the library on the south. When the library needed more room after World War II, one thought was to build that twin, connecting it underground to the original, but the library deemed it impracticable. When state government decided to relocate the Colorado History Museum in the 2000s, it also briefly considered the twin idea.

Proctor Bronzes

South-central Civic Center

The two most significant of Civic Center's many sculptures, from both artistic and historical perspectives, are by Alexander Phimister Proctor (1860–1950), who had created statuary for the Chicago World's Fair and had worked with Augustus Saint-Gaudens, master of Beaux-Arts sculpture. *Bucking Bronco* (1920), a cowboy on a bucking horse, is west of the promenade. *On the War Trail* (1922), sited east of it, depicts a spear-carrying Native American warrior astride his horse. Critics consider both to be outstanding examples of Proctor's work. Proctor had spent part of his childhood living nearby.

Voorhies Memorial

North end of Civic Center

Symmetrically balancing the Greek Theater, the Voorhies Memorial serves as gateway between Civic Center and downtown. William and Arthur Fisher modeled the arch and curving colonnade, built of Turkey Creek sandstone and Tennessee marble, after the 1893 Chicago fair's Water Gateway.

Construction funds came from the estate of mining and banking magnate John H.P. Voorhies, an enthusiastic supporter of Speer's Civic Center plans. Until his 1915 death, Voorhies had lived on Cleveland Place directly opposite the site. Denver rerouted Colfax around the memorial so it could be joined to Civic Center. Within the colonnades' embrace, an oval pool features bronze sea lions surmounted by cherubs, spouting water in warmer months. Allen True painted two small murals for the arcade, depicting a bison and an elk.

COLORADO CAPITOL

200 East Colfax Avenue (Capitol Hill)
colorado.com/articles/colorado-history-colorado-state-capitol-denver; free; closed on weekends

Like the U.S. Capitol, Colorado's consists of two symmetrical wings and a central entrance surmounted by a pediment, the whole capped by a dome, in Federal Revival style. Unlike the national one, however, this dome is covered in .999 pure gold, symbolizing Colorado's original source of wealth. The building is 383 feet wide, 313 feet deep and 252 feet tall. Its architect, Elijah E. Myers, also designed the Michigan and Texas capitols, as well as the demolished Arapahoe (later Denver) County Courthouse. Frank Edbrooke later took over as supervising architect.

The capitol's location resulted from real estate speculation. Henry Brown donated ten acres to Colorado Territory in 1868 hoping that a future capitol would enhance property values for his adjacent development on "Brown's Bluff." Construction commenced in 1886, five years after Denver was made permanent capital (beating Golden); it opened in 1894. More than 5 million bricks support exterior walls of gray Colorado granite from Gunnison. Inside, walls are in Colorado Yule marble and Beulah onyx, a variegated pink stone quarried in Beulah, Colorado; all known supplies went into this building. The first two hundred ounces of gold were applied to the original copper dome in 1908. With gold susceptible to weathering, re-gildings occurred in 1950, 1980, 1991 and 2014. In the twenty-first century, Colorado, tapping the State Historical Fund and private money, spent significant sums to repair its cast iron, which had deteriorated.

The west steps feature a marker one mile above sea level. This has moved upward; in 2009, Metropolitan State University surveying students determined that the step just below the top was correct. After entering through the north doors, visitors can take guided tours on weekdays; House, Senate and Supreme Court chambers, restored to their historic splendor, are highlights. Allen True's rotunda murals, captioned by Thomas Hornsby Ferril and painted between 1934 and 1940, illustrate historical themes and Colorado's relationship with water. Climbing to the dome allows for up-close views of sixteen stained-glass windows honoring Colorado historical figures. Along the way, Mr. Brown's Attic, an educational gallery, details the building's history. The only way to visit the dome is to take the tour.

The most impressive of the grounds' many statues and memorials are *Civil War Soldier* (1909), by Civil War veteran Jack Howland, and *The Closing Era*, depicting a slain bison surmounted by a Native American. The University of Denver's Dean Powers sculpted this bronze, which was shown at the 1893 Chicago fair and was meant to raise capital for a much larger stone version (unrealized). The block between Lincoln Street and Broadway is home to the Colorado Veterans Monument, a fifty-foot red sandstone obelisk dedicated in 1990.

DENVER MOUNTAIN PARKS SYSTEM

Various locations
(720) 865-0900; denvergov.org/content/denvergov/en/denver-parks-and-recreation/
parks/mountain-parks; mountainparksfoundation.org
DL, NR (various sites)

The twenty-two accessible parks and twenty-four conservation areas comprising the city-owned Denver Mountain Parks System encompass 14,000 acres across four counties, providing necessary outdoor amenities for Denverites, other Front Range residents and tourists. Impetus for its creation came in 1910 from entrepreneur John Brisben Walker, who owned Red Rocks Park. Tourists tended to gravitate toward Colorado Springs; Walker knew that Denver could not compete without a major draw and promoted his plan for parks spreading across 41,000 acres, connected by well-built and maintained "boulevards." Mayor Speer initially hesitated, worried about political implications of acquiring land far outside city limits. The chamber of commerce and Denver Real Estate Exchange immediately got on board, along with the Motor Club. Businessmen Warwick Downing and Kingsley Pence publicized a Mountain Parks Amendment establishing a mill levy, approved by voters in 1912. The system opened its first park in 1913 and continued buying or receiving donated lands until World War II. Denver hired Frederick Law Olmsted Jr. to make recommendations. After horseback touring between Golden, Morrison and Evergreen, he recommended 41,310 acres of parks, similar to Walker's plan, and proposed two hundred miles of roads; ultimately, while Denver's system includes just 14,000 acres, other park systems—including Jefferson County Open Space, Colorado State Parks, U.S. Forest Service and town park districts—own most other parcels, so Olmsted's plan eventually came to fruition.

Although Denver constructed some facilities, much of the parks' built legacy comes from 1930s New Deal programs, including Civilian Conservation Corps (CCC), Works Progress Administration (WPA) and other agencies. Denver architects, including J.J.B. Benedict and the Fisher brothers, designed picnic shelters and other structures, generally built of logs and stone found on site. The parks vary in size, use and terrain and cover all Front Range ecosystems, including prairie, lower and upper montane, subalpine and alpine tundra. Human activities range from hiking and horseback riding to picnicking, fishing and camping. Mountain Parks suffered from city neglect from the 1970s through the 1990s, but Coloradans have rediscovered them, with 2 million visitors annually. Mayors have pledged reinvigoration, guided by a 2008 master plan and aided by Denver Mountain Parks Foundation. Thanks to Walker, Speer and Olmsted, these parks continue to provide vital respite and relaxation.

DENVER PARKWAY SYSTEM

Thirty-five thoroughfares
DL (eighteen), NR (sixteen)

Although associated with Speer, the parkway idea predates his administration. John Evans championed beautifying parkways in the early 1890s. In 1894, the public works department produced an Edward Rollandet–drafted map, likely influenced by Reinhard Schuetze, showing landscaped parkways linking established and proposed parks, thriftily utilizing existing routes on the grid rather than cutting through diagonally on the Paris/Washington, D.C., model. Although city council adopted it, public opposition and straitened finances following the Panic of 1893 tabled it. Charles Mulford Robinson, hired by Speer's Art Commission, produced a plan based on the 1894 one. Speer ultimately hired Kansas

City landscape architect George Edward Kessler to develop it further. He envisioned "single drive" parkways, with extra-wide tree lawns framing roadways, and "double drive," with twin roadways divided by wide, park-like medians. Work began immediately, and by October 1909, *Municipal Facts* was able to publish the 1909 Adopted Plan, showing completed parkways in east and south Denver; construction would continue through Speer's second term. Some parkways, predominantly in the politically less powerful northwestern quadrant, remained unrealized—the city only built one, on West 46th Avenue linking Rocky Mountain Lake and Berkeley Parks. Later, Saco DeBoer refined the 1909 plan with additional routes and worked to landscape built parkways with stately trees and flowerbeds.

The system's jewels include East 1st Avenue from Downing Street to University Boulevard, East 6th Avenue from Colorado Boulevard to Quebec Street, East 7th Avenue from Williams Street to Colorado Boulevard, East 17th Avenue from Colorado Boulevard to Monaco Street, Monaco Street from Smith Road to 1st Avenue, Montview Boulevard from Colorado Boulevard to Syracuse Street and Speer Boulevard from Interstate 25 to Downing Street. Smaller parkway gems include Bonnie Brae Boulevard from South University Boulevard to South Steele Street, Clermont Street from East 3rd to East 6th Avenues, Forest Street from East 17th Avenue to Montview Boulevard, Richthofen Place from Monaco Parkway to Oneida Street and the Country Club parkways on Franklin, Gilpin and High Streets and East 3rd and East 4th Avenues.

EAST HIGH SCHOOL

1600 City Park Esplanade (City Park); exterior only
(720) 423-8300; east.dpsk12.org
DL

The grandest of Denver's high schools, East is also the oldest, descending from Denver's first 1859 log cabin school; the first East Side High School opened in 1875. It is one of four "directional" high schools and one of three built from a 1923 bond issue, which also provided for junior high and elementary schools. Like other 1920s schools, it follows City Beautiful principles through its park-adjacent siting, as well as by visually terminating 16th Avenue. East formerly occupied a downtown block, between 19th and 20th and Stout and California Streets, in an 1882 Robert Roeschlaub building. He inadvertently gave East its mascot, the Angel, by holding a competition for a model to pose for a cornerstone sculpture. Six-year-old winner Ella Matty had "the face of an angel" (when that East was demolished, the cornerstone was preserved). George Hebard Williamson, an 1893 graduate, designed the new East in 1924; his English Jacobean composition, particularly the 162-foot clock tower, takes inspiration from Philadelphia's Independence Hall. Like other 1923 bond issue schools, it features extensive glazing, due to the school board's mandate that windows should equal 25 percent of floor area. East's colors are red and white. Notable Angels include Judy Collins, Bill Frisell, Jack Swigert, Paul Whiteman, Sidney Sheldon, Philip Bailey, Larry Dunn, Andrew Woolfolk, Harold Lloyd, Hattie McDaniel, Ward Bond, Pam Grier and Don Cheadle. East's most noted faculty member was Justin W. Brierly, who hobnobbed with Beat Generation figures Neal Cassady (who attended East), Jack Kerouac and Allen Ginsberg; Brierly appears, fictionalized ("Denver D. Doll"), in *On the Road*.

MANUAL HIGH SCHOOL

1700 East 28th Avenue (Whittier); exterior only
(720) 423-4661; manual.dpsk12.org

Manual has played a vital role in its students' lives since its 1892 founding. Initially proposed by former governor James Grant, school board member Chester Morey and East Side High School assistant principal Charles Bradley, Manual Training High School was housed at old East for two years until its own facility at East 28th Avenue and Franklin Street opened. Bradley had seen the need for teaching manual arts—metalworking and woodworking for boys and sewing, cooking and domestic arts for girls—alongside preparing students academically. When Manual opened, about two-thirds of students' time was devoted to traditional classwork and one-third to manual arts; the student body was always multiracial. The original building burned down in 1953, replaced by a new facility in 1954. Manual's colors are blue and red, and its athletic teams are Thunderbolts. Its notable alumni include Denver's first two African American mayors, Wellington E. Webb and Michael B. Hancock; "Corky" Gonzales; Ted Conover; Scott Horsley; and Seattle's first African American mayor, Norman Rice.

NORTH HIGH SCHOOL

2960 Speer Boulevard (Highland); exterior only
(720) 423-2700; north.dpsk12.org
DL

Ashland School, North's original name, opened in 1874 in a small all-grades schoolhouse on today's West 29th Avenue, on land donated by the Highland Park Company. A larger William Quayle–designed building replaced the first, and after Denver swallowed the town of Highlands in 1896, upper grades became "North Side High School." The present North opened in 1911, a Beaux-Arts composition by David W. Dryden; 1912 brought a wing for "Manual Training Shops." The lobby features Nordic-themed Art Deco murals painted in 1934 by Frank "Pancho" Gates as part of the New Deal's Public Works of Art Project (PWAP). Originally North, unlike other directional high schools, faced businesses and residences, but in the 1980s, Denver purchased the triangular block across Speer Boulevard to create Viking Park, giving North its City Beautiful setting. North's colors are purple and gold, and its teams are Vikings. Its most famous alum, Israeli prime minister Golda Meir, attended but graduated elsewhere. Other notable alumni include Spring Byington, Burnham and Merrill Hoyt and Rhoda Krasner. North student Margaret Overbeck won a citywide contest to design Denver's official flag, adopted in 1926.

PIONEER MONUMENT

Broadway and West Colfax Avenue, NE corner (Downtown)
DL

The corner of today's Colfax Avenue and Broadway was the terminus of Smoky Hill Trail from Kansas. Occupying the site of an early firehouse at that intersection, this fountain and sculpture assemblage commemorates Colorado's pioneers. Denver Real Estate Exchange members, including some descended from 1858–59 arrivals, launched the project in 1907, dedicating it in 1911. The design, by Beaux-Arts sculptor Frederick MacMonnies, features three sculptures near the base representing "the hunter," "the prospector" and "the pioneer mother"; uppermost a statue of frontiersman Kit Carson rides a prancing horse. MacMonnies had originally intended for this figure to be a nearly nude Indian, but locals refused to pay for it, so he substituted Carson, whose granddaughter participated in the dedication.

RED ROCKS MOUNTAIN PARK AND RED ROCKS AMPHITHEATRE

18300 West Alameda Parkway (Morrison)
(720) 865-2494; redrocksonline.com; friendsofredrocks.org
DL, NR

The most visited and most famous Denver Mountain Park, Red Rocks is also closest to Denver and lowest in elevation, at 6,450 feet. Its geology is part of the Fountain Formation, which includes Boulder's Flatirons and Colorado Springs' Garden of the Gods. During the Cretaceous period (145–65 million years ago), it uplifted and tilted; weathering exposed rocks and oxidized iron, causing their red coloration. Native Americans revered the site and often gathered at its natural amphitheater for ceremonies. Leonard Eicholtz bought Red Rocks in 1878 and built roads, trails and picnic grounds. In 1905, he sold it to John Brisben Walker, who marketed it as "Garden of the Titans" and, recognizing the marvelous acoustics in the amphitheater between Creation Rock and Ship Rock, built a stage. In financial difficulty, he sold off most of the park to John Ross, who donated 530 acres to Denver Mountain Parks in 1927. The city subsequently bought other tracts, bringing total acreage to 868.

Benjamin Stapleton, after regaining the mayoralty in 1935, appointed campaign manager George Ernest Cranmer as manager of improvements and parks, and thanks to Cranmer's ambition to create an amphitheater on par with ancient European ones, Denver possesses one of the world's finest outdoor concert venues. Stapleton frowned on Cranmer using city funds, but with New Deal programs providing CCC and WPA labor, the federal government paid for most of Red Rocks' construction, including the amphitheater, Indian Concession House, roads and parking lots. Cranmer hired architect Burnham Hoyt; his design features continental seating (no center aisle) and juniper-landscaped planter boxes lining both sides. Red Rocks Amphitheatre held its grand opening on June 8, 1941, and since then, countless great musical artists have performed here, many naming it their favorite venue anywhere. In addition to concerts, the amphitheater hosts

Left: The Tivoli-Union Brewery, now Tivoli Student Union. *Photograph by author.*

Below: Larimer Square at night. *Photograph by Ryan Dravitz.*

The Buckhorn Exchange. *Photograph by Ryan Dravitz.*

Rockmount Ranch Wear, interior. *Photograph by author.*

The Denver Gas & Electric Building. *Photograph by Ryan Dravitz.*

Allen Tupper True mural at the Mountain States Telephone and Telegraph Building. *Photograph by author.*

Denver and Rio Grande Western Railroad locomotive at Colorado Railroad Museum. *Photograph by author.*

The Denver Tramway Company Power House, now an outdoor goods store (*center*), and Confluence Park's Shoemaker Plaza. *Photograph by Ryan Dravitz.*

The Brown Palace Hotel. *Photograph by Ryan Dravitz.*

Union Station. *Photograph by Ryan Dravitz.*

Above: Civic Center; the McNichols Civic Center Building and the Voorhies Memorial are at left. *Photograph by Ryan Dravitz.*

Left: The Colorado Senate Chamber. *Photograph by author.*

Above: The Colorado State Capitol. *Photograph by Ryan Dravitz.*

Right: Under the capitol dome. *Photograph by author.*

The Kirkland Museum of Fine & Decorative Art. *Photograph by Ryan Dravitz.*

The City and County Building, illuminated for the Denver Broncos. *Photograph by Ryan Dravitz.*

The Denver Art Museum's Frederic C. Hamilton Building (*left*) and Denver Public Library (*center*). *Photograph by Ryan Dravitz.*

City Park Pavilion and Ferril Lake, with electric fountain. *Photograph by Ryan Dravitz.*

Su Teatro. *Photograph by author.*

La Alma mural by Emanuel Martinez on the La Alma–Lincoln Park Recreation Center. *Photograph by author.*

Red Rocks Amphitheatre. *Photograph by Ryan Dravitz.*

The Denver Performing Arts Complex, with the Helen G. Bonfils Theatre Complex at left and Boettcher Concert Hall at right. *Photograph by Ryan Dravitz.*

The Denver Dry Goods Building. *Photograph by Ryan Dravitz.*

The Dennis Sheedy Mansion. *Photograph by Ryan Dravitz.*

Cathedral Basilica of the Immaculate Conception. *Photograph by Ryan Dravitz.*

The Molly Brown House Museum. *Photograph by Ryan Dravitz.*

The Boettcher Memorial Conservatory at Denver Botanic Gardens. *Photograph by author.*

The Mayan Theatre. *Photograph by Ryan Dravitz.*

The 2700 block of Larimer Street in the River North Arts District. *Photograph by Ryan Dravitz.*

The Bonfils-Lowenstein Theatre, now the Tattered Cover Book Store. *Photograph by Ryan Dravitz.*

The Denver Museum of Nature and Science. *Photograph by Ryan Dravitz.*

Mile High Stadium, formerly Sports Authority Field at Mile High. *Photograph by Ryan Dravitz.*

morning yoga, movie nights and Easter sunrise services. In recent years, Red Rocks has become almost too popular, and Denver Arts and Venues has nearly succumbed to concert promoters' requests to pave over Hoyt's planters for reserved box seating and sell naming rights. In response, a nonprofit organization, Friends of Red Rocks, formed in 1999 to guard the park's legacy, performs monthly volunteer cleanups and prevents over-commercialization.

During the April–October season, check redrocksonline.com for schedules, as amphitheater access is impossible prior to and during concerts. Group tours (fee) are available.

Trading Post

17900 Trading Post Road
(303) 697-4939 x108
DL, NR

Predating the amphitheater and located below it, the Trading Post opened in 1931 as the Indian Concession House. The Pueblo Revival building, designed by W.R. Rosche, complements the setting. It originally housed a dining room, a luncheonette, an "Indian curio" shop and a museum; today, it still serves food and sells souvenirs.

Colorado Music Hall of Fame

17900 Trading Post Road
(303) 320-7599; cmhof.org; free

Opened within the Trading Post in 2011, this small museum seeks to "honor musicians, individuals and organizations who have made outstanding contributions to Colorado's musical legacy, to preserve and protect historical artifacts, and to educate the public regarding everything that's great about Colorado music," per its website. The hall has inducted more than fifty Colorado artists to date, including Glenn Miller, Paul Whiteman, Max Morath, Lannie Garrett, Chris Daniels, Judy Collins, Dianne Reeves, Dan Fogelberg and the man who so loved Colorado he changed his last name, John Denver.

Visitor Center

Top of amphitheater
Free

Interactive educational displays here describe the geological and musical history of Red Rocks, including concert footage. A Performers Hall of Fame display complements the Colorado Music Hall of Fame.

SLOAN'S LAKE PARK

1700 Sheridan Boulevard (Sloan's Lake)
denvergov.org/content/denvergov/en/denver-parks-and-recreation/parks/find-a-park

Legend says that farmer Thomas Sloan created Sloan's Lake by accident in 1866. He dug a well, and the next morning his land was underwater. It may be true; artesian wells dot the area. Denver's second-largest park focuses on the 177-acre lake, which was originally two water bodies; the southeastern portion was Cooper's Lake, joined to Sloan's by the WPA. The park's northwest corner was once Manhattan Beach, an amusement park opened in 1890. Because Manhattan Beach was located in the town of Highlands, it was "dry"; across Sheridan Boulevard in Edgewater, saloons soon sprang up to serve "wet" park-goers. Manhattan Beach went through changes in management and ownership, as well as a name change to Luna Park in 1909, before closing during World War I. The Speer administration began acquiring surrounding land in 1906 to create the public park. Each summer, it hosts Colorado Dragon Boat Festival (www.cdbf.org), a two-day celebration of Asian culture with boat competition, performing and visual arts, an Asian marketplace and Asian foods.

SOUTH HIGH SCHOOL

1700 East Louisiana Avenue (Washington Park); exterior only
(720) 423-6000; denversouth.dpsk12.org
DL

Descending from an Auraria schoolhouse that opened in 1862 and the later Grant School that opened in the town of South Denver in 1890, South, built

South High School. *Photograph by author.*

in 1925, is the youngest of the four directional high school buildings. William and Arthur Fisher, following City Beautiful ideals of incorporating art into architecture, hired sculptor Robert Garrison to adorn the Romanesque Revival building, which is partly based on Milan's Basilica of Sant'Ambrogio and possibly Rome's Basilica of Santa Maria in Cosmedin. Garrison's frieze above the entrance, *Faculty Row*, shows a row of medieval teachers who, new students are told, represent South's earliest instructors. Gargoyles and griffins supervise grounds from fourth-floor perches and at the roof's peak, and zodiac symbols substitute for numerals on tower clocks. The school's mascot used to be the Confederate "Johnny Reb," since replaced by a gargoyle. School colors are purple and white. Notable Rebels include Gene Amole, Stan Brakhage and Congresswoman Diana DeGette.

SOUTH PLATTE RIVER GREENWAY

South Platte River from southern to northern city limits
(303) 455-7109; thegreenwayfoundation.org

Robert Speer was long dead on June 16, 1965, when a wet spring and massive upstream cloudburst combined to deluge Denver with more water than it had ever seen, washing out bridges, destroying businesses and ruining lives, but he would have been pleased by Denver's eventual response. The flood forced Denver to reimagine what the river, long a polluted industrial channel, could be. In 1974, Republican state senator Joe Shoemaker and Democratic Denver mayor William McNichols established the Platte River Development Committee. Two years later, this became the Greenway Foundation, and since then, it and the city have transformed the river into a verdant ribbon linking new parks, providing recreational opportunities, cleaning up pollution sources and reorienting Denver's geography away from its streets. The 10.5-mile Greenway is nucleus of a metropolitan trail system; one can follow the South Platte from Chatfield Reservoir in Douglas County deep into Adams County or enjoy trails that connect along its tributaries, including Bear Creek, Cherry Creek, Sand Creek, Clear Creek and minor streams.

WASHINGTON PARK

701 South Franklin Street (Washington Park)
denvergov.org/content/denvergov/en/denver-parks-and-recreation/parks/find-a-park

Stretching a mile north–south and a quarter mile east–west, with three water bodies, a great lawn, flower gardens, tennis courts, playgrounds, picnic areas, trails and other facilities, Washington Park reigns as Denver's most popular. It is also the only place in Denver where City Ditch is visible—most of its course now runs underground. This man-made stream, completed by John W. Smith in 1867, carried South Platte water from upstream of Littleton through today's east Denver, terminating in City Park; it allowed barren Denver to relieve its brown monotony. Smith also built a reservoir for summer water storage and winter ice harvesting. In 1891, the Town of South Denver bought Andrew Whitehead's farm south of it for parkland. Denver annexed South Denver in 1894, retaining the park idea. In 1898 Reinhard Schuetze began designing the park, and work began in 1902. Washington Park reached its full 160-acre size in 1916.

The reservoir, now Smith Lake, features two historic structures. On the southern shore, the 1913 two-level Boat House designed by J.J.B. Benedict once housed a boat rental concession; the upper level is a picnic shelter. Denver was enamored of electricity, so Benedict outlined it with lightbulbs. On the northwestern shore, the 1911 Arts and Crafts–style Dos Chappell Bathhouse once served swimmers with showers and lockers. After the 1950s polio scare ended swimming, it was unused until converted to office space in the 1990s; it currently houses Volunteers for Outdoor Colorado. Near Smith Lake, facing Franklin Street, a small 1875 wooden house was once occupied by journalist-poet Eugene Field. Editing the *Denver Tribune* between 1881 and

Washington Park after an early autumn snowstorm. *Photograph by Ryan Dravitz.*

1883, Field lived in it when it stood at 317 West Colfax Avenue. In 1927, with demolition immanent, Margaret Brown bought it and paid to move it to the park; it served as Denver Public Library's Eugene Field branch until 1970 and has since been headquarters for the Park People. Near it the *Wynken, Blynken, and Nod* sculpture by Coloradan Mabel Landrum Torrey illustrates Field's famous poem, "The Dutch Lullaby."

South of the Great Lawn, Grasmere Lake is named for an English Lake District village that was home to William Wordsworth and Samuel Taylor Coleridge—its name was chosen in hopes that this part of town would become a center for high culture. It, like Smith Lake, is man-made, completed in 1906. The Martha Washington Mount Vernon Garden, designed by Saco DeBoer in 1926, is nearby. DeBoer, a Dutchman who had migrated to Colorado to cure his tuberculosis, took over landscaping after Schuetze's death, and his garden closely adheres to the Virginia original. DeBoer also designed gardens near Franklin Street and Ohio Avenue, as well as the serene rock garden and pond in the park's northwestern corner. Frederick Olmsted Jr. contributed the grove of evergreens, home to a sculpture, *Colorado Miner*, at Washington Park's northern end.

WEST HIGH SCHOOL

951 Elati Street (La Alma–Lincoln Park); exterior only
(720) 423-5460; westleadershipacademy.dpsk12-org
DL

West's history began with the one-room Eleventh Street School, opened in 1865 and replaced by Central School at West 12th Avenue and Kalamath Street in 1880. With neighborhood population booming, Benjamin Franklin School at West Colfax Avenue and Lipan Street opened in 1884 to augment Central. The first West Side High School opened in 1893 at West 5th Avenue and Fox Street. The current West, designed by William Harry Edwards in Collegiate Gothic style, opened in 1926 opposite Sunken Gardens Park, which then featured a pavilion and pool reflecting West's seven-story central tower. West's famous Singing Christmas Tree, with its choir arranged as a *tannenbaum*, began in 1941. By 1969, West's largely Latino student body had long resented instructors' lack of respect for their culture, and when a social studies teacher reportedly disparaged Hispanic foods, mispronounced students' surnames and said that if they were stupid it was "because their parents are stupid," their anger boiled over into the "West Blowout," a protest inspired by Crusade for Justice leader Rodolfo Gonzales's activism; it was violently suppressed by police after several days. This was seminal for *El Movimiento*, the Chicano movement. West's colors are orange and brown, and its teams are Cowboys. Notable West alumni include Gene Fowler and Mary Coyle Chase.

CITY OF NEIGHBORHOODS

Streetcars provided critical links between downtown and residential districts; without this technology, which arose just when Denver began growing into a city, Denver's physical form would have likely evolved very differently. Denverites have long enjoyed the ability to live in verdant settings and commute to jobs farther away than walking distance. As Denver's fortunes grew, mining and business barons constructed monuments to their wealth, building an impressive legacy of residences that impressed contemporaries and those alive today—at least, the surviving mansions do. Denver lost much of its Victorian residential legacy in the 1950s and 1960s, when the past seemed unimportant. As much as downtown sights impressed visitors, guided tour routes often included Grant Avenue (now Street) and its neighbors Sherman, Pennsylvania and Pearl, the heart of Capitol Hill's millionaire district. This residential chapter covers a representative sampling of Denver's many historic houses and historic districts, which could easily fill an entire book. In fact, they do—several are listed in the bibliography. Thomas J. Noel's *Denver Landmarks and Historic Districts* is particularly useful.

BAKER HISTORIC DISTRICT

West 5th to West Alameda Avenues, Bannock to Fox Streets (Baker)
DLD, NRD

With Denver's largest concentration of Queen Anne houses, including many by the masterful William Lang, Baker could be called Byers, for William Byers and his wife, Elizabeth, who homesteaded the southern portion and in 1874 platted its streets. Or it could be called Dailey, for Byers's business partner, John Lewis Dailey, who homesteaded the northern portion. Instead, it is named for a former school (now Denver Center for International Studies) honoring James Hutchins Baker, an early East High School principal and University of Colorado president. After William A.H. Loveland's Denver Circle Railroad connected it to downtown via Inca Street in 1882, followed by Denver City Railway's extending its Broadway line across Cherry Creek in 1884, Baker, then called "the South Side," grew rapidly, its homes favored by the upper middle class. Following the Panic of 1893, remaining undeveloped lots saw less elaborate Denver Squares (foursquares), classic cottages and Craftsman bungalows built. Two Denver mayors, Marion Van Horn and Thomas McMurray, resided in Baker, and later Mary Coyle Chase, a *Rocky Mountain News* reporter and Pulitzer Prize–winning playwright (*Harvey*, 1944), lived at 532 West 4th Avenue (DL). Middle-class residents largely left after World War II, replaced by the less affluent and nonwhite. Baker was among the first neighborhoods to see young middle-class whites return in the 1970s, intent on renovating houses; gay couples particularly favored Baker.

Broadway emerged early as a commercial strip, thanks to its one-hundred-foot width (originally engineered by Englewood farmer Thomas Skerritt in 1864 as an alternative to Santa Fe Drive) and streetcar lines. The 1906 First Avenue Hotel anchored the district, and both sides of Broadway from 6th Avenue south past Alameda Avenue saw one- and two-story buildings erected, housing every imaginable business, including F.W. Woolworth and J.C. Penney. The 1917 Webber Theatre at 119 South Broadway, recently renovated as a distillery, filled Baker's entertainment needs, as did the 1930 Mayan at 110 Broadway. Today, most businesses—including shops, bars, restaurants and galleries—are locally owned.

BELCARO

3400 Belcaro Drive (Belcaro); exterior only
DL, NR

Designed by New York architect Charles Adams Platt working with locals William and Arthur Fisher, Belcaro (Italian for "beautiful dear one") is possibly Denver's finest house. U.S. Senator Lawrence Cowle Phipps commissioned the 33,123-square-foot, fifty-four-room Georgian Revival mansion, built of red brick with Indiana limestone trim and slate roof, as his personal seat and ornament to the surrounding neighborhood his investment company platted and developed. Phipps was nephew to industrialist Henry Phipps Jr., the second-largest shareholder in friend Andrew Carnegie's steel company, and Lawrence, after rising to treasurer of Carnegie Steel, relocated to Denver in 1901. Phipps's budget benefited from the Depression's onset—both labor and materials were cheaper than they might have been, and total cost was $301,063 (about $5.2 million today) at its 1932 completion. It was furnished with a pipe organ, and paneling in the billiard and dining rooms, purchased in England, predates the United States. On the eight-acre grounds (since reduced to five), Phipps built a glass-roofed tennis house, with its own kitchen, soda fountain and lounge. On the lounge's walls, Allen True painted murals depicting Phipps family members at Winter Park ski area, which they helped develop. After his 1958 death, widow Margaret Rogers Phipps donated the tennis house, and later the mansion, to the University of Denver, which operated it as a conference center. In 2010, DU sold it to software developer/philanthropist Tim Gill, who lives here with his husband. Phipps's two younger sons, Gerald and Allen, became notable businessmen and philanthropists, buying the then-failing Denver Broncos football team in 1964 to prevent its move to Atlanta.

BOSLER HOUSE

3209 West Fairview Place (West Highland); exterior only
DL

One of Denver's few "Territorials" (houses built before statehood), this 1875 mansion at Highland Park's western end was thoroughly restored in 2016–18. Ambrose Bosler, owner of Union Ice Company at Rocky Mountain

Lake and a town of Highlands founder, built the Italianate home, selling it in 1888 to prominent banker William H. Yankee, who sold it in 1915 to Dr. John Henry Tilden. Although an MD, Tilden was far outside his profession's mainstream, counseling patients that their ills, which he lumped together as "toxemia," could be cured only through proper nutrition. He established Tilden Health School, with this house as headquarters, publishing *Philosophy of Health* magazine from it. Harry Edbrooke designed three residential sanatoria, built between 1918 and 1924, on adjacent properties; patients stayed several weeks to learn proper habits. Two of these buildings, with the Bosler House, form the Tilden School for Teaching Health Historic District. Restoration, partly underwritten by the State Historical Fund, replicated the original cupola from early photographs. This came after a previous owner had removed the roof, leaving it open to rain and snow; its survival and rehabilitation is miraculous.

BYERS-EVANS HOUSE

1310 Bannock Street (Civic Center)
(303) 620-4933; historycolordo.org/center-colorado-womens-history-byers-evans-house;
admission fee
DL, NR

Renamed in 2018 as the Center for Colorado Women's History at Byers-Evans House, this house museum's oldest section dates to 1883, with subsequent additions in 1895 and 1905. William and Elizabeth Byers built the Italianate house but lived here only six years before selling to William Gray Evans and his wife, Cornelia, who christened it Victoria. Evans amassed great wealth while living here, from banking, railroads, Denver Gas & Electric Company, Denver Union Water Company and Denver Tramway Company, of which he was president. With his businesses making him a political power player, the *Denver Post* dubbed him "Napoleon Evans," with editorial cartoons depicting him wearing a bicorn hat. The Evans family included children John, Josephine, Margaret and Katherine; later, Evans's mother, Margaret, and sister, Anne, joined them, necessitating a large addition. Anne contributed greatly to Colorado's fine arts, cofounding Central City Opera House Association in 1932. Family members occupied the home until Margaret's 1981 death; heirs donated it to the State Historical Society, which opened it in 1990. The family modernized Victoria only slightly over the years, and more than 90 percent of the furnishings belonged to them.

The Byers-Evans House Museum. *Photograph by Ryan Dravitz.*

COUNTRY CLUB HISTORIC DISTRICT

East 1ˢᵗ to East 4ᵗʰ Avenues, Downing Street to University Boulevard and
East 4ᵗʰ to East 6ᵗʰ Avenues, Race Street to University Boulevard (Country Club)
DLD, partially NRD

Encompassing four subdivisions built from 1905 through the late 1920s (with some lots not occupied until much later), these nearly three hundred residences comprise Denver's densest concentration of mansions. John Reithmann owned land between 4ᵗʰ and 1ˢᵗ Avenues and a larger property south of 1ˢᵗ. After his 1901 death, his executor sold the southern piece to Denver Country Club, a society institution founded in 1887 that had occupied Overland Park and was seeking new quarters. Simultaneously, some club members, including Frederick Ross and Robert Speer, formed Fourth Avenue Realty Company to develop land north of 1ˢᵗ into a luxury neighborhood finer than anything previously attempted in Denver. Hiring William Fisher as planner and architect, the company platted Park Club Place between Downing and Humboldt Streets in 1905 and Country Club

Place between Franklin and High Streets in 1906. While Park Club Place aligns with Denver's grid, Country Club Place is more expansive, with wide landscaped parkways, massive lots and homes set far back. Fisher designed Mediterranean-style gates on 4th Avenue, marking the development's prestige. Fisher encouraged architects to adopt Mediterranean modes, which he deemed appropriate for Denver's sunny climate, but some preferred other styles. The third subdivision, Country Club Annex, platted in 1924 east of Country Club Place and running to University Boulevard, lacks wide parkways, but lots are large and its homes manorial. Developers platted Park Lane Square in 1926, working with Saco DeBoer. He disregarded the grid entirely, creating a romantic English-style layout of curving streets isolated from the city.

Several architects built their own homes in Country Club, including Maurice Biscoe at 320 Humboldt, William Fisher at 110 Franklin and James Sudler at 180 High. Others who worked in Country Club but lived elsewhere included J.J.B. Benedict, Burnham and Merrill Hoyt, Willis Marean, Albert Norton, Frederick Sterner, George Williamson and Temple Hoyne Buell. Mayor Speer lived at 300 Humboldt Street until his 1918 death, and Kate Speer remained there until hers in 1954. The 1931 Tudor Revival mansion at 475 Circle Drive in Park Lane Square, designed by Harry Manning for Mary Reed, widow of Verner Reed, is Country Club's largest mansion. Four massive chimneys dominate its skyline, rising above steep slate roofs and glazed tapestry brick walls. DeBoer designed its grounds.

CROKE-PATTERSON-CAMPBELL MANSION

420 East 11th Avenue (Capitol Hill)
(303) 955-5142; pattersoninn.com
DL, NR

This three-story 1891 Isaac Hodgson–designed home built of Manitou red sandstone takes inspiration from the Loire Valley's Château d'Azay-le-Rideau, completed in 1522. With its steeply raked slate roof and French Renaissance elements, complete with matching carriage house, the mansion is one of Capitol Hill's most distinctive—and is purportedly haunted. Thomas Bernard Croke, former Daniels and Fisher carpet department manager and later owner of his own carpet emporium, flush with a fortune made in railroads, commissioned it. A widower, he decided after six months

Country Club Historic District gateway on 4th Avenue. *Photograph by author.*

The Croke-Patterson-Campbell Mansion, now the Patterson Inn. *Photograph by Ryan Dravitz.*

to trade it for Thomas MacDonald Patterson's ranch, where he ran cattle and bred plants experimentally. *Rocky Mountain News* owner Patterson, who later served as U.S. senator, had emigrated from Ireland during the potato famine and became a successful attorney. A Democrat in a then largely Republican state, he used the *Rocky* to expose corruption, of which there was plenty, and during his ownership its long-running feud with the *Denver Post* began.

One morning in 1907, Patterson left the mansion to walk downtown, encountering *Post* publisher Frederick Bonfils, who physically assaulted him for the *News'* characterization of him as a blackmailer. Patterson's daughter, Margaret, and her husband, Richard C. Campbell, lived in the mansion with him for a time. After Patterson's death, Margaret sold it to a realtor, who leased it to Joe Mann School of Orchestra and later a radio station, ultimately converting it to apartments. Seeing it threatened with demolition in the early 1970s, realtor Mary Rae bought it and had it landmarked. In 2003, architect Brian Higgins bought the mansion, renovated it and opened the Patterson Inn.

CURTIS PARK HISTORIC DISTRICTS

Park Avenue West to Downing Street, Arapahoe to California Streets (Five Points)
curtispark.org/historic-districts
DLDs, NRDs

Comprising forty-four city blocks (or portions), this mostly contiguous set of eight historic districts, designated between 1995 and 2011, form Denver's first suburb, developed from 1868 to 1893. Frederick Ebert and Frank Case saw its potential early. Believing that railroads would transform Denver and that flat terrain would steer growth naturally northeastward, they bought land, platting blocks aligned with downtown streets. To attract residents, they deeded a Curtis Street block as parkland, giving the neighborhood its name. Public transportation arrived on January 2, 1872, when Denver City Railway began horsecar service from 7th and Larimer Streets, across Cherry Creek via Larimer, up 16th to Champa and then out to 27th Street. By this line's tenth birthday, most of Case and Ebert's subdivision had filled in with fine brick homes, with more added up to the Panic of 1893.

Case and Ebert did not market lots to any one class, resulting in a heterogeneous mix of laborers, clerks, schoolteachers, doctors, builders, bankers and entrepreneurs. Those with limited means built small houses,

Italianate homes in Curtis Park Historic Districts. The home at center belonged to John Jay Joslin. *Photograph by author.*

those with more built larger ones and everyone rode the streetcar (later electrified) downtown together. After wealthier residents recovered from 1893, however, most moved away, joining financial peers in Capitol Hill, far from noxious industries clustering north of town. If after 1893 Curtis Park was less economically mixed, it remained diverse. Although most practiced Christianity, many German Jews settled, building synagogues and businesses; Scandinavians were another early group. In the 1920s, both African Americans and Hispanic people began moving in; by the 1940s, both groups represented significant shares of Curtis Park's demography. After World War II, Japanese, freed from internment camps, settled in Curtis Park; Japanese Methodists obtained a vacant church for services.

This diversity seemed foreign to Denverites living elsewhere, perceiving Curtis Park as unsafe and blighted; mortgage lenders redlined it together with Five Points. Denver Housing Authority built projects in 1941 and 1952, and in 1956 rezoning allowed commercial and industrial uses and high-density residential. Yet despite setbacks, Curtis Park remained mostly physically intact. When young, middle-class whites began looking for interesting history at low prices in the 1970s they liked Curtis Park's walking distance from downtown. Young couples, gay and straight, began renovating, and while longtime residents were not always sure about newcomers' motives, they appreciated declines in crime along with beautification. Forty-three low-income homeowners joined with renovators, receiving exterior restorations through Historic Denver Inc.'s FACE Block Rehabilitation Program. Curtis Park, despite gentrification, retains some diversity today, which Denver respected in its 1987 park renaming to Mestizo Curtis Park, formalizing what Chicanos had been calling it for years.

Curtis Park's building stock is old, and because so little was demolished, it comprises one of America's largest concentrations of 1870s and 1880s homes. That period's Italianate style—combining symmetry, evenly spaced windows with carved stone "caps" and generous front porches—is well represented, as is the Queen Anne style, more ornate, with elaborate "gingerbread" trimming. Some designs came from architects' drafting boards, but most did not, produced by talented builders and craftsmen, some utilizing popular pattern books. The oldest Curtis Park house is likely David Crowell's, built in 1873 at 2816 Curtis. Merchant John Jay Joslin and wife Mary built 2915 Champa in the early 1880s, where he remained until 1926. Fellow department store founder David May lived briefly at 2546 Champa before moving to Capitol Hill. Jewish leader Louis Anfenger lived in a large Italianate at 2900 Champa until his 1900 death; he helped found Temple Emanuel and National Jewish Hospital, and his son, Milton, later owned the Denver Bears baseball team. In the 1990s, Dana Crawford lived in it, and when she showed it to architectural critic Vincent Scully, he called it "one of the best examples of Italianate design in the United States." One of Curtis Park's quirkiest houses is at 2418 Stout, designed by John J. Huddart and built in 1891 for railroad conductor Cole Lydon. William A. West, who has worked since the 1970s to ensure Curtis Park's preservation, owns it.

DOUD HOUSE

750 Lafayette Street (Country Club); exterior only
DL, NR

John and Elivera Doud had no idea when they moved into this 1905 Edwin Moorman–designed foursquare that their daughter, Mamie Geneva Doud, would become First Lady of the United States. John Doud had made money in meatpacking and could afford to winter in San Antonio, which is where Mamie met Second Lieutenant Dwight Eisenhower, stationed at Fort Sam

Houston. He proposed on Valentine's Day 1916, and they wed in Denver on July 1. Sources vary as to venue—some say it was 750 Lafayette's living room, while others cite nearby Corona Presbyterian Church, where the Douds worshiped. When Ike won the presidency in 1953, passersby knew when he and Mamie were visiting, which they did frequently, by the Secret Service agent in front.

EAST SEVENTH AVENUE HISTORIC DISTRICT

Logan Street to Colorado Boulevard, 6th to 8th Avenues (narrower east of Steele Street)
(Capitol Hill, Speer, Cheesman Park, Country Club, Congress Park)
DLD

Denver's largest designated landmark district includes 927 buildings, cataloguing the work of sixty-four architects and anonymous builders. The parkway on 7th Avenue runs east from Williams Street, where it connects with Cheesman Park via the full-block Cheesman Esplanade (nicknamed "Little Cheesman") to Colorado Boulevard. Saco DeBoer designed the median, and Frederick Law Olmsted Jr. specified rows of elms on either side. Generally, homes near its western end, from Downing to Logan, are larger and more historic, while those east of York tend to be smaller. Predominant styles include Neoclassical, Colonial Revival and Mediterranean, with houses dating mostly from the twentieth century's first three decades, contemporaneous with municipal City Beautiful efforts.

Three of the most historic homes—Governor's Residence, Grant-Humphreys and Doud House—are discussed elsewhere; what follows samples the district's historic riches. Harry Mellon Rhoads, the longest-tenured newspaper (*Rocky Mountain News*) photographer in American history, lived in a duplex at 636 Logan. At 707 Washington, the 1911 Maurice Biscoe– and Henry Hewitt–designed French Mediterranean built for Cripple Creek gold millionaire Gilbert Wood later belonged to *Denver Post* heiress Helen Bonfils and husband George Somnes—still later, it housed the Mexican Consulate (now condominiums; DL, NR). Adolph Zang constructed his Frederick Eberley–designed mansion at 709 Clarkson in 1904 (DL, NR). The George Louis Bettcher–designed house at 685 Emerson, built in 1900 for mining millionaire Harry Crowe James, later was home to Dr. John Tilden, who vacated the Bosler House after conflicting with his eponymous school's board. In 1967, John and Dana

Crawford bought it after their previous home at 629 Humboldt proved too small to raise four sons. Across the street at 680 Emerson lived their friend David French, who in 1980–82 restored the Daniels and Fisher Tower. Claude Boettcher and his wife, Edna, hired Frederick Sterner for their 1902 Mediterranean home at 701 Emerson, where they lived before buying the former Cheesman mansion in 1923. Ralph L. Carr lived at 747 Downing when he served as governor. American Furniture president Samuel Kohn and wife Aimee lived at 770 High in a 1925 J.J.B. Benedict Mediterranean Revival with landscaping by Saco DeBoer; architect Peter Dominick Jr. later lived there. Attorney and western history enthusiast Fred Mazzula lived at 1930 East 8th Avenue, where he hired Herndon Davis to paint murals in his basement. William Edmund Barrett and wife Christina moved into the 1912 Baerresen Brothers–designed foursquare at 770 York in 1945, where he wrote *The Left Hand of God*, adapted into a Humphrey Bogart movie, and *The Lilies of the Field*, the basis for the 1963 Sidney Poitier film.

GOVERNOR'S RESIDENCE AT BOETTCHER MANSION

400 East 8th Avenue (Capitol Hill)
(303) 866-5344; colorado.gov/pacific/governor-residence; free
DL, NR

This twenty-four-thousand-square-foot, twenty-seven-room Colonial Revival house completed in 1908 is popularly known as the "Governor's Mansion"; Governor Bill Owens changed its name by proclamation in 2003. Walter Cheesman had bought the property late in life. Before his planned Aaron Gove– and Thomas Walsh–designed mansion could rise Cheesman died, and after his widow, Alice, worked with Willis Marean and Albert Norton on the Cheesman Memorial Pavilion, she replaced Gove and Walsh with them. Built of red brick, each façade is different, but all are symmetrical with Neoclassical ornamentation. Alice, daughter Gladys and Gladys's husband, John Evans II, lived here together at first. They planted formal gardens designed by George Kessler and added the Palm Room, a south-facing solarium floored in Colorado Yule marble. John and Gladys eventually moved elsewhere, with Alice living here until her 1923 death. Claude Boettcher, son of Charles, then bought it, and over three decades he and wife Edna hosted high-society events. The

The Governor's Residence at Boettcher Mansion. *Photograph by Ryan Dravitz.*

Boettchers traveled frequently, returning with valuable antiques and art; their most notable addition was a Waterford crystal chandelier that had hung in the White House in 1876, when President Ulysses Grant signed the bill admitting Colorado to the Union. The Boettchers also expanded the Palm Room and altered upstairs rooms. One upstairs bedroom they added came to be called "Charlie's Room," after their son's friend Charles Lindbergh, who frequently stayed in it. Dwight Eisenhower also stayed in the mansion.

Claude and Edna Boettcher died in 1957 and 1958, respectively, and Boettcher Foundation donated it to Colorado as a governor's mansion. Legislators and state employees were reluctant to accept an aging house with potentially high upkeep costs, and regarded the land underneath it as more valuable than the house. After nearly two years of failing to persuade the state, the foundation planned to auction its contents, prior to likely demolition. Governor Stephen McNichols, who had grown up nearby, was happy to accept it, however, once the legislature passed a law, by a single vote, authorizing acceptance. He took up residence in 1960. Most subsequent governors have lived in private quarters upstairs. The home is open for docent-led tours on Tuesday afternoons; check the website.

GRANT-HUMPHREYS MANSION

770 Pennsylvania Street (Capitol Hill); exterior only
(303) 894-2505; historycolorado.org/plan-event/grant-humphreys-mansion-plan-event
DL, NR

Located adjacent to the Governor's Residence and Governor's Park, this forty-two-room Neoclassical mansion with grounds covering nearly a block dates to 1902. Built by former governor (1883–85) and Grant Smelter owner James Benton Grant, the Theodore Boal– and Frederick Harnois–designed house remained in his family after his 1911 death, until his widow sold it in 1917 to oil and mining tycoon Colonel Albert E. Humphreys. Nicknamed "King of the Wildcatters," Humphreys enjoyed the high life, adding a ten-car automobile garage, but became enmeshed in the Harding presidency's Teapot Dome scandal. He died under mysterious circumstances—accident, suicide or murder—on May 8, 1927, just before his scheduled testimony in the trial of former interior secretary Albert Fall, implicated in Teapot Dome. In 1976, his son Ira Boyd Humphreys died, leaving the property to the state historical society, which still owns it, making it available for events. The house was one of the first large Denver mansions to employ terra-cotta ornamentation instead of carved stone, and its western front features a two-story portico supported by four Corinthian columns of this material.

HILL MANSION

969 Sherman Street (Capitol Hill); exterior only
DL, NR

Named the Crawford Hill Mansion, this twenty-two-room, seventeen-thousand-square-foot 1906 French Revival edifice by Theodore Boal and Frederick Harnois should be called the Louise Hill Mansion, as former Memphis belle Louise Bethell Sneed Hill was far more outgoing and influential than her quiet husband. Crawford's father, Senator Nathaniel P. Hill, had arrived in Colorado in 1865, developing its smelting industry; both father and son later owned the *Denver Republican* newspaper. Louise adored the spotlight, and after her 1895 marriage to Crawford, she became Denver's answer to Mrs. Caroline Astor, whose ballroom famously

The Crawford
Hill Mansion.
*Photograph by
Ryan Dravitz.*

held four hundred people, inspiring the "Four Hundred" list of New York society. Louise could seat thirty-six women in her ballroom for whist games, at nine tables of four, and these became known as the "Sacred Thirty-Six," Denver's first A-list. In 1908, she formalized it by publishing *Who's Who in Denver Society*, the city's first *Blue Book*, with her portrait, captioned "Arbiter of Denver Society," as its frontispiece. In 1911, she hosted President William Howard Taft. During a visit to England, Louise was presented to King Edward VII.

In about 1914, Louise met and was captivated by one of Crawford's business acquaintances, Bulkeley Wells. The two commenced an affair, apparently with Crawford's tacit acceptance. Louise commissioned a large portrait of Wells, far larger than her husband's, to hang in her entry. In 1918, Wells's wife divorced him, claiming desertion, and four years later, Crawford died, freeing up Louise to marry her paramour. Instead, Wells married a younger woman rather than fifty-eight-year-old Louise. Stung by his sudden rejection, Louise vowed revenge. His main financial resource was Harry Payne Whitney of the New York Whitneys, husband to Gertrude Vanderbilt, and Louise convinced him to withdraw his backing. Unable to rebuild his fortune, Wells shot himself in 1931. Louise continued her reign atop Denver's social world, moving into the Brown Palace in 1944. She died in 1955, and heirs sold the house to the Town Club, a Jewish organization that occupied it until disbanding in 1989. In 1990, a law firm renovated it for use as offices.

HUMBOLDT ISLAND HISTORIC DISTRICT

Humboldt Street between East 10th and East 12th Avenues (Cheesman Park)
DLD, NRD

Denver's second designated historic district consists of twenty-six homes lining two Humboldt blocks. They date from 1895 to the 1920s, and while styles vary, they share a common characteristic: conservative formality reflecting Denver's maturation during the City Beautiful era. The word *Island* came into general use in the 1960s, when appalled residents watched developers demolishing nearby mansions, most infamously the Leopold H. Guldman/Frederick G. Bonfils residence at 10th Avenue and Humboldt. These historically minded homeowners lobbied Denver to establish the district in 1972.

The largest house at more than sixteen thousand square feet, the Willis Marean– and Albert Norton–designed Stoiberhof at 1022, dates to 1907. Edward G. Stoiber had made his mining fortune in Silverton, where he met and married Lena Allen. In Silverton, she had been gossiped about as possibly a former prostitute, and these rumors followed her to Denver. In response, she erected a twelve-foot wall around her property to shut out society. Her husband died during construction, and she married lumber baron Hugh Rood, who went down on the *Titanic*. Stoiber later sold it to Verner and Mary Reed, who once hosted John D. Rockefeller Jr. here. After Vernor's death, she sold Stoiberhof to Albert Humphreys Jr., who was married to Ruth Boettcher, Charles Boettcher's daughter and member of the Sacred Thirty-Six.

The Sweet-Miller House at 1075 (Frederick Sterner and George Williamson, 1906) was home to Governor William Ellery Sweet, a one-term (1923–25) Democrat who lost reelection to Republican Clarence Morley, a virulently anti-Catholic Ku Klux Klan member. Harry Heye Tammen, co-publisher of the *Denver Post*, built his Edwin Moorman–designed home next door at 1061 in 1907. Sweet—no fan of the sensationalistic, often lurid *Post*—did not fancy Tammen as a potential neighbor and tried to keep him out. Tammen, who also owned the Sells-Floto Circus, threatened to build an elephant barn instead, quieting Sweet.

MOLLY BROWN HOUSE MUSEUM

1340 Pennsylvania Street (Capitol Hill)
(303) 832-4092; mollybrown.org; admission fee
DL

Debbie Reynolds and Kathy Bates have portrayed Molly Brown in movies (1964's *The Unsinkable Molly Brown* and 1997's *Titanic*), but Margaret Tobin Brown was never called "Molly" during her lifetime—she was always Mrs. J.J. Brown. Meredith Willson and Richard Morris decided that Molly sounded more fun than Margaret when they created the 1960 Broadway musical that became the 1964 movie, and "Molly" has stuck. Perhaps it is well that it did, as when this house was threatened with demolition in 1970, the musical's popularity made it easier to build awareness and momentum toward saving it.

Born in Hannibal, Missouri, to Irish immigrants, Margaret came to Leadville in 1885 at age eighteen. There she met and married mining engineer James Joseph Brown. In 1893, the Browns came into sudden wealth when J.J.'s work at Little Jonny Mine resulted in a major gold strike. In 1894, they and their two children relocated to this 1889 house, purchasing it from original owners, Isaac and Mary Large. Architect William Lang combined Queen Anne and Richardsonian Romanesque styles in pink and gray rusticated rhyolite. Inside, the house is restored to its 1910 appearance, using photographs the Browns had taken for posterity that year.

Margaret, with her Irish roots, was not popular with Denver's elite; Louise Hill's Sacred Thirty-Six parties excluded her. Yet she found ways of making impacts locally, nationally and internationally. Locally, she partnered with Judge Benjamin Lindsey to create Denver's first-in-the-nation juvenile justice system. She cofounded Denver Dumb Friends League for animal adoption, and she helped fund the Cathedral of the Immaculate Conception. She ran for U.S. Senate six years before women's suffrage became official nationally. Margaret was Denver's first historic preservationist when she bought Eugene Field's cottage and moved it to Washington Park. She negotiated with John D. Rockefeller for coal miners' rights after the 1914 Ludlow Massacre. Frequently traveling, she made friends among European elites and learned several languages. France later awarded her the *Légion d'Honneur* for her Great War volunteer work.

Brown entered national consciousness when she survived the 1912 sinking of the RMS *Titanic*. After assisting people into lifeboats, she was persuaded to join Lifeboat 6. She strongly urged its quartermaster to return to where *Titanic* had sunk to search for survivors. After rescue by RMS *Carpathia* and arrival in New York, she created a survivors committee to raise funds for steerage passengers traveling as immigrants. Gene Fowler popularized her story in *Timberline* (1933), his not terribly factual history of the *Denver Post*, likely inspiring the Broadway musical. Caroline Bancroft later published a semifictional biography, adding to the mythology. After Margaret died in 1932, the home served as boardinghouse, apartment house and home for wayward girls until Historic Denver Inc. formed in 1970 to acquire it and open the museum. In addition to tours, the museum offers special events.

MONTCLAIR HISTORIC DISTRICT

Olive and Oneida Streets between East 7ᵗʰ and East 12ᵗʰ Avenues
DLD

Baron Walter B. von Richthofen came to Denver in the 1870s; pleased to find many Germans living here, he stayed. In 1885, he and Matthias Cochrane established Montclair Town and Improvement Company to build a suburb five miles east of downtown. Cochrane named it for his native Montclair, New Jersey, and the baron, despite its French etymology, agreed to it—five hundred feet higher than downtown, the site boasted mountain views and clear air. Richthofen, uncle to World War I flying ace the "Red Baron" Manfred von Richthofen, established a moral atmosphere, even prohibiting vulgar language. To attract wealthier families, he stipulated that houses must be three stories high and their designs subject to approval. The isolated town, incorporated in 1888, required transportation, so the developers established horse-drawn carriage service until a streetcar line reached Montclair. Growth was slow, with about one house per block, until the 1893 Panic ended development entirely. Richthofen regrouped, marketing Montclair to tuberculosis sufferers. He announced a "Colorado Carlsbad" spa, which never left the drawing board, and died in 1898 of appendicitis. Denver annexed Montclair in 1902.

In 1901, Baroness Louise built Richthofen Fountain at Richthofen Parkway and Oneida Street, memorializing the baron; Montclair mayor Harlan Thomas designed it. Between 1907 and 1911, Charles Kittredge and Dennis Tirsway built several "TB houses" in Montclair, with screened porches, large windows and open floorplans for superior air circulation,

The Montclair Civic Building ("the Molkery"). *Photograph by Ryan Dravitz.*

thought to aid in tuberculosis recovery. Four of these survive, at 928, 940 and 956 Olive and 791 Newport. Montclair Civic Building (6820 East 12th Avenue; DL, NR) sits in Montclair Park. Designed by Alexander Cazin, Richthofen built this around 1888 to serve as cattle barn, dairy, lodging, restaurant and sanatorium. The first two floors are of Castle Rock rhyolite, with wooden construction above. Dubbed Montclair Molkery (milk house) and Hotel, it offered fresh milk for the "milk cure" and sunny verandas. In 1908, the city bought it, enclosed the porches and opened it as Denver's first community center. After a period of disuse, the city renovated it in 2004, reopening the porches.

Montclair's crown jewel is the baron's 1887 residence, Richthofen Castle (7020 East 12th Avenue; DL, NR). Cazin designed it as a German castle built of rhyolite, complete with three-story crenelated turrets and a wall-mounted bust of twelfth-century Holy Roman Emperor Frederick Barbarossa. Richthofen filled it with tapestries and artwork, but his wife found it isolated and bleak. After his death, in 1903 mining equipment manufacturer Edwin Hendrie bought it and, in 1910, hired Maurice Biscoe to design a west wing and generally soften its lines. Biscoe's addition, along with another in 1924 by J.J.B. Benedict, added English Tudor elements to its Germanic character; with these additions, the home now boasts thirty-eight rooms.

MORGAN'S ADDITION HISTORIC DISTRICT

East 8th Avenue to Denver Botanic Gardens, York Street to Cheesman Park (Cheesman Park)
DLD

These forty-five homes by Denver's best architects practicing between 1906 and 1930—including several by J.J.B. Benedict, William and Arthur Fisher, Maurice Biscoe, Aaron Gove and Thomas Walsh and Burnham Hoyt—fill the southern twenty acres of onetime Mount Calvary Cemetery. Samuel P. Morgan platted the neighborhood after buying land from the Catholic diocese in 1887, a transaction that proved controversial, as the city had donated the property as a burying ground. Denver filed suit against Morgan and the diocese, with the U.S. Supreme Court ruling in Morgan's favor in 1903. After Cheesman Park's completion, its high elevation and distance from downtown appealed greatly to the younger generation of blue bloods. One house is no longer residential: the 1926 Benedict-designed Richard Campbell mansion at 909 York (DL). In 1958, Ruth Porter Waring, living in another Benedict house next door at 910 Gaylord Street, bought it and donated it to Denver Botanic Gardens, then beginning to prepare Mount Calvary's northern twenty acres as its new home. The 1917 Gove and Walsh Georgian Revival design at 2109 East 9th Avenue (DL) was built for Great Western Sugar Company president William Lloyd Petrikin.

POTTER HIGHLANDS HISTORIC DISTRICT

Zuni Street to Federal Boulevard, West 32nd to West 38th Avenues (Highland)
DLD, NRD

Potter Highlands is named for First Baptist Church's founding pastor, Reverend Walter McDuffie Potter, who homesteaded it in 1863. He died in 1866, and his sister, Lucy, contested with both First Baptist and Boston-based Home Missionary Society for title. By the early 1870s, the land, surrounded by new subdivisions, was too valuable not to develop, and in 1872, J.E. Ayers and Henri Foster bought and platted it into thirty-six square blocks with houses fronting on all four sides, each block containing an interior lot where residents could create common gardens. In 1875, Foster and others, including Denver and Rio Grande Railroad founder General William Jackson Palmer and his business partner, Dr. William A. Bell, incorporated

The Dr. James J. and Ruth Porter Waring Mansion, Morgan's Addition, designed by Jules Jacques Benoit Benedict. *Photograph by author.*

The John Mouat Mansion, now the Lumber Baron Inn. *Photograph by author.*

the town of Highlands, encompassing this and other subdivisions, ultimately stretching from West Colfax to West 38th Avenues, from Zuni Street to Sheridan Boulevard. Highlands, where churchgoing, temperate citizens held themselves superior to Denver's supposed sinners, merged with Denver in 1896 after the 1893 Panic destroyed its financial viability.

Potter Highlands' oldest structure is Henri Foster's 1874 masonry house at 2533 West 32nd Avenue (DL). Foster worked closely with Palmer and Bell not only on founding Highlands but also on their land development, Highland Park, platted in the picturesque enclave style with romantically curving thoroughfares, south of West 32nd Avenue between Zuni and Federal Boulevard; today, their subdivision is informally called Scottish Highlands for its Caledonian-named streets, including Caithness, Argyle and Fife.

John Mouat's three-story, ten-thousand-square-foot residence at 2555 West 37th Avenue is Potter Highlands' largest. Lumber miller Mouat ("mow-it") was president of North Side Building and Loan. He used the house as sales tool, inviting customers to see how he used various woods, including walnut, oak, sycamore and cherry, to trim rooms; the third floor contains a ballroom. After Mouat sold it, the mansion housed a business school and, later, apartments. It deteriorated, and in 1970, two young women were murdered, a still-unsolved case. In 1991, Denver condemned it, but Walt Kelly saw its potential. He bought it, spent a fortune on restoration and won a National Trust for Historic Preservation award. He opened it as the Lumber Baron Inn; it has since changed hands but continues operating. Longtime Denverites will recognize the three-dimensional mirrored metal star that rests atop the corner tower as a relic from Celebrity Sports Center's sign on South Colorado Boulevard.

SHANGRI-LA

4150 East Shangri-La Drive (Hilltop); exterior only

Denver's finest example of residential Streamline Moderne, this 7,474-square-foot home, completed in 1938 for movie theater mogul Harry E. Huffman and wife Christine, is Raymond Harry Ervin's design. However, Ervin based his work, which also incorporates Art Deco elements, on that of Stephen Goosson, Oscar-winning art director of Frank Capra's 1937 Columbia Pictures film *Lost Horizon*. The Huffmans had loved it, and Harry, with his Hollywood connections, obtained Goosson's plans for its lamasery of the High Lama, set in the idyllic valley of Shangri-La in Tibet's Kunlun Mountains. With three wings and large main floor rooms, it was built for entertaining, and the Huffmans' guests delighted in its glamour. Huffman had bought the land from Franklin Burns, whose will donated the triangular plot across Leetsdale Drive from Shangri-La to Denver for a park (which bears his name), thus preserving the view. Huffman, originally a pharmacist, opened the Bide-a-Wee movie theater on West Colfax Avenue in 1909 and eventually owned or managed several Denver theaters, including the Bluebird, Broadway, Paramount, Tabor, American, Rialto and others. In the 1950s, he briefly owned KLZ Radio, establishing KLZ-TV, now KMGH-TV, before selling them. Huffman died in 1969, and in 1974, philanthropists Barry and Arlene Hirschfeld bought Shangri-La.

SHEEDY MANSION

1115 Grant Street (Capitol Hill); exterior only
DL, NR

Most Grant Street "Millionaire's Row" mansions are gone, lost to twentieth-century "progress" imperatives and neglect, but some remain, including this 1892 three-story red brick behemoth built by Dennis Sheedy. Architect E.T. Carr took advantage of its corner setting by gracing it with a sweeping first-floor veranda and round corner tower. Sheedy engaged carpenter John Joseph Queree for fine woodwork and custom furniture, each room featuring a different species. By 1892, Irish immigrant Sheedy was vice-president and part owner of Colorado National Bank and proprietor of Globe Smelter. In 1893, he and bank president Charles Kountze won at auction the assets of McNamara Dry Goods after it went bankrupt; in May 1894, they renamed it The Denver Dry Goods Company. After Sheedy's 1923 death, his widow sold the mansion, which became the Fine Arts Building, housing music studios and small apartments for music teachers; later, Helen Bonfils assumed its management. In the 1970s, new owners converted the house to office space.

DIVERSE DENVER

The Cheyennes, Arapahos and Utes were here first. Traditionally, Denver's historiography concentrated on those who displaced them: whites, mainly Protestant. That has begun to change, as stories of the nonwhite, non–northern European, non-male and non-heterosexual have begun to be appreciated for their importance to Denver's story. Formerly enslaved African Americans came simultaneously with whites, including Barney Ford, who conducted thriving hospitality businesses. Denver was not a major destination during the Great Migration, but some came, and Five Points became known nationally for its rich African American cultural scene, inspiring Jack Kerouac to write in *On the Road*, "At lilac evening I walked with every muscle aching among the lights of 27th and Welton in the Denver colored section, wishing I were a Negro, feeling that the best the white world had offered was not enough ecstasy for me, not enough life, joy, kicks, darkness, music, not enough night."

How Denver's African Americans felt about the white Kerouac (or his fictional alter ego, Sal Paradise) wandering their neighborhood is not recorded. What is recorded is a legacy of discrimination, countered by efforts to fight back, including a 1932 incident when African Americans attempted to swim at Washington Park and were attacked by a mob of angry whites. The Denver Dry Goods Company only began employing African American sales clerks in 1962, after the Congress of Racial Equality picketed. These are just two examples; for decades, Denver's whites kept African Americans confined to Five Points, encountering them infrequently. In the early 1920s, the Ku Klux Klan thrived, its membership including Denver's mayor and Colorado's governor.

Colorado's mines attracted Cornish and Welsh, with many settling in Denver. Germans also arrived in the 1860s. With railroads came workers to build and operate them: Irish and Chinese at first, followed by Italians, who settled in "the Bottoms" near the South Platte before climbing the hill to populate North Denver. Chinese clustered in Lower Downtown's "Hop Alley," dispersing after 1880s anti-Chinese riots. Poles, Slovenes, Lithuanians and Russians settled in Globeville, employed by Denver's three smelters—dirty work that shortened lives. Denver's Greeks eventually numbered enough to support a Greek Orthodox Metropolis. German Jews arrived early, many forming a merchant class and mixing within non-Jewish neighborhoods; in the 1880s, Russian and eastern European Jews followed, clustering along West Colfax Avenue, opening yeshivas, synagogues and mikvehs. Japanese and Koreans have long resided in Denver; many early Japanese businesses clustered near today's Sakura Square. Vietnamese refugees arrived after South Vietnam's 1975 collapse, opening businesses and restaurants along South Federal Boulevard and West Alameda Avenue. More recently, Denverites' cosmopolitanism and generally welcoming attitudes have embraced people from Africa, the Americas, the Middle East and southern and eastern Asia. Due to Denver's higher housing costs, Aurora has attracted many of the newest immigrants.

Today, Denver's largest ethnic group—self-identifying as Hispanic, Mexican American, Latino, Mestizo or Chicano—began small. Although Colorado was once part of the Spanish empire, no European ever lived permanently in Denver until 1858. Early Denver attracted migrants from New Mexico and the San Luis Valley, but they remained few until the twentieth century. Colorado's sugar beets and other crops attracted seasonal workers, and some began living permanently in Auraria and Lincoln Park. More have since arrived, residing in North Denver, southwest Denver and, most recently Globeville, Elyria, Swansea and suburbs. Hispanic communities lacked political power, but in the 1960s, Rodolfo "Corky" Gonzales founded Crusade for Justice, combining cultural expression with civil rights organizing. Today, Hispanic elected officials are not uncommon. Beginning also in the 1960s, Chicano artists celebrated culture and educated people through elaborate wall murals in La Alma–Lincoln Park and other neighborhoods. Some were suppressed, but more recently, the larger Denver community has come to appreciate the murals for their artistry and cultural impact.

ARTS DISTRICT ON SANTA FE

Santa Fe Drive between 5th and 12th Avenues (La Alma–Lincoln Park)
(720) 773-2373; denverartsdistrict.org; lincolnparkneighborhood.org

South of Colfax Avenue and west of Cherry Creek, Lincoln Park is one of Denver's oldest neighborhoods and the heart of the West Side. Early on, it housed Denver's working class, who favored its proximity to jobs at Denver and Rio Grande Western Railroad's Burnham Yards and industries that developed along the South Platte. While Lincoln Park's early inhabitants were ethnically mixed, many of them immigrants, it evolved into a largely Latino community, with waves following the 1910–20 Mexican Revolution and after DURA demolished Auraria in the 1970s. In the 1960s and 1970s, Chicano activists began calling the park on Mariposa Street "La Alma Park" ("spirit" or "soul") instead of Lincoln Park, and in 2013, city council formally respected this by designating the neighborhood and park as La Alma–Lincoln Park.

The neighborhood's main drag has always been Santa Fe Drive; prior to Interstate 25's construction, it was the primary route south to New Mexico. In the 1870s and 1880s, Santa Fe developed into a commercial strip with shops, services, cafés and other businesses interspersed with houses, which later saw storefronts added. In the twentieth century, movie theaters and automotive businesses opened. Santa Fe thrived until the 1950s, when Denver's inner-city neighborhoods lost population and people with means moved away. By 1969, transportation planners hoped to turn Santa Fe Drive into "Columbine Freeway," but community protests led by Chicano activists scuttled the plan, saving Santa Fe Drive and La Alma–Lincoln Park from ruination. In the early twenty-first century, Santa Fe Drive saw numerous art galleries open, several relocating from the more expensive LoDo, where they had previously concentrated. In 2003, the nonprofit Art District on Santa Fe formed, promoting the concentration of arts and artists and launching a popular First Friday gallery walk.

Byers Library

675 Santa Fe Drive (La Alma–Lincoln Park)
(720) 865-0160; denverlibrary.org/content/byers-branch-library
DL

Opened in 1918 as part of Denver's second wave of Andrew Carnegie–funded libraries, the Byers branch, DPL's smallest, is named for William Byers. Designed by Ernest and Lester Varian, its architecture is Mediterranean, blending well with Santa Fe Drive's several buildings inspired by Hispanic styles. DPL threatened to close Byers three times, in 1952, 1979 and most recently 2011. Each time, neighborhood activists and politicians fought to keep it open. Byers Library has responded to La Alma–Lincoln Park's particular needs by conducting adult literacy programs and stocking books and media in Spanish. In 1975, Denver artist Carlota Espinoza painted a twenty-foot mural behind the checkout desk, *Pasado Presente, Futuro*, a panorama of Hispanic history.

Museo de Las Americas

861 Santa Fe Drive (La Alma–Lincoln Park)
(303) 571-4401; museo.org; admission fee

Founded by Jose Aguayo and a group of community members in 1991, Museo de las Americas, the Rocky Mountain region's premier Latino art museum, opened in 1994 in a twelve-thousand-square-foot space. In addition to frequent shows by contemporary Latino artists, the *museo* holds more than 3,500 artworks, including the Irving and Eleanor Tragen Collection of Latin American Folk Art, and more than one thousand volumes on Latin American art, history and culture in its basement library. The *museo* runs educational programs, including Sin Fronteras (traveling exhibitions), Los Jovenes Leadership Lab (leadership building through art and technology for young teens), Culture Lab (multicultural professional teacher training) and summer cultural camps for children.

Su Teatro Cultural and Performing Arts Center

721 Santa Fe Drive (La Alma–Lincoln Park)
(303) 296-0219; suteatro.org; admission fee

As America's third-oldest Chicano theater, Su Teatro ("Your Theater") was formed in 1971 at University of Colorado–Denver when drama students broke away from standard forms and repertory to present politically charged original short plays and skits to engender social justice and empower Chicano audiences. In the 1980s, it began presenting full-length original plays that continue to rouse audiences. Su Teatro and longtime executive artistic director Tony Garcia have won many awards and national reputations, with productions playing at New York's Public Theater, San Antonio's Guadalupe Cultural Arts Center and Los Angeles's Plaza de la Raza. It bought its first permanent home, the former Elyria School, in northeast Denver in 1989, opening El Centro Su Teatro as an arts center, hosting educational programs and arts festivals along with plays. These continue at its current home; Su Teatro hosts an annual Chicano Music Festival (with Chicano Music Hall of Fame Awards) and the XicanIndie Film Festival, screening Chicano independent films and foreign fare.

In 2010, Su Teatro bought the former Denver Civic Theatre. Producer Henry Lowenstein had founded the Civic in 1993 after his namesake community theater, formerly Bonfils Memorial Theatre on East Colfax, closed in 1986. He honored community theater tradition by re-creating Denver Civic Theatre, ancestor to the Bonfils. Lowenstein remodeled the onetime Cameron Theater, a cinema built by Fred Cameron in 1921, creating two spaces, a 322-seat proscenium theater (now Martinez Performing Arts Hall) and a 134-seat black box (now Frank Trujillo Salon de Arte). Su Teatro has kept Denver Civic Theatre's name on the façade and marquee, engaging Chicano artist and Metropolitan State University of Denver educator Carlos Fresquez on a "Surround Mural," guided by him and painted by his students, transforming the exterior to reflect the cultural life within.

BABI YAR MEMORIAL PARK

10451 East Yale Avenue (Hampden)
mizelmuseum.org/exhibit/babi-yar-park-a-living-holocaust-memorial; free

On September 29, 1941, German forces occupying Kiev, USSR, began systematically killing Jews at the Babi Yar ravine. Over two days, they machine-gunned about 33,771 Jewish men, women and children. Killings continued for two years: Jews, Roma, Ukrainian nationalists and others, ultimately more than 100,000. The Soviets later erected a memorial but excluded any mention of Jews. Denver's Committee of Concern for Soviet Jewry decided that Jewish victims and others must remain alive in memory. The committee concluded that a living memorial would be more poignant than a sculpture and formed Babi Yar Park Foundation, led by Helen Ginsburg. In 1969, city council voted unanimously to appropriate land bordering Aurora, adjacent to a ravine the foundation purchased to add to the park. Mayor Bill McNichols and Holocaust survivor Elie Wiesel dedicated Babi Yar Park, designed by Lawrence Halprin and Satoru Nishita, in 1971.

Babi Yar Park. *Photograph by Ryan Dravitz.*

In 2011, the Mundus Bishop landscape architectural firm restored its prairie ecosystem and upgraded some elements. Visitors enter between two black monoliths and then encounter a circular amphitheater, People's Place, where each year on the Sunday nearest September 29, Mizel Museum hosts an annual Babi Yar Remembrance. The amphitheater's center is one point on a Star of David pathway. Following it rightward leads to the Grove of Remembrance, with one hundred linden trees planted to represent more than 100,000 people murdered, and following it leftward leads to the Wooden Bridge across the ravine. High black walls enclose this narrow crossing, reminding visitors of train cars that hauled Holocaust victims. At either end, polished granite monoliths stand, inspiring self-reflection. Babi Yar Park is ecumenical. In Helen Ginsburg's words, "be they Christian or Jew, whatever their color, whether in Europe, the Mid-East, at Hiroshima, Vietnam, Belfast, Wounded Knee, or Watts…Babi Yar must be a national, if not international effort to create a powerful coming together."

DENVER TURNVEREIN

1570 Clarkson Street (Uptown)
(303) 831-9717; denverturnverein.com
DL

Now devoted to social dancing and dance education, Denver Turnverein dates to 1865, when German immigrants began meeting to practice gymnastics. Turnverein is a German term combining *turnen*, to practice gymnastics, with *verein*, club or union. The American Turners organization, whose motto is "A Sound Mind in a Sound Body," began in 1848, when Turners fled their homeland after the 1848–49 German Revolutions. Denver Turnverein focused on fitness originally, with one member introducing physical education to Denver schools. Membership declined in 1917–18 after America entered World War I against Germany but bounced back afterward. The organization bought the current building in 1922, a year after it opened as the short-lived Coronado Club, whose organizers aimed to provide an alternative venue for young people to meet for dancing. George Bettcher employed Spanish Colonial Revival elements in its design. Denver Turnverein lost members again during World War II but hung on until the 1990s, when Tango Colorado began renting the hall for dances. This led to its current emphasis, which has allowed this old organization to thrive again.

FIVE POINTS HISTORIC CULTURAL DISTRICT

24th to 30th Streets, California Street to Glenarm Place
Denver Landmark Cultural District

As the historic heart of Denver's African American community, this district should not be confused with the larger Five Points neighborhood designation on city maps, which includes Curtis Park and RiNo. Named for the five-point intersection of Welton Street, 27th Street, 26th Avenue and Washington Street, Five Points transitioned into an African American neighborhood early in the twentieth century. This accelerated after Denver extended Broadway north from 20th Avenue, cutting through previously rectangular blocks largely populated by African Americans. With realtors, banks and landlords enforcing segregation by refusing to sell or lease to African Americans elsewhere, by the mid-1920s Five Points was majority African American and rapidly becoming the "Harlem of the West."

In Five Points' prime, Welton Street, from 22nd Street to its terminus at Downing, boasted not just the Rossonian Hotel but also every sort of business and institution: restaurants, shops, groceries, barbers and salons, funeral homes, theaters, pharmacies, veterans' halls, fraternal lodges and recreational facilities. Welton's cultural landmarks include Roxy Theater (at 2551), opened in 1934 as the only cinema where African Americans were not restricted to the balcony; the Cousins Building next door, named for community pillar Charles "Brother" Cousins Jr. and once home to Elvin R. Caldwell and Earl M. West's Equity Savings and Loan; the Radio Drugs building (at 26th, northern corner) where Oglesvie "Sonny" Lawson dispensed pharmaceuticals and incubated African American political culture from 1924 to 1963; the onetime Rhythm Records and Sports Shop (at 2615), where Leroy Smith, Denver's first African American disc jockey and first African American member of the chamber of commerce, sold music and rifles; Pullman Porters and Waiters Club (at 2621, upstairs), a union hall established in 1938; and Casino Cabaret (at 2637), opened by Benny Hooper, unofficial "Mayor of Five Points" in the 1930s. This two-level club boasted a forty-foot bar, a dance floor and balcony seating. Denver's George Morrison Orchestra performed here, as did Jimmy Lunceford and, later, Ray Charles, Fats Domino, B.B. King and James Brown; in 2003, it became Cervantes' Masterpiece Ballroom. The next block hosts two other important sites: the onetime Atlas Drugs (at 2701), the only white-owned Denver drugstore that allowed African Americans to enjoy its soda fountain;

and the Douglass Undertaking Building (at 2745; DL), where brothers Lewis H. and Frederick Douglass Jr., sons of the abolitionist, dispatched deceased community members toward their final resting places.

Although Five Points is no longer solidly African American, it remains dear to community members. From 1953 on, Denver has celebrated Juneteenth in Five Points, with a parade from Manual High School followed by food and music. Five Points Jazz Festival, held each May, remembers the Rossonian, Casino Cabaret and other musical legacies. In 1994, RTD opened a light-rail line on Welton, connecting to downtown, and developers have recently embraced Welton for large, upscale apartment buildings. These threaten to erase what is left of Five Points' African American heritage, which is why Denver designated its first "Landmark Historic *Cultural* District."

Black American West Museum & Heritage Center

3091 California Street (Five Points)
(720) 242-7428; bawmhc.org; admission fee
NR

When Paul Wilbur Stewart was growing up in Clinton, Iowa, his white playmates always made him the "Indian" when they played cowboys and Indians—there was no such thing as a black cowboy, they said. When adult Paul Stewart visited his Denver cousin Earl Mann in the early 1960s, he saw an African American dressed in cowboy attire and said, "Look at that drugstore cowboy. Who's he trying to fool? Everybody knows there are no black cowboys." Mann corrected him, explaining that he was a rancher and that, indeed, African American cowboys existed. Stewart moved to Denver, opening a Five Points barbershop, and while cutting hair he asked customers if they knew of any black cowboys. Stewart collected oral histories (archived at University of Northern Colorado), and as word spread that he was interested in African Americans in the Old West, people brought him artifacts and family heirlooms. His collection outgrew his shop, so in 1971 Stewart established the museum, which moved several times until this location opened in 1989. It now holds more than thirty-five thousand objects in its collections.

The museum's building played an important historical role long before Paul Stewart arrived, as home of Dr. Justina Ford, Denver's first licensed African American female doctor. After graduating from medical college

The Black American West Museum. *Photograph by author.*

in Chicago, Ford and husband John moved in 1902 to Denver, where he would lead Zion Baptist Church. Six years later, he moved on, while Justina remained. They divorced in 1915, but after she remarried, she kept Ford's name for professional reasons. In 1912, she occupied this house, living upstairs, with downstairs rooms for her practice, which specialized in gynecology, obstetrics and pediatrics. Ford remained Denver's only African American female doctor until her death in 1952; her patients were African Americans, Latinos, poor whites and non-English-speaking immigrants. She estimated she had delivered more than seven thousand babies. In the 1980s, the house, then at 2335 Arapahoe Street, was slated for demolition. Numerous "Ford babies," led by Moses Valdez, explored rescue options; ultimately, Historic Denver Inc. paid to move it to this site for repurposing as this museum. A statue of Ford stands across the street at the 30th and Downing light-rail station.

The sidewalk features a "Black Cowboy Hall of Fame," with bronze plaques inset into concrete. Exhibits inside include Dr. Ford's office, complete with her original equipment and furnishings, as well as rooms devoted to roles played by African Americans in the West, including Buffalo Soldiers, Tuskegee Airmen, cowboys, farmers, ranchers, miners and Five Points residents.

Blair-Caldwell African American Research Library

2401 Welton Street (Five Points)
(720) 865-2401; history.denverlibrary.org/about-blair

This Denver Public Library branch opened in 2003, honoring Omar Blair, the first African American Denver Board of Education president, and Elvin Caldwell, the first African American person on Denver City Council. Blair, a Tuskegee Airman, served Denver schools from 1972 to 1984, a contentious period during which he and other board members received threats for implementing court-ordered busing for desegregation. A politician and businessman, Caldwell fought for equal housing and for teaching African American history. The library, largest of DPL's branches, is a legacy of Wellington Webb's mayoral administration. Webb and his wife, Wilma, sought to create a research library and museum to highlight African American contributions to Denver and the West. The first floor is a lending library, while the second floor houses historical archives and a reading/research room. The third floor features the Western Legacies Museum and Charles R. Cousins Gallery.

Rossonian Hotel

2650 Welton Street (Five Points)
DL, NR

Designed by George Bettcher and built in 1912 as the Baxter by cigar manufacturer Robert Baxter, this three-story, flatiron-shaped hotel evolved into the secular heart of Denver's African American community. In 1929, its original white patronage waning, a group led by A.W.L. Ross took over management, coining its new name. Ross divided the first floor, opening the Grill restaurant in the northern corner and the live-music Lounge filling the rest. From 1929 until the mid-1950s, this lounge was one of America's great jazz clubs. Ella Fitzgerald, Duke Ellington, Lionel Hampton, Billie Holiday, Nat King Cole, Count Basie and others stayed upstairs after playing late-night sets that came after performances for white audiences downtown. The scene declined in the 1950s, as cover charges grew higher than many African Americans could afford, downtown hotels began desegregating and Five Points lost population. Since then, the Rossonian

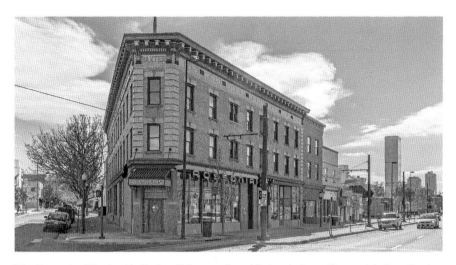

The Rossonian Hotel, with Casino Cabaret reflected in its windows. *Photograph by Ryan Dravitz.*

has had many owners; one used city loans to renovate in the early 1990s, but promises of bringing back the glory years by reopening the jazz club came to naught. In 2019, a developer, partnering with Denver native and basketball legend Chauncey Billups, has begun renovating the Rossonian into a boutique hotel with a ground-floor restaurant and a basement jazz lounge to be named for Billups.

JEWISH CONSUMPTIVES' RELIEF SOCIETY

1600 Pierce Street (Lakewood)
NRD

East Denver's National Jewish Hospital catered to tuberculosis patients who could prove means of support and who were not at death's door; because it was nonsectarian, it did not keep kosher. West Denver Jews, mostly eastern European and working class, wanted a sanatorium open to all, even the very ill, where Jews could keep kosher, speak Yiddish and feel comfortable. In 1903, a group formed Jewish Consumptives' Relief Society (JCRS) and, in 1904, after hiring Dr. Charles Spivak as director, opened an administration building and rows of tent-cabins, designed for maximum fresh air and sunshine ("heliotherapy"). JCRS's motto, from the Talmud, was "He who saves one life saves the world." Although JCRS had initially managed to raise only $1.10 in funding, word spread, and ladies' auxiliaries formed in synagogues across the United States (particularly in New York and Texas) to help.

Through the 1920s, JCRS grew into a campus, with a post office ("Sanatorium, Colorado," later "Spivak, Colorado"), a dining hall, a library, medical buildings and, to keep hands busy while lungs healed, a print shop and a bookbindery. The 1926 Moorish-style Isaac Solomon Synagogue (NR) by William and Arthur Fisher catered to patients' spiritual needs. A ten-by-twelve-foot tent-cabin stands nearby, restored. JCRS used its southern acreage as a farm, dairy and chicken-raising operation, as Spivak and his successor, Dr. Philip Hillkowitz, believed in the nutritive value of fresh poultry, eggs and milk. JCRS treated more than seven thousand patients during its fifty-year history, but once science found a tuberculosis cure, its directors closed it, opening in 1954 the cancer-focused American Medical Center. AMC sold off the Colfax-facing southern portion where JCRS Shopping Center opened in 1957. AMC eventually closed, and in 2003, Rocky Mountain College of Art and Design bought most of the campus; the New York Building at the eastern end is a separate, private facility.

MARTIN LUTHER KING JR. MEMORIAL

City Park

This 2002 Martin Luther King Jr. sculpture by noted African American sculptor Ed Dwight centers a circle designed for contemplating King's life and African American history. After reading extensive interpretive displays south of the circle (across the roadway), visitors proceed north across the bronze slave ship diagram, proceeding counterclockwise to contemplate the carved granite panels "Slavery," "Struggle," "Justice" and "Living the Dream," featuring Dr. King's words. On each corner are statues of other key civil rights figures: Frederick Douglass, Mahatma Gandhi, Sojourner Truth and Rosa Parks. Dwight, a Denverite, was also the first African American astronaut candidate.

The Martin Luther King Jr. Memorial in City Park. *Photograph by author.*

MIZEL MUSEUM

400 South Kearney Street (Washington Virginia Vale)
(720) 785-7300; mizelmuseum.org; admission fee; appointment only

Founded in 1982 by Rabbi Stanley Wagner and philanthropists Carol and Larry A. Mizel, the Mizel Museum of Judaica (its original name) first occupied part of a synagogue before opening its present building in 2004. Its mission includes "fostering cross-cultural understanding, combating racism and promoting social justice" through "educational programming, events and exhibits that connect universal Jewish values to the larger world." Its permanent exhibit, "4,000 Year Road Trip: Gathering Sparks," surveys Jewish culture from biblical times to the present through artifacts, art, photography and digital media.

MOTHER CABRINI SHRINE

21089 Cabrini Boulevard (Lookout Mountain)
(303) 526-0758; mothercabrinishrine.org
NR

Honoring the first canonized naturalized American, Frances Xavier Cabrini—patron saint of immigrants, hospital administrators, impossible causes and India—the Mother Cabrini Shrine is highly visible to travelers due to its white, twenty-two-foot *Sacred Heart of Jesus* sculpture mounted on an eleven-foot pedestal at the site's highest point. Mother Cabrini, sent by Pope Leo XIII to America in 1889 to aid Italian immigrants, founded sixty-seven institutions in the United States and elsewhere to care for poor, abandoned, uneducated and sick people. Bishop Nicolas Matz and Father Mariano Lepore of Our Lady of Mount Carmel Church invited her to Denver in 1902. She founded Mount Carmel School and Queen of Heaven Orphanage. In 1910, seeking a mountain retreat for orphans, Cabrini obtained land on Lookout Mountain. It lacked water, and the sisters complained of hauling water from the bottom of Mount Vernon Canyon. Cabrini said, "Lift that rock over there and start to dig. You will find water fresh enough to drink and clean enough to wash." This spring, now housed in a grotto, continues flowing today. Cabrini died in 1917, was beatified in 1938 by Pius XI and was canonized in 1946 by Pius XII. In 1948, Denver's

Italian community formed a committee to honor her and, with the Knights of Columbus, created the shrine. The *Sacred Heart of Jesus*, by Santa Fean Maurice Loriaux, was erected in 1954. A 373-step stairway leads to it following the path trod by Cabrini when she first encountered the site, with Stations of the Cross and stone benches for rest and contemplation. Also on site is a convent of the Missionary Sisters of the Sacred Heart of Jesus, the order cofounded by Cabrini in 1880.

OUR LADY OF GUADALUPE CATHOLIC CHURCH

3565 Kalamath Street (Highland)
(303) 477-1402; ologdenver.org
DL

Established in 1936 as a storefront mission by St. Cajetan's, the present church named for Mexico's patron saint dates to 1948. John Monroe designed it in Spanish Mission Revival style. A center of community life, the church has long fought for social justice, particularly when Father José Lara and then Father Marshall Gourley led it between 1969 and 1998. Lara, who instituted mariachi masses and established a food bank, actively supported César Chávez and the United Farm Workers in the 1970s, even donning a chasuble emblazoned with the UFW's Aztec eagle. Gourley raised money for victims of the 1985 Mexico City earthquake and, dismayed by frequent funerals for victims of gang-related shootings, worked to reduce violence by urging people to surrender their guns. In recent years, a 1975 mural of La Virgen de Guadalupe disappeared behind a wall built by a more conservative leadership concerned that the parish had become too focused on Mary and not enough on Jesus; the intra-congregational dispute received wide news coverage.

OUR LADY OF MOUNT CARMEL CATHOLIC CHURCH

3549 Navajo Street (Highland)
(303) 455-0447; ourladyofmountcarmel.com
DL, NR

Mount Carmel's history began in 1894 when Father Joseph P. Carrigan of nearby St. Patrick's convinced the diocese to establish a specifically Italian parish. After its first wooden church building burned in 1898, Father Mariano Felice Lepore engaged Frederick William Paroth to design this red brick Romanesque Revival–style church; it was dedicated on December 18, 1904. Lepore did not live to see its completion; late in 1903, he suffered gunshot wounds in the church's rectory. His assailant also received bullets, possibly after Lepore wrestled the gun away; both died the next day. Numerous theories arose regarding the assailant's motive, as Lepore was not only divisive, with some congregants disliking him enough to form a new church, but also quite handsome (some have speculated that a jealous husband killed him). Each August, Mount Carmel hosts the Feast of San Rocco. Since 1926, the Società Nativi di Potenza Basilicata (nearby Potenza Lodge) has administered the feast, auctioning the right to carry the San Rocco statue, carved in Potenza, Italy, along a parade route that begins and ends at Mount Carmel. In the 1950s, it was common for several thousand to attend, and most politicians made appearances; it is smaller today but remains a link to old, Italian North Denver.

ST. JOSEPH'S POLISH CATHOLIC CHURCH

517 East 46th Avenue (Globeville)
(303) 296-3217; swietyjozef.org
DL, NR

One of three eastern European churches clustered in Globeville (the others are Holy Rosary Slovenian and Holy Transfiguration Russian Serbian Orthodox), St. Joseph's opened in 1902 serving Polish immigrants and continues to conduct some services in Polish today, the only church doing so in the western-central United States. Its first pastor, Father Theodore Jarzyński, began the church's annual Boże Ciało Corpus Christi procession, with celebrants singing Polish songs, carrying portraits and banners and stopping at front-lawn home altars. He also established English classes for parishioners working industrial jobs at nearby smelters, stockyards and meatpacking plants. In late August, St. Joseph's hosts a Polish Food Festival (polishfoodfestival.org), with folk dances, folk singing and pierogi-eating and beer-drinking contests. Holy Transfiguration Orthodox Church at 349 East 47th Avenue stages the Orthodox Food Festival and Old Globeville Days (globevilleorthodoxfoodfestival.org) each July, with food and libations from Greece, Russia, Romania, Serbia, Ukraine and Italy, along with entertainment and tours of its historic church.

ST. PATRICK'S MISSION CHURCH

3325 Pecos Street (Highland)
DL, NR

Denver attracted Irish immigrants with the railroads' arrival, and while they never formed an enclave, there were enough in North Denver that the diocese established a specifically Irish parish in 1881. The first St. Patrick's opened on Osage Street in 1884. In 1906, Father Joseph Carrigan, after touring California mission churches, decided that St. Patrick's needed a new building, obtained land for it and hired Harry Manning and Francis Wagner to design a fine Mission Revival church. Carrigan's superior, Bishop Nicolas Matz, then spearheading Cathedral of the Immaculate Conception's construction and seeing no need for a new St. Patrick's, ordered Carrigan to stop. Carrigan refused, and Matz excommunicated him for "open rebellion," outraging Denver's Irish community. Intervention by a papal representative restored Carrigan to the Church, but Matz transferred him away from Denver. Prior to the fracas, Carrigan had been one of Denver's best-known clergymen, agitating for a 20th Street viaduct across the railyards to connect his neighborhood with downtown and helping organize Denver's St. Patrick's Day parade. The new St. Patrick's opened in 1909. After serving for decades, it closed as the neighborhood became majority Hispanic. The building is now a cloister for Capuchin Poor Clare nuns, closed to the public.

SAKURA SQUARE

1255 19th Street (Downtown)
(303) 295-0305; sakurasquare.com

Sakura Square opened in 1973, built by Tri-State Buddhist Church, which had occupied a portion of its block since 1947. The area had long been home to Japanese businesses, although many had dispersed by the 1960s. DURA had included the block in its 1967 Skyline Urban Renewal Plan, and Tri-State bought the remaining properties from DURA for $188,800, hiring Bertram A. Burton to design the project, which included Tamai Tower with subsidized seniors' apartments, retail space and a parking garage. Original tenants included Pacific Mercantile Company, Granada Fish Market (named for the Colorado town near Camp Amache Japanese internment camp) and

Kyoto and Akebono restaurants. Today, Pacific Mercantile, founded in 1944 by former internee Yukata Inai, survives.

The corner plaza on 19th and Larimer features statues of three people important to Colorado's Japanese American history. Ralph Carr was Colorado's Republican governor in 1942 when President Roosevelt signed Executive Order 9066 authorizing internment for West Coast residents of Japanese ancestry, and Carr, alone among governors, welcomed the Japanese to his state and decried the near-universal racism directed against them, dooming his future political career. Attorney Minoru Yasui headed the mayor's Commission on Community Relations, working closely with African American and Hispanic communities, and chaired the Japanese American Citizens League's Committee for Redress, which obtained reparations payments for World War II internees. Reverend Yoshitaka Tamai led Tri-State during the Depression, working to pay its debts. Each June, Sakura Square hosts the two-day Cherry Blossom Festival (cherryblossomdenver. org), celebrating all things Japanese, featuring taiko drumming and other entertainment, foods, exhibits, demonstrations and a marketplace.

TEMPLE EMANUEL

1595 Pearl Street (Uptown)
(303) 777-1102; denverchurch.org
DL, NR

Jewish pioneers organized in 1860 to provide for proper burial of the dead and to hold holiday prayer services. In 1873, this first Jewish society reorganized as Temple Emanuel, and in 1874, it opened its first permanent synagogue at 19th and Curtis Streets. In 1882, it built a second temple at 24th and Curtis; fire gutted it in 1897. Moving to Capitol Hill, Temple Emanuel bought property at 16th Avenue and Pearl Street and engaged architect John J. Humphreys. His Islamic-influenced design features two copper dome–crowned octagonal towers and a Moorish arch entry, its opening filled with stained glass, including three Stars of David. A 1924 addition by his former apprentice, Thielman Robert Wieger, largely duplicates his design. The dark oak interior features a double-vaulted ceiling and Saracen-inspired floral and geometric motifs. After Temple Emanuel relocated, it was home to First Southern Baptist Church and then Lovingway Pentecostal. A private developer bought it in 1982, and demolition loomed until Denver purchased

Sakura Square. *Photograph by Ryan Dravitz.*

Temple Emanuel, now Denver Community Church. *Photograph by author.*

it in 1986, hiring a private company to operate it as an events center. Most recently, Denver Community Church has operated a house of worship again in what is surely Denver's most ecumenical building.

Temple Emanuel moved to Hilltop in 1957. It has always been active in Denver community affairs. William Friedman, its historically best-known rabbi, served for more than forty years, working for mutual understanding between faiths and races and even exchanging pulpits with Christian ministers. In 1890, Frances Wisebart Jacobs, "Mother of Charities," honored today with a stained-glass window in the Capitol, inspired Friedman to found National Jewish Hospital for Consumptives, which opened in 1899. Friedman, Jacobs and other community leaders banded together in 1887 to form Denver Charity Organization Society. Later renamed Community Chest, it is known today as United Way.

ZION BAPTIST CHURCH

933 East 24th Avenue (Five Points)
(303) 861-4958; zionbaptistchurchdenver.org
DL

Founded on November 16, 1865, by freedmen, including Barney Ford, Zion is one of the earliest African American congregations west of the Mississippi and Colorado's oldest. Initially meeting at 18th and Market Streets, by 1867 Zion had bought land at 20th and Arapahoe, where it built a wooden sanctuary, replaced by a masonry building in 1883. It vied with Shorter African Methodist Episcopal Church, founded 1868, to minister to African Americans, although when Denver's public school would not allow their children to enroll, the rival churches jointly operated a private one. Zion's congregation grew, and as Five Points became African American, white congregations' churches became available. In 1911, Zion bought Calvary Baptist, built in 1893, where it has remained. Its pastors have been community pillars. The longest serving was Reverend Wendell T. Liggins, who led Zion from 1941 to 1991; his voice boomed, audible from a block away. Civil rights icons have spoken from Zion's pulpit, including James Weldon Johnson, A. Philip Randolph, Martin Luther King Jr. and Jesse Jackson. Wellington Webb, Denver's first African American mayor, worships here, along with his wife, Wilma, a former state legislator.

LESS IS MORE

Denver has not been a hotbed of architectural experimentation; for most of its history, its powerful, culturally conservative upper crust preferred traditional styles. Denver has also not preserved its Modernist buildings, viewing them as disposable. The most infamous example was the 1996 demolition of the concrete-and-glass hyperbolic paraboloid main entry to the May-D&F department store, designed early in his career by internationally regarded master I.M. Pei. When an out-of-town hotelier applied for demolition, Modern architecture lovers rallied to save it. City council refused to grant landmark status, and down it came, along with Pei's adjacent Zeckendorf Plaza, a sunken ice-skating rink. Pei's other major Denver work, Mile High Center, stands, but his plaza has disappeared under a glass atrium designed by a lesser architect.

In recent years, Modernist design has come to be better appreciated for its elegance and simplicity, and newer projects have boldly revived the idea that "less is more," the minimalism popularized by Ludwig Mies van der Rohe. This chapter celebrates Modern, Neo-Modern and Postmodern architectural sites with historical significance. Mary Voelz Chandler's *Guide to Denver Architecture* and *Denver: The Modern City*, by Michael Paglia, Rodd L. Wheaton and Diane Wray, are valuable guides.

ARAPAHOE ACRES

East Bates to East Dartmouth Avenues, South Franklin to South Marion Streets
(Englewood); exteriors only
NR

Built between 1947 and 1957, this thirty-acre subdivision is the first post–World War II housing development listed in the National Register of Historic Places. Denver native Edward B. Hawkins had built homes in Chicago, where he came to love Frank Lloyd Wright's works, and after World War II he completed several Modernist houses in northeast Denver before embarking on a grander vision, a unified neighborhood. Hawkins hired Eugene Sternberg as architect and planner, and his plat takes advantage of the site's forty-foot elevation change with broad, sweeping streets. Sternberg also designed the initial twenty houses, which he sited at various angles to maximize privacy, take advantage of mountain views and create the sense of living in a park. House plans varied in size, so the neighborhood's social aspect would not become economically homogenous—doctors and lawyers would live alongside salesmen and secretaries. Sternberg's style was International, influenced by Marcel Breuer, but he and Hawkins fell out,

Homes in Arapahoe Acres. *Photograph by author.*

and Hawkins, later working with Joseph G. Dion, designed Arapahoe Acres' other homes, which are more varied but generally reflect Wright's Usonian influence. The Hawkins/Dion homes were also more elaborate than Sternberg's. What unites Arapahoe Acres' houses are all three designers' use of natural materials—including stone, brick, wood and glass—earth-tone colors and horizontal designs.

CLYFFORD STILL MUSEUM

1250 Bannock Street (Civic Center)
(720) 354-4880; clyffordstillmuseum.org; admission fee

Clyfford Still (1904–1980) never lived in Denver, but it is home to 95 percent of his life's work, about 825 paintings and 1,575 works on paper. In 2004, his widow, Patricia, chose Denver over nineteen other cities after then mayor John Hickenlooper promised the city would honor Still's will, which stipulated that his work be kept in a museum exclusively devoted to it, with no other artists. The 28,500-square-foot, two-level facility, tucked behind Denver Art Museum's Hamilton Building, is by Portland's Brad

The Clyfford Still Museum. *Photograph by Ryan Dravitz.*

181

Cloepfil, who worked in textured concrete, even for the perforated ceilings. The attenuated light coming from above creates serenity, and the building's simple rectangular design contrasts with its neighbors—Cloepfil decided that "some silence" was needed amid architectural cacophony. Still was one of the first to shift from representational styles to Abstract Expressionism, which dominated art after World War II. He greatly influenced peers Mark Rothko, Jackson Pollock, Willem de Kooning, Robert Motherwell and others. In the 1950s, Still came to despise big museums and private galleries, calling them "a cesspool of insidious and poisonous matter," and grew estranged from fellow artists for their willingness to play by those institutions' rules. Since the museum's 2011 opening, many people have come to recognize his central role—Still got his wish.

DENVER ART MUSEUM

100 West 14ᵗʰ Avenue Parkway (Civic Center)
(720) 865-5000; denverartmuseum.org; admission fee

Denver Art Museum occupies three connected, iconic buildings across two city blocks. It originated in 1893 as Denver Artists Club and received its first permanent home in 1917, when Jean Chappell and husband George Cranmer donated 1300 Logan Street, dubbed Chappell House; the club then renamed itself Denver Art Association. In 1932, it obtained space in the City and County Building, becoming Denver Art Museum. With the growing city needing that space, in 1949 DAM relocated to a former automobile showroom on Bannock Street south of Civic Center. It acquired nearby properties and, in 1954, opened a Burnham Hoyt–designed gallery at 13ᵗʰ Avenue and Acoma Street. By 1965, the museum owned most of its block and was planning an expansion.

The resulting 1971 seven-story tower by Italy's Gio Ponti (exterior) and Denver's James Sudler (interior) was immediately either loved or hated—there was no middle ground. Ponti's only completed U.S. work, the twenty-eight-sided structure resembles a medieval fortress, its narrow slit windows seemingly designed for archers defending the keep. More than 1 million gray, sculptural glass tiles custom-manufactured by Corning Glass cover it. Each floor houses two ten-thousand-square-foot galleries; Otto Karl Bach, its then director, believed that ten thousand square feet ideally suited average museumgoers' attention spans. The tower was renamed the J. Landis and Sharon Martin Building, honoring their donation, for its 2017–21 renovation. In 2006, DAM opened a second building, named for Frederic C. Hamilton, across 13th Avenue, linked by enclosed bridge. Designed by Daniel Libeskind with Denver's Davis Partnership, the Hamilton is a sculpture inspired by Colorado's mountains and, per Libeskind, "the wide-open faces of the people of Denver." Its pointed shards are sheathed in titanium panels, their gray matching the tower. Its four floors are linked by a twisting, sloping atrium. Libeskind's design polarizes; some love its exuberance, and others find its galleries, with their sloped walls and odd floor plates, off-putting. DAM's newest element is the Anna and John J. Sie Welcome Center, a largely transparent structure, oval in plan, at the 13th and Acoma corner replacing the Hoyt building. Designed by Boston's Jorge Silvetti with Denver's Curt Fentress Architects, it provides a main entrance and space for visitor amenities.

DAM's collection is spread across eleven curatorial divisions: African; American Indian; architecture, design and graphics; Asian; European and American; modern and contemporary; pre-Columbian; photography; Spanish Colonial; textiles and fashion; and western American. Lacking a deep pool of wealthy donors, its European holdings are fewer, compensated for by strengths elsewhere, particularly Native American, pre-Columbian and modern and contemporary. The European and American Department includes the Berger Collection of British Art, covering five centuries. The Spanish Colonial collection, spanning between 1492 and 1850, is one of the world's most comprehensive. The twenty-thousand-piece American Indian Department is encyclopedic. The Petrie Institute of Western American Art curates work related to the historical and contemporary American West, with strengths in bronze sculptures and the Taos Society of Artists.

DENVER BOTANIC GARDENS

1007 York Street (Cheesman Park)
(720) 865-3500; botanicgardens.org; admission fee

Occupying twenty-four acres of the former Mount Calvary Cemetery, Denver Botanic Gardens showcases plants, but Modern architecture lovers will find it compelling for its 1964–66 Claude K. and Edna C. Boettcher Memorial Conservatory for tropical plants (DL). Funded by a Boettcher Foundation grant, architects Victor Hornbein and Edward D. White Jr.

created a fifty-foot-high inverted basket of thin concrete ribs, reflecting Claude Boettcher's association with Ideal Cement. The ribs form a lattice, its openings filled with diamond-shaped Plexiglass panels. So impressive was it that city council voted it landmark status just nine years after it opened. Gardens are devoted to flora from Colorado and around the world. Notable are the Shofu-en Japanese Garden by Koichi Kanawa and the Roads Water-Smart Garden. Designed by Lauren Springer Ogden, it highlights xeric plants that thrive in dry Colorado, demonstrating that xeriscaping can be as beautiful as more water-intensive gardens.

Prior to occupying its current home, Denver Botanic Gardens, which had formed in the late 1940s from the Colorado Forestry and Horticultural Association, had attempted in 1953 to create botanical gardens in City Park. Relics—including a lilac grove, rose beds and a box canyon—remain there, but the organization, which included Saco DeBoer and society figures, soon realized that it needed land that it could enclose to prevent damage to plants. In 1959, DBG focused on Mount Calvary, owned by Denver since 1950 and (mostly) empty of bodies. After a period when Denver Botanic Gardens maintained both installations, it consolidated its efforts at York Street.

DENVER PUBLIC LIBRARY

10 West 14th Avenue Parkway (Civic Center)
(303) 865-1111; denverlibrary.org
DL, NR (older portion)

Officially named Central Library to distinguish it from branches, this seven-story complex, America's eighth-largest public library, occupies a city block, forming, with Denver Art Museum, Civic Center's southern wall. DPL's history dates to the 1885 opening of the chamber of commerce's Mercantile Library; Roger W. Woodbury drove its founding. Four years later, Denver hired John Cotton Dana to helm a free library inside Denver High School (later East). Dana's vision broke new ground: he pioneered open stacks with patrons browsing shelves rather than librarians retrieving books from closed stacks. Dana also created a children's library, the nation's first; after leaving Denver in 1898, Dana influenced library development nationally.

The libraries merged, and in 1910, DPL's first major building, a Greek temple partly funded by Andrew Carnegie, opened at Colfax Avenue and Bannock Street. As Denver grew, this structure became inadequate. Voters approved a bond issue in 1947, and in 1956, the new four-story library opened. Burnham Hoyt designed this, his last completed work, with Fisher and Fisher. Although Modernist, it recognizes its setting with a classical hemicycle facing Civic Center. In 1990, voters approved expansion. Postmodernist Michael Graves, working with Denver's Klipp Colussy Jenks DuBois, designed a structure that incorporated the landmarked Hoyt building. Graves took inspiration from medieval Italian hill towns, clustering masses and colors that contrast with, and respond to, the medieval fortress–like Denver Art Museum. His dramatic interior spaces include a three-story, block-long atrium and circular reference and reading rooms on three floors, in a drum-like rotunda. The fifth-floor Gates Western History Reading Room serves as the centerpiece to DPL's greatest resource, the Western History and Genealogy Collection, established in 1935, archiving more than 600,000 photographs, more than 4,000 manuscripts, more than 250,000 books, pamphlets, maps, newspapers (including the *Rocky Mountain News* archives), clipping files, paintings and other resources covering the American West.

In July 1997, the library hosted the twenty-third G-7 Summit, also billed as Summit of the Eight, at which President Bill Clinton welcomed world leaders, including the United Kingdom's Tony Blair, Germany's Helmut Kohl, France's Jacques Chirac and Russia's Boris Yeltsin. The library still owns the round table custom-fabricated for the occasion.

HISTORY COLORADO CENTER

1200 Broadway (Civic Center)
(303) 447-8679; historycolorado.org/history-colorado-center; admission fee

The State Historical Society of Colorado's third home opened in 2012. A five-level facility designed by David Tryba, faced in golden limestone and glass, it feels suitably Colorado-casual rather than museum-formal. A full-height atrium features a topographical map of Colorado rendered in terrazzo. Permanent exhibits on Colorado's history occupy spaces on three levels; it also hosts temporary and traveling exhibits. The Stephen H. Hart Research Center (open to qualified researchers), State Historical Fund and Office of Archaeology and Historic Preservation are also here. This building replaced a 1977 museum one block north, demolished in 2009 for the Ralph L. Carr Colorado Judicial Center.

The History Colorado Center. *Photograph by Ryan Dravitz.*

KIRKLAND MUSEUM OF FINE & DECORATIVE ART

1201 Bannock Street (Civic Center)
(303) 832-8576; kirklandmuseum.org; admission fee

Ohioan Vance Kirkland (1904–1981) was a Colorado artist from 1929 until his death. He founded the University of Denver's School of Art, ran his own art school and painted about 1,200 works over five decades. This museum displays his paintings, which progressed through five periods, from early "Designed Realism" to brilliantly colored "Dot Paintings" of his elder-hood. Kirkland could "hear" colors through music and sound, an ability called synesthesia, and Bartók, Mahler, Prokofiev and other composers inspired his color juxtapositions. In addition to Kirkland's works, the museum houses an important collection of international decorative art, ranging from early twentieth-century Arts and Crafts and *art nouveau* periods to 1980s Postmodernism, as well as collections of Colorado and regional art. Contrasting with typical museum galleries, items are displayed "salon style," with fine and decorative arts juxtaposed. The main building, designed by Seattle's Olson Kundig, opened in

2018. Of historical interest is Kirkland's studio, a 1911 brick building by Maurice Biscoe and Henry Hewitt that stood at 1311 Pearl Street and was originally home to Henry Read's Students' School of Art. It opened as the Kirkland Museum in 2003 and was moved eight blocks in 2016 and attached to the new museum. Kirkland occupied it from 1932 until 1981, and visitors can see how he suspended himself over his dot paintings, which had to lie flat.

KRISANA PARK

East Louisiana to East Florida Avenues, South Dahlia to South Fairfax Streets
(Virginia Village); exteriors only
krisanapark.community

Comprising 177 homes built in 1954 and 1955, this is one of Denver's best concentrations of California Contemporary style. Father-and-son developers Hiram B. and Brad Wolff had greatly admired Joseph Eichler's Bay Area subdivisions, and their architect, Frenchie Gratts, closely followed Eichler's designs, adapting them for Colorado's colder climate yet keeping their essence intact. Key features of Krisana Park homes include post-and-beam construction, low-pitch rooflines, open plans, Philippine mahogany paneling and carports. Vertical slot windows and horizontal glass bands below eaves provide privacy. Yet interiors are not dark: larger windows and sliding glass doors face backyards and private lanais, for indoor/outdoor living. The Wolffs marketed the "3-D Contemporary" three-bedroom homes as affordable; eligible ex-servicemen paid $50 down and $104.02 monthly under the GI Bill. Buyers snapped up Krisana Park's houses, and the Wolffs followed with similar projects, including nearby Lynwood (East Mexico to East Jewell Avenues, South Holly to South Jasmine Streets). Residents are protective and have worked with Historic Denver Inc. on a pattern book and with the City and County of Denver on conservation overlay zoning to protect Krisana Park's impossible-to-replicate character. The name comes from farmers Christian and Ann Noe, who sold their alfalfa field to the Wolffs.

MUSEUM OF CONTEMPORARY ART DENVER

1485 Delgany Street (Lower Downtown)
(303) 298-7554; mcadenver.org; admission fee

Displaying only recently created art with no permanent collection, MCA Denver's black glass building is the first museum by British Ghanaian architect Sir David Adjaye. Sue Cannon and a group of art lovers founded the institution in 1996, and it occupied a former Sakura Square fish market prior to the present building's 2007 opening. Its location away from the museum district near Civic Center is due to trustees Mark Falcone and Ellen Bruss's donation of land they already owned, but it also reflects MCA Denver's independent spirit. The twenty-seven-thousand-square-foot building contains five galleries on two floors, filled with natural light from hidden skylights. Adjaye's design engenders a sense of discovery, compelling visitors to explore around corners. The glass-walled rooftop café/bar provides a peaceful perch with great views.

The Museum of Contemporary Art Denver. *Photograph by author.*

WASHINGTON WEST

Metropolitan residents are proud that Denver and suburbs are home to what some call "Washington West," although the enduring belief that Denver is second only to Washington, D.C., in federal jobs is difficult to substantiate. Denver has had a long history of federal employment, both civilian and military. Although the Bureau of the Mint has owned a Denver Mint since 1862, it did not manufacture coins here until 1906. Fort Logan's 1887 establishment got the federal ball rolling, followed by Fitzsimons Army Medical Hospital in 1918. By the late 1930s, federal government employed more than seven thousand local civilians, and Franklin Roosevelt's administration, gearing up for world war the president knew would come, established Lowry Field and contracted with Remington Arms to open the Denver Ordnance Plant. World War II saw openings of Rocky Mountain Arsenal and Buckley Field. The Office of Price Administration fully leased downtown's Kittredge Building. The Cold War saw America's primary nuclear "trigger" plant built at Rocky Flats and the conversion of Remington Arms to Denver Federal Center, employing thousands. The U.S. Air Force opened its Finance Center in Denver, administering retirement and other programs. Subsequently, federal presence has grown with suburban office parks near the Federal Center home to various agencies, as well as the 1974 establishment of the National Solar Energy Research Institute (now National Renewable Energy Laboratory). The Denver area may or may not be second in federal jobs, but government continues to make a significant impact on Denver.

BYRON WHITE U.S. COURTHOUSE

1823 Stout Street (Downtown); exterior only
(303) 236-0944; gsa.gov/about-us/regions/welcome-to-the-rocky-mountain-region-8/
buildings-and-facilties/colorado/denver-federal-district/byron-white-us-courthouse
DL, NR

This Neoclassical building opened in 1916 as Denver's main post office and federal courthouse. The post office, with its block-long lobby and twenty-eight-foot barrel-vaulted ceilings, occupied the main and basement levels, with district courtrooms on upper floors. After postal operations decamped in 1991, the General Services Administration spent $28 million to restore it to its Beaux-Arts glory, reopening it in 1994 as the U.S. Court of Appeals for the Tenth Circuit and renaming it to honor Coloradan Byron White, U.S. Supreme Court associate justice, appointed by President John F. Kennedy in 1962.

Egerton Swartwout of New York firm Tracy, Swartwout and Litchfield designed it. Exterior walls are of Colorado Yule marble, with Latin inscriptions related to the building's legal functions and names of cities related to its postal persona; sixteen fluted, three-story Ionic columns march across its Stout Street front. Built-in marble benches feature somewhat puritanical inscriptions; one reads, "If Thou Desire Rest, Desire Not Too Much." On the 18th Street side are two Rocky Mountain sheep sculptures, rendered in Indiana limestone by Gladys Caldwell Fisher in 1936 through the New Deal's Treasury Relief Art Project. In 2002, Justice White donated memorabilia now housed in the Justice White Museum and Judge's Chambers on the first floor; these include

The Byron White United States Courthouse, with the Byron G. Rogers Federal Building in the distance. *Photograph by Ryan Dravitz.*

his University of Colorado football jersey. During his college years, he earned the nickname "Whizzer," which dogged him throughout his subsequent legal career. The courthouse is generally closed to the public, but the GSA sometimes opens it to visitors.

Across 19th Street, the Byron G. Rogers Federal Building and U.S. Courthouse (1961 Stout Street; NR) hosted the 1997 criminal trial and conviction of domestic terrorist Timothy McVeigh, perpetrator of the 1995 Oklahoma City bombing.

COLORADO FREEDOM MEMORIAL

756 Telluride Street (Aurora)
(303) 248-3990; coloradofreedommemorial.com

Honoring Colorado-resident military service members killed in action or dying from direct injuries suffered in action from the Spanish-American War to the present, the Colorado Freedom Memorial resulted from an "aha!" moment that KEZW-AM 1430 radio host Rick Crandall felt in 2000 while broadcasting on Memorial Day from Normandy, France. Discovering that eighty-eight Coloradans lay buried there, he wondered how many others had died in America's wars. After establishing a nonprofit foundation to build a memorial, it took several years to raise funds and secure a site. Aurora suggested this four-acre plot near Buckley Air Force Base, and the memorial, designed by Kristoffer Kenton, was dedicated on Memorial Day 2013. Its centerpiece, reached after passing several flags flown at half-staff, is a jagged glass wall, echoing the shapes of Colorado's mountains and inscribed with thousands of names. A second monument, a Colorado Gold Star Families Memorial, is planned.

DENVER FEDERAL CENTER

West Alameda Avenue and South Kipling Street (Lakewood)
(303) 236-5374; gsa.gov/dfcmuseum

Denver Federal Center occupies land once owned by Jacob Downing, who bought it in the 1860s to raise Arabian horses. In 1913, Thomas S. Hayden bought it from Downing's estate and incorporated it into a larger ranch, and in

1940, the Hayden family sold 2,040 acres to the federal government. With skies darkening, the Roosevelt administration aimed to move some arms production away from coasts, choosing this site for a massive plant producing small arms ammunition. It was close enough to Denver that finding employees would not pose problems, but because ammunition is volatile, the site needed to be away from built-up areas. The Denver and Interurban Railroad, in partnership with other railroads, built a spur from D&I's Denver-to-Golden interurban line to ship products via railcar. The government began construction in March 1941 and opened Denver Ordnance Plant, operated by Remington Arms, in September. By 1943, at peak production, it employed more than twenty-two thousand people, working three shifts.

After the war, the government converted the plant to peacetime uses. Today, twenty-eight agencies employing more than 6,200 people occupy 4 million square feet across forty-four buildings within the Federal Center's 670 acres; these include the Interior Department's Bureau of Land Management, Bureau of Reclamation, U.S. Geological Survey and the General Services Administration. It houses the National Science Foundation Ice Core Laboratory. Tours are unavailable, but visitors (who must use Gate 1 on Kipling Street and bring valid government identification) may tour the Denver Federal Center Museum in Building 41 by appointment. It holds more than 360 historic artifacts dating back to the site's previous incarnation as a ranch.

FEDERAL RESERVE BANK OF KANSAS CITY, DENVER BRANCH

1020 16th Street (Downtown)
(303) 572-2300; kansascityfed.org/moneymuseum?location=1; free

After President Woodrow Wilson signed the 1913 Federal Reserve Act, Denver bankers tried landing one of its regional banks but lost to Kansas City; Denver had to content itself with a branch. Initially occupying rented quarters it built a white marble Neoclassical *palazzo* at 17th and Arapahoe Streets in 1925. By the 1960s, it was woefully inadequate; as a check clearinghouse, it could not keep up with increased volume as Colorado's population grew. Nearby, Park City Realty Company had assembled most of the block bounded by 16th, 15th, Arapahoe and Curtis Streets, demolishing structures in anticipation of a multi-tower apartment project. Park City and Central Bank, a Denver Branch member, shared common board members. Worried that the Fed might decamp to suburbia, Park City sold its assemblage to it, keeping the Denver Branch safely close to member banks. The Brutalist-style facility designed by William C. Muchow opened in 1968. Although operations are not public, the bank houses a Money Museum, open on weekdays. Visitors view exhibits on American currency dating to 1775, learn how to manage personal finances and create their own currency.

FITZSIMONS ARMY MEDICAL HOSPITAL

13001 East 17th Place (Aurora)
ucdenver.edu/academics/colleges/medicalschool/administration/history/pages/
eisenhower-suite.aspx; free

A centerpiece of the University of Colorado's Anschutz Medical Campus and Fitzsimons Innovation Campus, this eight-story Art Moderne former hospital serves as the medical school's administration building. The U.S. Army established Hospital Number 21 here in 1918 to treat tuberculosis and other lung ailments, taking over a tree nursery after locals raised money to buy it and lease it for one dollar per year, hoping the hospital would boost the economy. It opened just before World War I ended, occupying eighty-six structures with total patient capacity of 1,400. In 1920, the army named it for Lieutenant William Thomas Fitzsimons, a doctor who was the first army officer killed in World War I. Fitzsimons nearly closed during the 1930s due to budget cuts, but instead, with the international situation worsening and Lowry Field opening nearby in 1937, it stayed open and was upgraded with this building.

Quartermaster Corps architect Luther Morris Leisenring oversaw its design in buff-colored brick with sandstone trim. For maximum sunlight exposure for pulmonary patients, who were still Fitzsimons's primary focus, Leisenring gave it projections, setbacks, outdoor decks and south-facing sunrooms. At its December 3, 1941 dedication, it was Colorado's largest building and, with 608 beds, the largest army hospital ever built. It accepted Pearl Harbor survivors as patients a few weeks later. By 1943, with additional structures, it had a 3,500-bed capacity and was the world's largest military hospital, serving American personnel, their dependents and even some Axis prisoners with lung ailments. That year, Fitzsimons treated Foreign Service officer Richard Kerry. On December 11, his wife, Rosemary, gave birth at Fitzsimons to John Forbes Kerry, who served as secretary of state under President Barack Obama.

The Fitzsimons Army Medical Center Hospital, now the University of Colorado Anschutz Medical Campus Fitzsimons Building. *Photograph by Ryan Dravitz.*

In 1955, Fitzsimons was home to President Dwight and Mamie Eisenhower for nearly eight weeks. Visiting Colorado and golfing too vigorously, Ike suffered a heart attack on September 24 and was admitted to Fitzsimons, where administrators set up an eighth-floor suite for him, the First Lady and his physician, Dr. Howard Snyder. Slowly recovering, he gradually reassumed presidential duties, receiving as visitors Vice President Richard Nixon and Secretary of State John Foster Dulles, among others. Not wanting the world to see him as weak, Eisenhower remained at Fitzsimons until he could climb stairs unaided, checking out on November 11. He won reelection handily in 1956, American voters having decided his health was fine. In 1965, Congress, apprehensive about presidential incapacitation, passed the Twenty-Fifth Amendment, which specifies how a vice president will succeed a president unable to perform the office's duties. The Kennedy assassination was the impetus, but Eisenhower's long Fitzsimons stay still colored memories.

Fitzsimons experienced a final busy period during the Vietnam War but afterward served only local personnel and dependents. With Lowry Air Force Base's 1994 closure, it lost its last large constituency. The army shuttered it in 1996, turning over most of the 578-acre campus to Fitzsimons Redevelopment Authority, comprising Aurora and the University of

Colorado. The authority has since transformed Fitzsimons into a medical treatment and research campus. In 2000, CU renovated the Eisenhower Suite to its 1955 appearance, and it can be visited by appointment.

FORT LOGAN FIELD OFFICER'S QUARTERS MUSEUM

3742 West Princeton Circle (Fort Logan)
(303) 789-3568; friendsofhistoricfortlogan.org; free

This house museum is one of sixteen Frank J. Grodavent–designed homes on Princeton Circle built as Fort Logan officers' quarters. Authorized by Congress in 1887, Fort Logan consolidated scattered army outposts across western prairies, as friction with Native American tribes had greatly declined. Lieutenant General Philip Sheridan selected the site, which Denver citizens paid for and donated to the army. It took the name Fort Logan in 1889, for Civil War general John Alexander Logan, who had died in 1888. Logan, whose name also marks a Chicago square and a Washington, D.C., circle, was the father of "Decoration Day," May 30, which became Memorial Day. The army acquired additional land in 1908, and in 1909, Fort Logan became a recruiting depot; one recruiting officer was Major Dwight Eisenhower, who worked in the building east of the museum. Among army posts in the 1920s and 1930s, when isolationist policies had greatly shrunk the armed forces, Fort Logan was a backwater, with army personnel dubbing it "Fort

The Fort Logan Field Officer's Quarters Museum. *Photograph by author.*

Fort Logan National Cemetery. *Photograph by author.*

Forgotten." In 1940, it became a subpost to Lowry Field, and after World War II, the army closed it. It opened Fort Logan National Cemetery in one portion and donated more than three hundred acres to Colorado, which in 1960 opened a mental health facility. The state also owns this museum building, restored beginning in 1995 and operated by Friends of Historic Fort Logan (check website).

FORT LOGAN NATIONAL CEMETERY

4400 West Kenyon Avenue (Fort Logan)
(303) 761-0117; cem.va.gov/cem/cems/nchp/ftlogan.asp
NR

When Fort Logan was established in 1887, the army set aside three acres for a post cemetery, and that year it accepted its first burial, the daughter of a private. In 1950, Congress authorized some of the former base's land for a new national cemetery, initially occupying 160 acres but since expanded to 214. Among its notable burials are seven twentieth-century Buffalo Soldiers; World War II hero Karl H. Timmerman, the first American officer to cross the Rhine after directing the assault on the Ludendorff Bridge during the Battle of Remagen; Tuskegee Airman Fitzroy Newsum; and George R. Caron, tail gunner on the *Enola Gay* on August 6, 1945, and thus the first American to see the atomic mushroom cloud over Hiroshima.

LOWRY AIR FORCE BASE

East 6th Avenue Parkway and Quebec Street (Lowry); former main entrance
(303) 344-0481; lowryfoundation.org

Named for aerial photographer Lieutenant Francis B. Lowry, the only Colorado pilot killed in combat during World War I, Lowry Air Force base trained 1.1 million service members over its nearly fifth-seven-year life. Its role, which evolved with technology, was training. In 1934, the U.S. Army Air Corps sought to relocate its photography and armament schools from Illinois, and Denver leaders wanted them. Agnes C. Phipps Memorial Sanatorium near 6th Avenue and Quebec, built in 1904 by Lawrence Phipps, abutted open land and had been closed since 1932. Denver voters approved a 1935 bond issue to buy and donate the properties to the U.S. Air Corps, and in October 1937, Lowry Field opened and began training students. Almost overnight, with war looming, Lowry's population mushroomed, from a few hundred to eight thousand by June 1941. The air corps made the sanatorium (demolished in 1963) its headquarters while it built classrooms, barracks, officers' quarters, hangars, runways and other military base accoutrements. At its peak during World War II, Lowry's population stood at twenty thousand, and instructors taught aerial photography, Norden bombsight operation and armaments.

After the war's end, training expanded to include rocket propulsion, missile guidance, nuclear ordnance, intelligence and other Cold War subjects. From 1953 to 1955, it frequently hosted President Dwight and Mamie Eisenhower. The president's plane, the *Columbine II* (not yet designated *Air Force One*), used Lowry, and the Eisenhowers often stayed on base. In 1953, Lowry hosted filmmakers and actors, including James Stewart and June Allyson, shooting *The Glenn Miller Story* (Universal-International, 1953). Two years later, Stewart, an Air Force Reserve colonel, returned to film *Strategic Air Command* (Paramount, 1955). In 1955, the newly chartered U.S. Air Force Academy admitted its first cadets at Lowry, which hosted the school until its permanent Colorado Springs campus opened in 1958.

Lowry Air Force Base Hangars No. 2 (*foreground*) and No. 1 (*in the distance*), which houses Wings Over the Rockies Air & Space Museum. *Photograph by Ryan Dravitz.*

Although flight operations ceased in 1966, Lowry continued operating until 1994. Lowry Redevelopment Authority then took over, master planning reuse of 3.3 square miles with residential and commercial development. The former temporary Air Force Academy campus serves as campus again, for Aurora Community College. While many air force structures are gone, key historic buildings remain. Lowry's street alignment reflects the base's street plan.

Eisenhower Chapel

293 Roslyn Street (Lowry)
(303) 344-0481; eisenhowerchapel.com
DL, NR

This New England–style chapel, clad in white-painted clapboard and dedicated in November 1941, was one of four on-base interdenominational worship facilities; the air force demolished the other three but retained this one for its historical associations with the thirty-fourth president. Here Ike and Mamie, sitting in the sixth pew on the left, worshiped on their Denver visits. After Lowry Redevelopment Authority transferred it to Lowry Foundation, a 2007 renovation lifted it up and turned it forty degrees to face a plaza. The foundation rents it for events and manages showings for visitors.

The Eisenhower Chapel at former Lowry Air Force Base. *Photograph by author.*

The Armament School at former Lowry Air Force Base. *Photograph by author.*

Lowry Technical Training Center

DLD

This historic district includes three buildings and two aircraft hangars central to Lowry's mission. The block-long Administration Building (200 Rampart Way) opened in 1940 as a 3,500-bed barracks, nicknamed "Buckingham Palace" by residents; the air force converted it to technical training school headquarters in the early 1960s, moving from the former sanatorium. It is now apartments. One block southeast, twin three-story Art Moderne classroom buildings (125 and 130 Rampart Way), originally housing the photography and armament schools, are restored and leased to office tenants. To their east, Hangar No. 1 is now an air and space museum, while Hangar No. 2 (7581 East Academy Boulevard) houses self-storage and other businesses.

Officer's Row

DLD

Northwest of the Administration Building, these identical houses along Rampart Way and East 5th Avenue Parkway, now privately owned, are built of buff-colored brick like other base buildings. Originally, the sanatorium/base headquarters stood northeast of them. This historic district includes the only sanatorium remnant, a 1904 house by Aaron Gove and Thomas Walsh at 7400 East 6th Avenue Parkway, built as the sanatorium superintendent's home and used by the air force as base commander's residence. Nearby the former officer's club at 350 Quebec Street is now Stanley British Primary School.

Wings Over the Rockies Air & Space Museum

7711 East Academy Boulevard (Lowry)
(303) 360-5360; wingsmuseum.org; admission fee

Completed in 1940, Hangar No. 1 houses Wings Over the Rockies, formed in 1994 as Colorado's official air and space museum. A Boeing B-52B Stratofortress greets visitors in front. The hangar is filled with more than fifty military aircraft, including a Douglas B-18A Bolo, Grumman F-14

B-52B Stratofortress in front of Wings Over the Rockies Air & Space Museum. *Photograph by Ryan Dravitz.*

Tomcat and Rockwell B-1A Lancer. The museum owns a piece of the Moon, brought back on Apollo 15. Denverites with memories of Stapleton International Airport will recognize its tile *Progress of Flight* mural. On long-term loan from Lucasfilm Ltd. is a three-quarter-scale model of an X-Wing Starfighter, built in 1996 to promote the original *Star Wars* trilogy's re-release and signed by several of its stars; Anakin Skywalker's podracer from *Star Wars Episode I: The Phantom Menace* is also on view. Noted flying enthusiast Harrison Ford narrates an eight-minute orientation film shown in the Harrison Ford Theater.

NATIONAL ARCHIVES AT DENVER

17101 Huron Street (Broomfield)
(303) 604-4740; archives.gov/denver

Dedicated in 2012, this 162,000-square-foot repository with 750,000 cubic feet of permanent records created by federal agencies and courts in seven Rocky Mountain states is open to researchers, but it contains no permanent exhibits. It offers group tours by reservation, subject to staff availability. Among its holdings are records from the Bureaus of Reclamation, Land Management and Indian Affairs; National Park Service; and naturalization documents. Genealogists will find it useful for homestead records, federal land leases, IRS tax assessments and other documents.

ROCKY FLATS NATIONAL WILDLIFE REFUGE

16170 West 120th Avenue (Jefferson County)
(303) 289-0930; fws.gov/refuge/rocky_flats; free

Opened to the public in 2018, this 5,237-acre wildlife refuge appears on its visitors' map as a giant doughnut, with the 1,300-acre hole in the center filled by a closed area called "Department of Energy Legacy Site." Originally settled by the ranching Scott family in 1868, this land was later bought by the Lindsay family and was known as the Lindsay Ranch; their barn and remnants of their house can be visited. The refuge has ten miles of trails, and visitors can experience a rare pocket of a tallgrass prairie ecosystem, home to much wildlife.

The site's primary historical interest lies in the restricted area controlled by the Department of Energy. With the Cold War in full swing by the early 1950s, the U.S. Atomic Energy Commission bought the Lindsay Ranch to build a facility for manufacturing plutonium fission "triggers," or cores, the mechanism inside atomic weapons that causes the explosion. Construction began in 1951, and the plant, operated under contract by Dow Chemical Company (Rockwell International after 1975), produced its first plutonium cores in 1953. Plutonium is spontaneously combustible, and two fires, in 1957 and 1969, resulted in plumes with plutonium particles spreading over wide areas east and northeast of the plant. For a time in the 1960s, Dow stored waste material contaminated with plutonium in barrels; leaks contaminated nearby soil, which was then transmitted offsite by wind. These releases of plutonium into Colorado's environment, originally kept secret, became known after the 1969 fire, and anti-nuclear activists staged numerous protests. One in 1979 resulted in 284 arrests, including of Allen Ginsberg and Daniel Ellsberg; a protest in 1983 drew ten thousand demonstrators. In 1989, the FBI and Environmental Protection Agency staged a joint raid seeking evidence of "environmental crimes," and they found it. The plant closed and production ceased. Cleanup, which involved demolishing about eight hundred structures and removing twenty-one tons of weapons-grade nuclear material, took more than a decade and cost more than $7 billion.

This plant, one of thirteen sites producing elements of America's nuclear arsenal, was responsible for the majority of the plutonium cores in the program. Opening the wildlife refuge, which comprises the plant's former buffer zone, was highly controversial, with activists and respected scientists concerned that hikers and other refuge trail users could possibly cause plutonium particles near the surface to be released. Whether the refuge remains open permanently remains to be seen. The author and publisher do not necessarily advocate visiting this site, but it is included here for its historical importance.

ROCKY MOUNTAIN ARSENAL NATIONAL WILDLIFE REFUGE

6550 Gateway Road (Commerce City)
(303) 289-0930; fws.gov/refuge/rocky_mountain_arsenal; free

Today one of America's largest urban wildlife refuges, this 15,988-acre site lies eight miles northeast of downtown. In 1942, the federal government purchased twenty-seven square miles and built a plant producing mustard agent, lewisite and a chlorine agent; it also produced napalm, some used in Tokyo's 1945 firebombing. After World War II, the government idled the plant, but the Korean War and Cold War brought reactivation and expansion to produce the Nazi-developed nerve agent sarin; between 1953 and 1957, it produced most of the non-Communist world's supply. None of these chemicals, other than napalm, was ever used in combat, but one Arsenal product found extensive peacetime use: rocket fuel. When NASA's Apollo 11 Lunar Module departed the Moon after its historic July 21, 1969 landing, it used Arsenal-produced fuel to lift off. Titan nuclear missiles also utilized Arsenal-produced rocket fuel. In 1961, operators began injecting toxic wastewater twelve thousand feet underground; scientists determined that this caused Denver-area earthquakes, and injections ceased in 1966. Chemical production, which also encompassed pesticides, ended in 1982. In 1992, Colorado representatives Patricia Schroeder and Wayne Allard co-sponsored a bill establishing the wildlife refuge. It opened in 2004; cleanup costs topped $2 billion. The Pat Schroeder Visitor Center features displays on the Arsenal's history and wildlife. Visitors can hike trails and navigate the eleven-mile Wildlife Drive. More than 330 species live here, including bison (reintroduced in 2007), bald eagles, deer, black-footed ferrets, coyotes, burrowing owls and prairie dogs.

UNITED STATES MINT

320 West Colfax Avenue (Civic Center)
(303) 572-9500; usmint.gov/about/mint-tours-facilities/denver/visiting-the-denver-
mint; free; ticket required
DL, NR

Thanks to Denver's early history as gold rush *entrepôt*, today it boasts one of four United States Mints—and one of two open to the public. In 1860, Austin Clark, Milton Clark and Emanuel Henry Gruber of Leavenworth, Kansas, established a mint and assay office at G (16th) and McGaa (Market) Streets to process gold arriving from mining camps. They began minting ten-dollar gold coins and later struck other denominations, but after the Civil War began the federal government discouraged private coinage; in 1862, Congress established the United States Mint at Denver to acquire the Clark, Gruber operation. The government discontinued coinage, using the mint primarily as assay office and for stamping gold bars for transport east.

The United States Mint, with the City and County Building at left. *Photograph by Ryan Dravitz.*

The current mint opened in 1906, after an 1895 Congressional act upgraded Denver Mint to a production facility. The Treasury Department, rather than expanding in Lower Downtown, bought a Colfax Avenue site, hiring New York architectural firm Gordon, Tracy and Swartwout, with James Knox Taylor as federal supervising architect. Inspiration came from Palazzo Medici Riccardi, the Florentine palace begun by Cosimo de' Medici in 1444 and associated ever after with banking and money. They utilized Colorado materials: gray Cotopaxi granite for walls and pink Pikes Peak granite for stairs and sidewalk-adjacent walls. Inside, Vincent Aderente painted murals illustrating mining, manufacturing and commerce. In 1922, the mint was robbed when Federal Reserve Bank staff loaded currency stored there onto a truck. The mint reached capacity in the 1970s and was nearly moved elsewhere. After political leaders prevailed to keep it in Denver, Rogers-Nagel-Langhart designed a 1987 expansion. Visitors should review the website prior to planning a visit.

ENTERTAINMENTS

In Denver's earliest days, people had gold fever, but they were also hungry for diversion from the town's hard realities. The city being hundreds of miles from the nearest theater, Jack Langrishe and his troupe commenced Denver's live entertainment history when they arrived in 1860. Early performances took place above saloons, but soon a Denver Theatre stood at 16th and Lawrence Streets. Horace Tabor gifted Denver with his Tabor Grand Opera House at 16th and Curtis Streets in 1881, the hub of what became a four-block entertainment district, with a dozen or more theaters with live entertainment and, later, movies. Singing, which anyone with a good ear could do, was immensely popular; merchant J. Jay Joslin cofounded the Haydn and Handel Society and accredited himself well, by all accounts, in a performance of *H.M.S. Pinafore*. Baseball developed early too, with the first recorded game played on April 26, 1862; businesses built employee morale by sponsoring baseball teams. Early baseball stadiums arose at John Brisben Walker's Riverfront Park (at today's Commons Park site), Colfax Avenue and Broadway, 6th Avenue and Broadway and the 1922 Merchants Park at Virginia Avenue and Broadway. This chapter highlights the histories of various performance groups, museums, athletic teams, amusement parks and other diversions Denverites enjoy today.

CASA BONITA

6715 West Colfax Avenue (Lakewood)
(303) 232-5115; casabonitadenver.com
Lakewood Landmark

Opened in 1973, Casa Bonita, "the world's most exciting restaurant," fills fifty-two thousand square feet on multiple levels, seats more than one thousand people and is famous across America thanks to its several appearances on the animated series *South Park*. Occupying a former Joslin's department store at JCRS Shopping Center (now Lamar Station Plaza), this was not the first Casa Bonita opened by Oklahoman Bill Waugh, but it has proven to be the most popular and longest lasting. Opened during a stressful era (Watergate, the 1973 oil embargo), its diversions proved immediately popular, with lines stretching down the center's sidewalk and two-hour waits; Ricardo Montalbán starred in television advertisements for it. The front façade boasts an eighty-five-foot-tall Spanish Colonial tower, rendered in pink stucco and topped by a gold-leafed dome and statue of Cuauhtémoc, the last Aztec emperor. After passing through the serving line, diners chose among myriad dining environments, each simulating some aspect of Mexico; the most coveted tables overlook the thirty-foot waterfall and its Acapulco-style divers. Strolling mariachis entertain, gorillas terrify and occasional gunfights break out. After dining, guests can wander through Black Bart's Cave, watch a puppet show or play Skee-Ball. Casa Bonita is a guilty pleasure for adults and a warm memory for the millions of children who have loved it.

COORS FIELD

2001 Blake Street (Ballpark/LoDo)
(303) 292-0200; mlb.com/rockies/ballpark

In 1991, Major League Baseball awarded an expansion slot to a Denver ownership group, and in 1993 and 1994, the Colorado Rockies played at the old Mile High Stadium. Coors Field, designed by HOK Sports Facilities Group, opened in 1995, during a wave of "old school" urban ballparks. Instead of being surrounded by parking, it hugs the sidewalk, relating to nearby historic warehouses. Its red brick façade nods to its team's home

Lower Downtown, with Coors Field in the distance. *Photograph by Ryan Dravitz.*

with the purple-blue columbine, Colorado's state flower, rendered in terra cotta by artist Barry Rose. At the 22nd and Blake Street corner, a historic warehouse incorporated into the ballpark houses Sandlot Brewery, the first microbrewery inside a major-league facility. Inside Coors Field, while most seats are in dark green, those on the upper deck's twentieth row are purple, marking one mile above sea level. This is the highest-altitude major-league ballpark, and while some believe thinner air aids hitters, others believe that Denver's dry climate is why Coors Field is "the most prolific offensive ballpark ever created," per the team's website. The Rockies' mascot, Dinger, is a triceratops; during Coors Field's construction, excavators discovered dinosaur fossils, including a seven-foot triceratops skull. Tours are available year-round but are limited during game days.

DENVER MUSEUM OF MINIATURES, DOLLS AND TOYS

830 South Kipling Street (Lakewood)
dmmdt.org; admission fee

Boasting a twenty-thousand-piece collection that includes miniatures in wood, ivory, silver and gold by renowned artisans; dolls, including Colorado's Japanese Friendship Doll, Miss Yokohama; and memory-evoking toys spanning the nineteenth to the twenty-first centuries, this museum, which first opened in 1981 in the Pearce-McAllister Cottage at 1880 Gaylord Street, closed in 2018 and as of this writing is raising funds to open its new Lakewood facility.

DENVER MUSEUM OF NATURE AND SCIENCE

2001 Colorado Boulevard (City Park)
(303) 370-6000; dmns.org; admission fee

Colorado's most popular museum, the Denver Museum of Nature and Science (DMNS) sprawls across 716,000 square feet on three public floors and nonpublic underground levels. Altogether, the museum owns more than 4.3 million artifacts. Its genesis dates to 1868, when naturalist Edwin Carter moved into a Breckenridge log cabin to study Colorado's native fauna. He built an extensive specimen collection, and in 1899, he offered it to either the state or to Denver. He died shortly thereafter; prominent Denverites paid his estate $10,000 and in 1900 formed Colorado Museum of Natural History. Items resided in the capitol's basement until 1908, when the museum opened in City Park. John Campion, its first board president, declared "a museum of natural history is never finished," and over time, newer construction has enveloped the original building, including matching wings in 1918 and 1929, followed by the Lawrence C. Phipps Auditorium in 1940. The museum built western wings after World War II, one hosting the Charles C. Gates Planetarium, followed by eastern wings in 1987 and the Morgridge Family Exploration Center in 2014. In 1948, the museum renamed itself Denver Museum of Natural History and in 2000 adopted its present name.

DMNH is known for its eighty-nine wildlife dioramas in the Wildlife Halls. Most date to the mid-twentieth century, when Director Alfred Bailey dispatched teams to six continents for specimens and hired artists to paint realistic backdrops. Other permanent exhibits include "Prehistoric Journeys," depicting the evolution of life; "Egyptian Mummies"; "Space Odyssey," spanning the universe and hosting a full-size replica of the Mars Exploration Rover; "Expedition Health," exploring the human body; "Gems and Minerals," inside a re-created mine; and "North American Indians." DMNS also hosts temporary and traveling exhibits. Gates Planetarium's shows explore space, while the Phipps IMAX Theater, housed in Phipps Auditorium, screens films on nature and scientific subjects.

DMNS has always pursued science. In 1927, a museum team proved that humans had lived in North America more than ten thousand years ago, discovering stone projectile points near bones from an extinct bison species near Folsom, New Mexico. In 2010, the museum gained international attention when it responded to a construction crew's discovery of Columbian mammoth remains in Snowmass Village ski resort in Pitkin County. During sixty-nine days of this "Snowmastodon Project" museum scientists and volunteers dug up thousands more fossils, aiding in understanding climate change impacts.

Sharp-eyed visitors will discover DMNH's "secrets." Among these are eight gnomes that artist Kent Pendleton painted surreptitiously in the 1970s in certain diorama backdrops. He was not fired, and DMNH has since gone along with the joke, adding a ceramic elf to Mars and, in the IMAX lobby, the *Millennium Falcon* and Yoda.

DENVER PERFORMING ARTS COMPLEX

1400 Curtis Street (Downtown)
artscomplex.com

Comprising four city blocks, Denver's arts complex, America's second largest by seat count, was the vision of attorney Donald Ray Seawell, who loved performing arts and had produced Broadway shows before coming to Denver in 1966. By 1972 controlling the Bonfils Foundation and publishing its *Denver Post*, he was a power broker. One day, stopped at 14th and Curtis Streets while returning from lunch, he gazed at the Auditorium Theatre and adjoining Auditorium Arena, and a performing arts complex presented itself in his mind. He sat on the curb, pulled out an envelope and penciled the basic plan. He returned to the *Post*, drafted legal papers to found Denver Center for the Performing Arts and telephoned Mayor Bill McNichols to pitch the idea. That fall, Denver voters passed a bond issue to fund its infrastructure, including a 1,700-car garage. Officials broke ground in 1974, and by late 1978, Boettcher Concert Hall had opened its doors, with other venues following. The project caused controversy, particularly as Seawell controlled Denver's largest newspaper. He maintained that he never used *Post* money on the complex, and in 1980, the foundation sold the newspaper.

Kevin Roche of Connecticut's Kevin Roche, John Dinkeloo and Associates created its master plan based on Seawell's envelope sketch. Roche used Curtis Street as its spine, covering it with a transparent vault, sixty feet wide, seventy-six feet above the galleria floor. In addition to large venues described in the following sections, the complex houses smaller ones, along with restaurants and shops. In 2014, the city presented plans to reimagine the complex, demolishing some parts, building new ones and integrating an educational component and residences, but as of this book's writing, the concept has not moved forward.

Boettcher Concert Hall

coloradosymphony.org

Named for Claude Boettcher, this 2,679-seat auditorium by New York's Hardy Holzman Pfeiffer Associates opened in 1978. The Denver Symphony wanted its audience close; 80 percent of seats are within sixty-five feet of the stage. To compensate acoustically for the configuration, undulating fascia front each curving audience section, and sound engineers raise or lower 108 translucent suspended disks to fine-tune it. Critics greeted America's first "in the round" symphony hall skeptically; some still maintain that Boettcher can never be "tuned" properly. If Denver's plan to remake the complex comes to fruition, a smaller traditional venue will replace it.

Denver Symphony Orchestra's roots dated to 1903, when Rafaello Cavallo established Denver Orchestra Association; in 1922, the semiprofessional Denver Civic Symphony formed to replace it but failed in 1934. Helen Marie Black, Jeanne Cranmer and Lucille Wilkin then founded Denver Symphony Orchestra, having decided that Denver needed a well-paid professional ensemble. In 1945, DSO hired Saul Caston as music director. Having worked with Leopold Stokowski and Eugene Ormandy at the Philadelphia Orchestra, he transformed DSO into a major institution locally and began building its national reputation. He toured the orchestra, established a Red Rocks concert series and brought music to schools. In 1949, he broke an unwritten racial code, employing Charlie Burrell to play bass viol, the first African American hired by any American symphonic orchestra, earning Burrell the nickname "the Jackie Robinson of classical music."

After 1970, conductor Brian Priestman further built DSO's popularity with summer park concerts. The DSO held annual "Marathon" fundraisers, with KVOD classical radio broadcasting from May-D&F department store windows, taking pledges and hosting symphony musicians playing mini-concerts for passersby. Ten years after moving into Boettcher, financially struggling DSO canceled its 1988–89 season. Sensing that it would not survive, several musicians established a smaller entity, Colorado Symphony Orchestra, which continues to play pops and classical concerts at Boettcher and elsewhere. It formally merged with DSO in 1990 and has grown to DSO's former size.

Helen G. Bonfils Theatre Complex

denvercenter.org

Seawell's 1972 performing arts plan encompassed more than buildings—he envisioned a professional repertory company to present plays, train actors and break new theatrical ground, similar to Minneapolis's Guthrie Theatre or Los Angeles's Mark Taper Forum. The Bonfils Foundation's previous theatrical establishment, Bonfils Memorial Theatre on East Colfax Avenue, produced community theater, not professional. Occupying a Kevin Roche–designed building, Denver Center Theatre Company (now DCPA Theatre Company) occupied three auditoriums: the 750-seat, thrust-style Stage; the flexible black box Space seating 380 to 550; and a 200-seat experimental lab, now Glenn R. Jones Theatre. Initially, it also housed the 250-seat Frank Ricketson Cinema, but with other options for fine films, DCPA converted it to another small theater. With more than four hundred productions to date, DCPA has won numerous accolades, including the 1998 Tony Award for Outstanding Regional Theatre. Some of its most lauded productions include *Black Elk Speaks* (1993); *The Laramie Project*; and the ten-play Trojan War cycle *Tantalus*, co-produced with the Royal Shakespeare Company. *TIME* named the latter two to its list of the ten best plays of 2000. The company offers ninety-minute tours of its venues, costume and scenery shops and design studios (reservations required).

Ellie Caulkins Opera House

operacolorado.org; coloradoballet.org
DL, NR

Impetus for a multipurpose Denver Municipal Auditorium began in the 1890s. Voters approved an 1899 bond issue, and in 1901, an Auditorium

Association, after examining fifteen sites, chose 14th and Curtis Streets. Little happened until 1904, when Robert Speer made its construction, "for the use of the people," a campaign issue. Opposition delayed groundbreaking until 1906, with the cornerstone not laid until September 18, 1907. Despite the slow start, it was ready by July 1908, when it opened with a free concert. Robert Willison designed it with domed corner cupolas; like privately owned theaters further up Curtis Street, its Neoclassical lines were brilliantly traced by seven thousand lightbulbs. Its walls enclosed a vast hall with room for 12,000 conventioneers, or a smaller 3,300-seat theater, created by a moveable proscenium and folding ceiling and wall panels. Three days after the concert, it hosted its first convention, the Democratic National Committee, which selected William Jennings Bryan to take on William Howard Taft for the presidency. This was the first presidential nominating convention west of the Mississippi for either major party. Speer inaugurated free public concerts, and managers booked myriad events, including automobile shows, prizefights, graduation ceremonies and agricultural fairs; it was hardly ever dark. In 1916, Speer raised funds for a thirty-five-ton Municipal Organ, which was operational by his 1918 funeral. In 1955, Denver closed the Auditorium for renovation, removing cupolas and converting the interior to single-purpose use, as the Auditorium Theatre; the organ disappeared. In 2002, renamed Quigg Newton Denver Municipal Auditorium, it was renovated again. Gutted to four walls, it reopened in 2005 as the 2,225-seat Ellie Caulkins Opera House, nicknamed "the Ellie" by fans. It boasts fine acoustics and four seating levels.

The Ellie's two principal tenants are Opera Colorado and Colorado Ballet. Opera Colorado was formed after interested and well-heeled opera lovers met in 1980 to create a company for "high-powered" opera after years of seeing underfunded groups fail. They hired Metropolitan Opera's Nathaniel Merrill as president and artistic director. He established Opera Colorado's standards from the beginning; in his first season (1983), he cast Placido Domingo as Rodolfo in Puccini's *La Bohème*. The company performed at Boettcher Concert Hall initially, staging "opera in the round," and later the Buell Theatre. Colorado Ballet's roots date to 1951, when Freidann Parker and Lillian Covillo established a dance school, followed by the Covillo-Parker Theater Ballet. In 1961, they renamed it Colorado Concert Ballet. Its 1961–62 season featured Denver's first full-length production of Tchaikovsky's *The Nutcracker*, and the company has performed it every holiday season since. In 1976, Colorado Concert Ballet professionalized, and in 1978, it dropped "Concert" from its name.

Temple Hoyne Buell Theatre

denvercenter.org

Like the Ellie, the Buell is a new venue inside an old shell. In 1941, Mayor Ben Stapleton began an Auditorium expansion. World War II halted construction after a steel skeleton arose, with 220-foot-long beams atop 110-foot-high columns. In 1947, voters approved funding for completion, and in 1952, the Auditorium Arena opened, its G. Meredith Musick– designed Streamline Moderne rounded corner entry facing 13th and Champa Streets. Inside, 7,500 seats surrounded an oval floor. In 1967, new National Basketball Association team the Denver Rockets (Nuggets after 1974) began playing. Denverites also came for all-star wrestling, high school graduations and religious revivals. After 1975's McNichols Arena opening, Auditorium Arena saw fewer bookings, and Denver Center Attractions, part of DCPA, eyed it for a large Broadway-style house. In 1984, Mayor Federico Peña and Governor Roy Romer raised money to supplement city funds, and in 1991 the 2,843-seat Buell opened. New York's Beyer Blinder Belle designed a glass-walled, three-level lobby and utilized gray, Lyons-quarried sandstone panels to give the theater a "Colorado look." A ten-week, sold-out production of *Phantom of the Opera* opened the Buell; that success, combined with other high-grossing productions, has earned it high regard from producers, who often book it to launch national tours of Broadway shows.

DENVER ZOO

2900 East 23rd Avenue (City Park)
(720) 337-1400; denverzoo.org; admission fee

Legend tells that the eighty-acre Denver Zoo was born in 1896 when Mayor Thomas McMurry received a black bear cub as a gift. In actuality, he was a surprise gift to a Colorado Midland Railroad employee named Bailey, from a colleague who had caught him near DeBeque, Colorado. Bailey's neighbors, amused at his predicament, christened the rambunctious bear "Billy Bryan," for William Jennings Bryan. Bailey gave Billy to Denver's park commissioners, who turned him over to City Park's manager, Alexander Graham, who housed him in his barn. After Billy consumed his chickens, Graham penned him at City Park's northern edge. Thus the zoo was born.

Billy and other donated animals languished in cages during early years, but Mayor Robert Speer supported improvements, hiring Frederick Law Olmsted Jr. to design a plan (never built). When Denver hired Victor Borcherdt as head animal keeper in 1912, he and Saco DeBoer planned a "Habitat Zoo," based on Carl Hagenbeck of Munich's then-revolutionary concept of naturalistic animal displays. Convincing city fathers proved difficult, but after Speer's 1916 mayoral win, he enthusiastically supported them, allocating $50,000 but expecting a private foundation to take over fundraising. The men identified a rugged outcropping on Dinosaur Mountain near Morrison. They spent weeks creating plaster castings of it, brought them to the zoo, built a steel skeleton and poured tinted concrete into the molds. With Bear Mountain's (DL; NR) 1918 completion, for the first time in America visitors could view wild animals without bars, safely isolated across a moat. The exhibit greatly influenced zoo design, but Borcherdt and DeBoer's additional plans remained unrealized after Speer's 1918 death, his successors failing to support the zoo. Its only improvement came with 1937's completion of the Works Progress Administration–funded Monkey Island. When Quigg Newton defeated Mayor Ben Stapleton in 1947, the zoo was moribund. Newton spearheaded revival, pushing for a Denver Zoological Foundation in 1950 and hiring Saco DeBoer for another plan. The foundation took over management in 1956 and, in 1957, enclosed the zoo with fencing, eliminating automobile access. Since then, it has created and implemented several master plans, each reflective of advances in zoological thinking, with the most recent approved by city council in 2018.

Following Billy Bryan, many zoo residents have captured Denverites' hearts. Between 1941 and 1961, female polar bear Velox ruled Bear Mountain, and the 31st Infantry Regiment ("Polar Bears") adopted her as mascot. The first elephant, Cookie, acquired in 1950, captivated a generation of children, greatly helping popularize the zoo. In 1978, lowland gorilla Maguba was stolen and abandoned, becoming the zoo's resident celebrity after recovery. Albino alligator Albert attracted national attention in 1981 when he escaped to Duck Lake. His presence attracted huge crowds for twenty-eight days until handlers captured him. Polar bear cubs Klondike and Snow were born at the zoo in 1994. Abandoned by their mother, Ulu, zoo staff nurtured them to adulthood, with Denver media covering every new development. When the zoo sold them to Sea World Orlando, thousands mourned their departure.

ELITCH GARDENS THEME & WATER PARK

2000 Elitch Circle (Central Platte Valley)
(303) 595-4386; elitchgardens.com; admission fee

Although its history dates to 1890, the present park is vintage 1995. John and Mary Elitch founded Elitch Gardens in a cherry orchard at West 38th Avenue and Tennyson Street, then semi-rural but accessible by streetcar. It featured clean family fun for generations, with a zoo in early years, a summer stock theater and the Trocadero Ballroom, home to big band–era greats. Families brought picnic lunches, enjoying them in pavilions near elaborate flower gardens. "Not to See Elitch's is Not to See Denver," advertising proclaimed. By the 1980s, Elitch's owner needed more room for thrill rides and moved it after 1994 to former downtown railyards. "New" Elitch's features the old park's merry-go-round with sixty-four hand-carved wooden horses, completed by Philadelphia Toboggan Company in 1928; its "Twister Two" roller coaster mostly replicates the old park's "Mister Twister." In 2018, Elitch's current owners announced plans to relocate and redevelop its valuable downtown acreage.

FILLMORE AUDITORIUM

1510 Clarkson Street (Uptown)
(303) 837-0360; fillmoreauditorium.org

Built in 1907 by Albert Lewin as Mammoth Roller-Skating Rink, this thirty-five-thousand-square-foot hall has seen more owners and disparate uses than nearly any Denver building. The rink failed after three years. In 1911, electric automobile manufacturer Oliver P. Fritchle converted it to a factory, ceasing production in 1920. It then served as an automotive garage and possibly a bootleg distillery. The Rocky Mountain Amusement Syndicate took over in 1935, converting it to an ice rink for casual skaters and hockey games; it also housed an illegal casino. In 1939, owners converted it back to roller-skating as Mammoth Garden Roller Club, and during World War II, it staged dances for soldiers and airmen. New owners in 1962 converted it to a warehouse. In 1970, it reopened as a concert venue, Mammoth Gardens, with new owners inspired by Bill Graham's Fillmore West in San Francisco. For less than a year, it hosted legends like Jimi Hendrix and the Grateful Dead before the city closed it as a public nuisance. It sat empty until 1976, when young Capitol Hill entrepreneurs opened The Market, a combination farmers' market and craft fair. This soon failed; the building reopened in 1981 as a sports venue, closing in 1982. In 1986, Manuel Fernandez opened Mammoth Events Center. In 1999, local promoter Chuck Morris and Bill Graham bought it from Fernandez and resurrected Graham's long-closed San Francisco venue's name.

HISTORIC ELITCH THEATRE

4655 West 37th Place (West Highland)
(720) 593-9395; historicelitchtheatre.org
DL, NR

As the centerpiece of former Elitch Gardens, this octagonal wooden theater was, per film director Cecil B. DeMille, a member of its 1905 company, "one of the cradles of American drama." Newly widowed Mary Elitch completed it as memorial to her late husband, John, in time for the 1891 summer season, the park's second, and remodeled it in 1902 to its current appearance. Initially booking traveling vaudeville acts, in 1897 she established a summer stock company. Its first season featured James O'Neill, Eugene O'Neill's father, the first of many famous names to trod the boards; portraits of many lined the outdoor lobby. "America's Oldest Summer Stock Theatre" ceased in 1987, and Elitch's booked traveling shows for a few years. After the park's 1995 relocation, developers demolished everything but the theater and nearby merry-go-round building, surrounding them with residential and commercial structures. In 2002, Historic Elitch Gardens Theatre Foundation formed to restore the theater and add systems and amenities to make it fully functional. To date, this work is incomplete. Check the website for events, tours and volunteer opportunities.

LAKESIDE AMUSEMENT PARK

4601 Sheridan Boulevard (Lakeside)
(303) 477-1621; lakesideamusementpark.com

Elitch Gardens did not serve alcohol. Adolph Zang, son of Zang Brewery founder Philip Zang, aimed to create a similarly respectable park while catering to those who enjoyed beer. In 1907, he and several associates formed Lakeside Realty and Amusement Company; bought land between Sheridan Boulevard, Harlan Street, West 44th and West 48th Avenues; and founded Lakeside; the park opened in 1908. Sylvan Lake covered most of Lakeside's northern half, and Zang planned a year-round town alongside his summer "resort" on the eastern shore. He hired architect Edwin Moorman, who worked in the Beaux-Arts style popularized by the 1893 Chicago World's Fair. That event was nicknamed "the White City" for its architecture, and so was Lakeside—early advertising billed it "Lakeside, the White City" (contrary to urban legend, it was never called simply "White City"). Moorman designed a boathouse, natatorium, ballroom and the 150-foot-high, lightbulb-encrusted Tower of Jewels with attached Casino Theatre. The latter once housed a ground floor German rathskeller, theater and roof garden café. The El Patio ballroom attracted hundreds nightly during the big band era, with Kay Kyser, the "Ol' Professor of Swing," frequently booked; Glenn Miller and Duke Ellington also played Lakeside.

In 1933, concession manager Benjamin Krasner bought Lakeside, and when daughter Rhoda was born, he renamed the lake for her. Krasner installed thrill rides; Lakeside had always featured a roller coaster, and Krasner built new ones, along with a racetrack. He hired architect Richard L. Crowther to update Lakeside's look with Art Moderne ticket booths, new buildings and remodels of old ones. Where Moorman had bathed buildings in white light from 100,000 bulbs, Crowther worked in color, utilizing neon and fluorescent. Over time, Lakeside, operating only in summer, aged, and Rhoda Krasner struggled to maintain buildings. Jefferson County forced her to demolish the ballroom and, to great dismay, the Fun House, with its creepy "Laffing Sal," a fat female mannequin who terrified children with insane laughter. Today, Lakeside continues summer operations, delighting new generations. People still board *Whistling Tom* and *Puffing Billie*, steam locomotives from the 1904 St. Louis World's Fair that power the one-and-a-half-mile-long miniature train ride encircling Lake Rhoda, they still bump into one another on Auto Skooters and they still seek thrills on four roller coasters.

MAYAN THEATRE

110 Broadway (Baker)
(303) 744-6799; landmarktheatres.com/denver/mayan-theatre
DL

"Mayan Deco" describes this themed movie house built in 1930 by Fox West Coast Theatres, replacing an earlier cinema. Architect Montana Fallis utilized pre-Columbian motifs, employing Denver Terra Cotta Company's chief artist Julius Ambrusch on its riotous façade. The Mayan served south Denver for decades, but by the 1970s, it was barely surviving on second runs and bargain prices. In 1984, its next-door neighbor and owner, a bank, announced demolition plans. Locals formed "Friends of the Mayan," Mayor Federico Peña vocalized strong support for its preservation and Denver Broncos owner Pat Bowlen contributed financially. Denver Landmarks Preservation Commission convinced city council to landmark it. After an ownership change, it underwent a $2 million renovation, which cleaned the façade and restored lavish interior terra cotta, wall stenciling and recessed neon lighting. It reopened in November 1986 as a three-screen art cinema (the original balcony divided into two smaller theaters), timed well to enjoy a boom in independent American and foreign film.

MILE HIGH STADIUM

1701 Bryant Street (Sun Valley)
(720) 258-3000; broncosstadiumatmilehigh.com

Opened in 2001, designed by HNTB with Denver's Fentress Bradburn Architects, Mile High seats 76,125. In addition to NFL games, it hosts Labor Day weekend's Rocky Mountain Showdown, season opener for University of Colorado Buffaloes and Colorado State University Rams and Major League Lacrosse's Denver Outlaws. The Broncos played the first regular season home game at Mile High against the New York Giants on Monday, September 10, 2001. On August 28, 2008, it hosted night four of the Democratic National Convention, when Senator Barack Obama accepted his party's presidential nomination. On the south end, the Ring of Fame Plaza honors former players and administrators. Colorado Sports Hall of

Fame, offering stadium tours (coloradosports.org/stadium-tour; fee), can be found just inside Gate No. 1.

Mile High replaced an earlier Mile High nearby; it opened in 1948 as Bears Stadium for the Denver Bears minor-league baseball team. When the Broncos formed in 1960 as one of eight American Football League teams, they played on the reconfigured baseball field. Initially clad in mustard yellow and brown, they adopted orange and blue in 1962. Bears Stadium became Mile High in 1968, and with 1976's construction of moveable east stands, the Broncos always sold all 76,082 seats. The south stands, which did not rise as high, acquired a rowdy reputation; the new stadium emulated this configuration. Another tradition carried over is "Rocky Mountain Thunder," with upper-deck fans stomping feet rapidly, creating a loud roar—louder in the old stadium, due to all-steel construction. Above the south stands, a twenty-seven-foot-high bucking bronco named Bucky, modeled after Roy Rogers's horse Trigger, topped the scoreboard; Bucky rears proudly today atop the new stadium's scoreboard. The Broncos performed poorly in early years, not boasting a winning season until 1973. Four years later, it made playoffs for the first time, thanks to the "Orange Crush Defense," and went on to play Super Bowl XII in 1978. That was the first of eight (so far) Super Bowl appearances, of which it has won three, in 1997, 1998 and 2015.

NATIONAL BALLPARK MUSEUM

1940 Blake Street (Lower Downtown)
(303) 974-5835; ballparkmuseum.com; admission fee

One half block from Coors Field, this nonprofit museum houses Bruce Hellerstein's baseball memorabilia, cited in Stephen Wong's *Smithsonian Baseball* as one of the world's finest private collections. Over three decades, Hellerstein has amassed myriad items, including seats, turnstiles and other pieces from Ebbets Field, Wrigley Field, Polo Grounds, Tiger Stadium, Forbes Field and Fenway Park. Denver teams are not left out, with the last pitching rubber used by the Rockies at old Mile High and a 1948 ticket to the first game at Bears Stadium. The collection also includes playing equipment, jerseys, programs, postcards and photographs.

PARAMOUNT THEATRE

1621 Glenarm Place (Downtown)
(303) 623-0106; paramountdenver.com
DL, NR

Built for Paramount Pictures' Publix circuit, the 1930 Paramount survives as Denver's last remaining downtown movie palace and finest Art Deco interior. Publix installed a Wurlitzer twin-console, 1,600-pipe organ to provide music and sound effects for silent films. Today, it is one of two still-operating Publix One models; the other survives at New York's Radio City. Architect Temple Buell employed Denver Terra Cotta Company–crafted white tile outside and worked with his former employer, Chicago's Rapp and Rapp, a movie palace specialist, inside. Its specific style is "Zigzag Art Deco," employing flamboyant decoration, Aztec figures, floral motifs, sunrays and ziggurats. Silk murals by Vincent Mondo depict *commedia dell'arte* characters, including Harlequin, Pierrot, Columbine and Pierrette. The Paramount reigned as a premier cinematic venue until the 1960s, eventually losing business to suburban cinemas and ceasing operations in the early 1980s. With the building potentially threatened, Historic Denver Inc. formed Historic Paramount Foundation to assume operations; later, a private entity succeeded the nonprofit. The 16th Street lobby, occupying rented space in the Kittredge Building, proved too expensive for the foundation and was leased to a restaurant. Today, the Paramount, its entrance now on Glenarm, hosts concerts, stand-up comedy and lectures. The Rocky Mountain Chapter of the American Theatre Organ Society occasionally plays Wurlitzer concerts.

RIVER NORTH ARTS DISTRICT

Burlington Northern Santa Fe Railroad to Arapahoe Street, Park Avenue West
to Interstate 70 (Five Points, Elyria, Globeville)
rinoartsdistrict.org

River North, or RiNo (its logo features a rhinoceros), is Denver's youngest neighborhood, having evolved in the 2000s and 2010s from three zones physically separate from one another, all home to innovative enterprises, including galleries, artists' studios, architectural offices, artisan furniture makers, restaurants, bars, performance spaces, shops, distilleries, vintners, brewpubs, coffee roasters, boutique hotels and food halls. The busiest locus is Larimer Street, lined with dining and shopping options, many inside former warehouses, east of RTD's A Line tracks. Between the tracks and the South Platte, a mile of Brighton Boulevard is transitioning from industry to mixed use; yet to come are riverside parks and a river-crossing pedestrian bridge. RiNo west of the South Platte is quieter, anchored by TAXI, a multibuilding development that formerly served as central dispatching for a taxicab company. RiNo is known for its murals, which seemingly cover every wall. Each summer, it hosts CRUSH WALLS (Creative Rituals Under Social Harmony; crushwalls.org), founded by Robin Munro. An urban art festival that attracts nationally known artists to create murals and street art, it transforms RiNo into a massive outdoor studio and gallery. Lonely Planet has named RiNo as a top-ten neighborhood to visit, praising it for "transform[ing Denver] into the cultural dynamo of the American West."

STREETCAR COMMERCIAL STRIPS

Various locations

Neighborhood commercial districts are an enduring legacy of decades of streetcar service. Merchants clustered together to capture trade from customers deboarding and walking home. Local chains sprouted up in these strips, including Lud Rettig and Lloyd King's Save-a-Nickel (King later founded King Soopers), Solitaire "Home Owned Stores" franchises and Se-Cheverell Pharmacies. Some boasted neighborhood cinemas or small J.C. Penney stores.

Although streetcar service ended in 1950 and rails have been pulled out or paved over (occasionally peeking through), in recent decades Denverites have begun appreciating these strips' interesting architecture and connection to Denver's history. Predominantly tenanted by locally owned shops, restaurants and services, they anchor neighborhoods and enhance their identities. Some strips are small, perhaps consisting of one or two buildings. Larger ones include:

- Highland Square: 32nd Avenue between Irving and Perry Streets (West Highland); visitdenverhighlands.com
- Historic South Gaylord Street: Gaylord Street between Mississippi and Tennessee Avenues (Washington Park); oldsouthgaylord.com

- Old South Pearl Street: Pearl Street between Buchtel Boulevard and Jewell Avenue (Platt Park); southpearlstreet.com
- Tennyson Street between 38th and 46th Avenues (Berkeley); shoptennyson.com

TATTERED COVER BOOK STORE COLFAX

2526 East Colfax Avenue (Congress Park)
(303) 322-7727; tatteredcover.com
DL, NR

This Art Moderne building opened in 1953 as Bonfils Memorial Theatre. Helen Bonfils, doyenne of Denver drama, built it for Denver Civic Theatre, honoring mother Belle and father Frederick Bonfils. The community-based company had begun in 1929 as University Civic Theatre, performing in DU's Margery Reed Hall with support from Bonfils and other socialites. It later occupied space near Civic Center before Bonfils commissioned John Monroe to design this theater at City Park Esplanade's southern terminus. The house sat 550, with a bar and intimate cabaret in the basement.

Henry Lowenstein oversaw more than four hundred Bonfils productions. His Jewish father and non-Jewish mother saved his life by sending him away from Nazi Germany to England via the *Kindertransport* rescue effort. After the war, his family, having survived, moved to Pennsylvania, and Henry enrolled at Yale, where Helen Bonfils, seeking a set designer, hired him. Lowenstein employed Jonathan Parker, an African American man, as custodian, and Bonfils supported him over some racist actors who demanded a white janitor. Lowenstein, deeming racism similar to Nazi anti-Semitism, cast Parker in a play, inaugurating an acting career; Parker's daughter, Cleo, later founded Cleo Parker Robinson Dance, an internationally known ensemble. Bonfils died in 1972, and Donald Seawell assumed control over Bonfils Foundation, embarking on his performing arts center and professional company. Initially, DCPA oversaw the community company and, in 1986, even renamed the facility for Lowenstein, but it soon closed it. Lowenstein re-created Denver Civic Theatre on Santa Fe Drive (today's Su Teatro), but the company eventually faded away. The Bonfils/Lowenstein Theatre sat vacant until 2006, when developer Charles Woolley renovated it as anchor for Lowenstein CulturePlex.

Tattered Cover opened in 1971 in a Cherry Creek storefront. In 1974, Joyce Meskis bought it and expanded several times. In 1986, she leased the vacant four-level Neusteters store on 1st Avenue, a bold move with Denver in recession. At its peak in the 1990s, Tattered Cover boasted more than 500,000 books on hand. In the early 2000s, facing a daunting rent increase, Meskis joined Woolley's project. Meskis, always a fierce First Amendment defender, has since retired, selling to new owners, and Tattered Cover continues thriving. Theatrical elements remain, including the orchestra pit and stage.

THE DEAD

As recounted in the City Beautiful chapter's Cheesman Park section, Denver's first repository for the departed was well southeast of town, with separate sections for Protestants, Catholics and Jews. It lost favor once Denver had its first "picturesque" cemetery, Riverside. These became fashionable after the Civil War, as funerary entrepreneurs sought to emulate verdant eastern cemeteries that established the type: Mount Prospect in Cambridge, Massachusetts; Greenwood Cemetery in Brooklyn; and Philadelphia's Mount Laurel. These burying grounds eschewed the old "boot hill" plots with graves dug willy-nilly, with no thought given to ambience, in favor of planned environments of graceful carriage drives and professional landscaping. They proved immediately popular not only for the dead but also for the living, who often treated them as parks, perfect for Sunday picnics in cities lacking park acreage. In Denver, Riverside started the trend, and in Fairmount, the picturesque cemetery achieved full expression, an environment more beautiful today than a century ago. This chapter covers those and two other historically important cemeteries, but smaller cemeteries often contain interesting sights too—Littleton Cemetery, for example, is the resting place for Alfred Packer, the so-called Colorado Cannibal.

CROWN HILL CEMETERY

7777 West 29th Avenue (Jefferson County)
(303) 233-4611; dignitymemorial.com/funderal-homes/wheat-ridge-co/olinger-
crown-hill-mortuary-cemetery
NR (portions)

Known for its 158-foot Tower of Memories (NR), Crown Hill, the vision of George Washington Olinger, opened in 1907. Olinger's parents, John and Emma, had opened their Denver mortuary in 1890 after moving from Santa Fe. With five partners, he formed Crown Hill Cemetery Association, buying 180 acres west of Wadsworth Boulevard from Henry Lee; in 1909, they bought additional property running west to Kipling Street but never used it. In 1978, Jefferson County Open Space, Lakewood and Wheat Ridge bought the excess land, establishing Crown Hill Park. Kansas City architect Charles Ashley Smith designed the Tower of Memories, begun in 1926, in Gothic Revival style. It evolved into stripped-down Modern Gothic after the Fisher brothers replaced Smith in 1928. The $1 million mausoleum's construction stalled in the Depression, and in 1948, Crown Hill hired John Monroe to complete it. The interior, more opulent than the exterior, houses a chapel, about six thousand crypts for bodies and five thousand niches for cremains.

Crown Hill's grounds form an arboretum, home to more than 1,700 trees and sixty-nine species. The oldest part of the cemetery, about fifteen acres, lies northeast of the tower and is in the National Register. It includes sections for Spanish-American War and Grand Army of the Republic veterans, including eighty-six who fought for the Union, as well as "Baby Lands," home to infants, and a Fitzsimons Army Medical Hospital plot. Crown Hill's first burial was Augusta Garson, relocated from Fairmount. Notable burials include brewer Adolph Coors and family members, Congressional Medal of Honor recipient Ernest Bjorkman, playwright Mary Coyle Chase and this land's onetime farmer, Henry Lee.

FAIRMOUNT CEMETERY

430 South Quebec Street (Windsor)
(303) 399-0692; fairmountheritagefoundation.org; free; admission fee for tours

During Denver's 1880s boom, Riverside Cemetery became surrounded by industries, and some feared that relatives would avoid visiting their graves. Sensing an opportunity, several businessmen formed Fairmount Cemetery

Left: The William Garrett Fisher family grave site, Fairmount Cemetery. *Photograph by author.*

Below: The mausoleum of Colorado Ku Klux Klan grand dragon Dr. John Galen Locke, with John Wesley Iliff's monument and Ivy Chapel in the distance, Fairmount Cemetery. *Photograph by author.*

Association in 1890, buying eight hundred acres about six miles southeast of Denver and one mile south of Montclair. Located on the High Line Canal, it was assured of water, founders believed. Fairmount engaged Reinhard Schuetze to plan its grounds and specify plantings to make it Denver's garden spot. Schuetze ordered more than four thousand trees, shrubs, vines, roses and other plants. Plots sold rapidly before Schuetze had even finished his design. Getting to Fairmount entailed a streetcar ride to 8th Avenue and Quebec, with a second streetcar for the final leg south to Fairmount. Water supplies proved fickle, as Colorado experienced severe droughts in 1893 and 1896, the latter year almost resulting in devastating plant loss after no water flowed for months. Fairmount engaged other water sources and built a reservoir, Windsor Lake.

Fairmount is home to three designated Denver Landmarks. Two, both by Henry Ten Eyck Wendell, date to 1890. The Richardsonian Romanesque–style Gate Lodge faces Alameda Avenue and formerly included caretaker living quarters. Built of gray sandstone, its Gothic entrance arch is twenty feet high; it houses Fairmount Heritage Foundation, which conducts cemetery tours. Nearby Ivy Chapel is thirteenth-century High French Gothic, with flying buttresses and an impressive spire. Due to sandstone's porosity, it no longer wears its namesake foliage. Fairmount's gray granite Mausoleum is one of America's largest, built in 1930 to a design by Frederick Mountjoy and Francis Frewan, expanded several times and the final home of nearly fifteen thousand. Four massive Doric columns greet visitors, who can gaze at an impressive stained-glass window collection by Colorado's Watkins Stained Glass Studio.

More Colorado historical figures reside at Fairmount than at any other cemetery; download checklists from the Heritage Foundation's website. "Millionaire's Row," the drive connecting Ivy Chapel with the Mausoleum, is a veritable "who's who" of Colorado history. Several Denver architects are buried here, including Robert Roeschlaub; Frank Edbrooke and Temple Buell designed their own mausoleums. Many other names discussed in this book can be visited at Fairmount, including John and Mary Elitch, Charles Boettcher, Claude Boettcher, Henry Brown, John Chivington, John Iliff (whose widow moved his body and monument from Riverside), Henry Buchtel, Robert Speer, Mattie Silks, Jennie Rogers (real name: Leah Wood), Nathaniel Hill, Emily Griffith, Ralph Carr, Justina Ford, William Friedman, William Byers, Frederick Bonfils, Helen Bonfils and Harry Tammen. More recent notables rest here too, including "Daddy" Bruce Randolph, Lloyd King, Elrey Jeppesen, Jerry Gart and Josiah "Joe" Holland. Special areas include the Emanuel Cemetery, affiliated with Temple Emanuel; a Nisei

Japanese American Memorial honoring World War II veterans who served in Europe while relatives resided in internment camps; a Denver Fire Department section; and a military section.

MOUNT OLIVET CEMETERY

12801 West 44th Avenue (Wheat Ridge)
(303) 424-7785; cfcscolorado.org

Dedicated in 1892 by the Denver diocese, Mount Olivet replaced Mount Calvary as the premier Roman Catholic cemetery. It occupies a portion of Bishop Joseph Machebeuf's 440-acre farm; he occupies a tomb in Gallagher Chapel alongside other Denver bishops and archbishops. After Mount Olivet opened, many families transferred their deceased from Mount Calvary, but some remained there until 1950, when the last of nearly 8,600 were disinterred and reburied here. Mount Olivet has seen about 150,000 interments. These include Apollo 13 astronaut John Leonard "Jack" Swigert, utterer of, "Okay, Houston, we've had a problem here"; once-wealthy Horace Tabor, who died penniless and converted to Catholicism on his deathbed; his second wife, Elizabeth Bonduel McCourt "Baby Doe" Tabor, who froze to death in a Leadville shack, which prompted history-minded Denverites to raise money for her interment next to Horace; Colorado's first territorial governor, William Gilpin; Colorado's thirty-fifth state governor, Stephen McNichols; his brother, William McNichols Jr., Denver's fortieth mayor; journalist Eugene Debs Cervi; and architect J.J.B. Benedict. The most spectacular of Mount Olivet's mausoleums belongs to mining and oil millionaire Verner Reed. Costing $250,000, it was inspired by Milan Cathedral and made of Carrara marble and bronze with stained glass and three altars inside; sculptor Raffaello Romanelli spent four years crafting it in his Florence, Italy workshop before shipping it to Colorado in 1923.

OLINGER MORTUARY/LOHI MARKETPLACE

1575 Boulder Street (Highland)

After opening Crown Hill Cemetery, George Olinger built a new mortuary in 1910. His architect made it resemble an elegant, Neoclassical-style home so mourners would not feel oppressed by gloom; it was later remodeled in Spanish Colonial style. The main floor featured a 150-seat chapel, and Olinger installed a basement cool room for storing bodies. In 1917, this was the five-month resting place of William Cody, prior to his burial on Lookout Mountain; Olinger hired guards to ensure that those who favored Cody, Wyoming, or North Platte, Nebraska, would not steal Buffalo Bill's body. In 1916, Olinger began sponsoring the Highlander Boys, a nonsectarian youth group. He opened other mortuaries, but this was always the flagship until its 2004 closure. Paul Tamburello bought and renovated the complex, which included the hearse garage on the hill above the mortuary, creating LoHi Marketplace, tenanted by restaurants and shops. Tamburello installed a custom-fabricated, twenty-eight-foot-tall "milk can" in the space between the mortuary and garage and opened Little Man Ice Cream, a busy neighborhood focal point.

RIVERSIDE CEMETERY

5201 Brighton Boulevard (Commerce City)
(303) 293-2466; friendsofriversidecemetery.org
NRD

Straddling Denver's border with Commerce City, mostly occupying the latter, and adjacent to the South Platte, Riverside opened in 1876 with a graceful, park-like design by Harvey Lowrie. Its seventy-seven acres are home to more than sixty-seven thousand deceased people. Among them are Augusta Pierce Tabor, Horace Tabor's long-suffering first wife; formerly enslaved man Barney Ford, the first African American person on Denver's Social Register; John Long Routt, Colorado's last territorial and first state governor; John Evans, Colorado's second territorial governor, and his wife, Margaret Gray Evans; Captain Silas S. Soule, who in 1865 testified honestly in court about the Sand Creek Massacre and was assassinated for it; "Aunt" Clara Brown, formerly enslaved, Denver pioneer and first African American woman to cross the Great Plains; Denver brewer Philip Zang; and Samuel Elbert, Colorado's sixth territorial governor and namesake of its highest peak. Union Civil War veterans are buried here, as are their Confederate opponents. Riverside boasts one of the world's largest collections of zinc ("white bronze") grave markers. The graveyard merged with Fairmount Cemetery in 1900 and has been operated by it

The Lester Drake "Cabin," marking three generations of men named Lester Drake, Riverside Cemetery. *Photograph by author.*

since 1925. Riverside lost water rights in 2001, subsequently losing most of its trees; weeds and native plants have supplanted bluegrass. The Friends of Historic Riverside Cemetery group educates visitors and maintains the cemetery; Fairmount has placed it in "caretaker only" status, providing no maintenance. In 2008, Colorado Preservation Inc. added Riverside to its list of "Most Endangered Places."

NEAR NEIGHBORS

Denver is more than the city and county. Suburbs—once isolated towns and some as old as Denver, or nearly so—boast rich histories. These historical societies, arts organizations and local museums tell those stories.

EAST OF DENVER

AURORA FOX ARTS CENTER
9900 East Colfax Avenue (Aurora)
(303) 739-1970; aurorafoxartscenter.org

AURORA HISTORICAL SOCIETY
aurorahistoricalsociety.org

AURORA HISTORY MUSEUM
15051 East Alameda Parkway (Aurora)
(303) 739-6660; auroragov.org/things-to-do/aurora_history_museum; free

ORIGINAL AURORA
East 21st to East 12th Avenues, Beeler to Hanover Streets (roughly)
aurorahistoricalsociety.org/historic-sites

SOUTH OF DENVER

CASTLE ROCK HISTORICAL SOCIETY AND MUSEUM
420 Elbert Street (Castle Rock)
(303) 814-3164; castlerockhistoricalsociety.org

CHERRY CREEK VALLEY HISTORICAL SOCIETY
ccvhsco.com

ENGLEWOOD HISTORIC PRESERVATION SOCIETY
(720) 254-1897; historicenglewood.com

HIGHLANDS RANCH HISTORICAL SOCIETY
(720) 507-1639; highlandsranchhistoricalsociety.org

HIGHLANDS RANCH MANSION & HISTORIC PARK
9950 East Gateway Drive (Highlands Ranch)
(303) 791-0177; highlandsranchmansion.com; free

HISTORIC DOUGLAS COUNTY INC.
historicdouglascounty.org

HISTORIC DOWNTOWN LITTLETON
South Santa Fe Drive to South Windermere Avenue, West Berry Avenue to
West Church Street (Littleton)
downtownlittleton.com

THE HUDSON GARDENS & EVENT CENTER
6115 South Santa Fe Drive (Littleton)
(303) 797-8565; hudsongardens.org

LITTLETON MUSEUM
6028 South Gallup Street (Littleton)
(303) 795-3950; littletongov.org/city-services/city-departments/museum;
free

PARKER AREA HISTORICAL SOCIETY
parkerhistory.org

SEDALIA MUSEUM AND GARDENS
4037-A North Platte Avenue (Sedalia)
(720) 336-9388 (answering machine); sedaliamuseumandgardens.org; free

SEVENTEEN MILE HOUSE FARM PARK
8181 South Parker Road (Centennial)
(720) 874-6540; arapahoe.co.us/facilities/facility/details/17-mile-house-farm-park-23; free
NR

TOWN HALL ARTS CENTER
2450 West Main Street (Littleton)
(303) 794-2787; townhallartscenter.org

WEST OF DENVER

AVOCA LODGE (MOLLY BROWN SUMMER HOUSE)
7595 West Yale Avenue (Lakewood)
(720) 253-8349; mollybrownsummerhouse.com; fee for tours; appointment only
NR

BAUGH HOUSE
11361 West 44th Avenue (Wheat Ridge)
wheatridgehistoricalsociety.org/baugh-house

BRADFORD WASHINGTON AMERICAN MOUNTAINEERING MUSEUM
710 10th Street (Golden)
(303) 996-2747; mountaineeringmuseum.org; admission fee

COLORADO SCHOOL OF MINES GEOLOGY MUSEUM
1310 Maple Street (Golden)
(303) 273-3815; mines.edu/geology-museum; free

DINOSAUR RIDGE
16831 West Alameda Parkway (Morrison)
(303) 697-3466; dinoridge.org; admission fee
National Natural Landmark

EVERGREEN MOUNTAIN AREA HISTORICAL SOCIETY
jchscolorado.org

FOOTHILLS ART CENTER
809 15th Street (Golden)
(303) 279-3922; foothillsartcenter.org; admission fee
NR

GOLDEN HISTORY MUSEUM & PARK
923 10th Street (Golden)
(303) 278-3557; goldenhistory.org; free

HISTORIC DOWNTOWN GOLDEN
visitgolden.com/places-to-go/historic-downtown-golden

HIWAN HOMESTEAD MUSEUM
28473 Meadow Drive (Evergreen)
(720) 497-7650; jcscolorado.org/33-2/museums
NR

LAKEWOOD HERITAGE CENTER
801 South Yarrow Street (Lakewood)
(303) 987-7850; lakewood.org/heritagecenter; free

MORRISON HISTORICAL SOCIETY
morrisonhistory.org

MORRISON NATURAL HISTORY MUSEUM
501 Colorado Highway 8 (Morrison)
(303) 697-1873; mnhm.org/246/morrison-natural-history-museum

OLDE TOWN ARVADA
Upham to Yarrow Streets, Ralston Road to Grandview Avenue (Arvada)
(303) 420-4769; oldetownarvada.org
NRD

WHEAT RIDGE HISTORICAL SOCIETY HISTORICAL PARK
4610 Robb Street (Wheat Ridge)
(303) 421-9111; wheatridgehistoricalsociety.org; admission fee

APPENDIX

NORTH OF DENVER

ADAMS COUNTY HISTORICAL SOCIETY & MUSEUM
9601 Henderson Road (Brighton)
(303) 659-7103; adamscountymuseum.com; free; fee for tours

BROOMFIELD DEPOT MUSEUM
2201 West 10th Avenue (Broomfield)
(303) 460-6824; broomfield.org/120/broomfield-depot-museum; free

BROOMFIELD VETERANS MEMORIAL MUSEUM
12 Garden Center (Broomfield)
(303) 460-6801; broomfield.org/121/broomfield-veterans-memorial-museum; free

COMMERCE CITY HERITAGE AND CULTURAL CENTER
6505 East 60th Avenue (Commerce City)
(303) 288-2590; cchistoric.com

HISTORIC BOULDER
(303) 444-5192; historicboulder.org

LAFAYETTE MINERS MUSEUM
108 East Simpson Street (Lafayette)
(303) 665-7030; cityoflafayette.com/463/miners-museum

LOUISVILLE HISTORICAL MUSEUM
1001 Main Street (Louisville)
(303) 335-4850; louisvilleco.gov/government/departments/home-museum; free

MUSEUM OF BOULDER
2205 Broadway (Boulder)
(303) 449-3464; museumofboulder.org

STONEHOCKER FARMHOUSE
10950 Fox Run Parkway (Northglenn)
northglennhistory.com/stonehocker-farmhouse
NR

WESTMINSTER HISTORY CENTER
7200 Lowell Boulevard (Westminster)
(303) 428-3993; westminstercohistory.com

WISE HOMESTEAD MUSEUM
11611 Jasper Road (Erie)
(303) 828-4561; eriehistoricalsociety.org/erie-wise-homestead-museum

SELECTED BIBLIOGRAPHY

Abrams, Jeanne E. *Jewish Denver, 1859–1940*. Charleston, SC: Arcadia Publishing, 2007.

Arps, Louisa Ward. *Denver in Slices*. Denver, CO: Sage Books, 1959.

Autobee, Robert, and Kristen Autobee. *Early Lakewood*. Charleston, SC: Arcadia Publishing, 2011.

———. *Lost Restaurants of Denver*. Charleston, SC: The History Press, 2015.

Bakemeier, Alice Millett. *Hilltop Heritage: A History and Guide to a Denver Neighborhood*. Denver, CO: Heritage Press, 1997.

Ballard, Jack Stokes, John Bond and George Paxton. *Lowry Air Force Base*. Charleston, SC: Arcadia Publishing, 2013.

Ballast, David Kent. *Denver's Civic Center: A Walking Tour*. Denver, CO: City Publishing Company, 1977.

Barnhouse, Mark. *Lost Denver*. Charleston, SC: Arcadia Publishing, 2015.

———. *Northwest Denver*. Charleston, SC: Arcadia Publishing, 2012.

Barrett, Daniel, and Beth R. Barrett. *High Drama: Colorado's Historic Theatres*. Montrose, CO: Western Reflections Publishing Company, 2005.

Beck, Rhonda. *Union Station in Denver*. Charleston, SC: The History Press, 2016.

Brettell, Richard R. *Historic Denver*. Denver, CO: Historic Denver Inc., 1973.

Bretz, James. *Mansions of Denver: The Vintage Years, 1870–1938*. Boulder, CO: Pruett Publishing, 2005.

Chandler, Mary Voelz. *Guide to Denver Architecture*. 2nd ed. Golden, CO: Fulcrum Publishing, 2013.

Coel, Margaret, Jane Barker and Karen Gilleland. *The Tivoli: Bavaria in the Rockies*. Boulder, CO: Colorado and the West, 1985.

Dallas, Sandra. *Gold and Gothic: Story of Larimer Square*. Denver, CO: Lick Skillet Press, 1967.

Etter, Carolyn, and Don Etter. *The Denver Zoo: A Centennial History*. Boulder, CO: Roberts Rinehart Publishers, 1995.

Etter, Don, and Carolyn Etter. *Forgotten Dreamer: Reinhard Schuetze, Denver's Landscape Architect*. Denver, CO: Denver Public Library, Western History Collection, 2001.

Faulkner, Debra. *Ladies of the Brown: A Women's History of Denver's Most Elegant Hotel*. Charleston, SC: The History Press, 2010.

Fetter, Rosemary. *Celebrating 20 Years of Innovation in Higher Education: A Brief History of Auraria*. Denver, CO: Auraria Higher Education Center, 1996.

Fisher, Steve, and Thyria K. Wilson. *University of Denver*. Charleston, SC: Arcadia Publications, 2018.

Forsyth, David. *Denver's Lakeside Amusement Park: From the White City Beautiful to a Century of Fun*. Boulder: University Press of Colorado, 2016.

Fowler, Gene. *Timberline: A Story of Bonfils and Tammen*. Reprint, Garden City, NY: Garden City Books, 1951.

Gibson, Barbara. *The Lower Downtown Historic District*. Denver, CO: Historic Denver Inc., 1995.

Goodstein, Phil. *Curtis Park, Five Points, and Beyond: The Heart of Historic East Denver*. Denver, CO: New Social Publications, 2014.

———. *The Denver Civic Center: The Heart of the Mile High City*. Denver, CO: New Social Publications, 2016.

———. *Denver's Capitol Hill*. Denver, CO: Life Publications, 1988.

———. *The Ghosts of Denver: Capitol Hill*. Denver, CO: New Social Publications, 1996.

———. *How the West Side Won*. Denver, CO: New Social Publications, 2015.

———. *North Side Story*. Denver, CO: New Social Publications, 2011.

———. *South Denver Saga*. Denver, CO: New Social Publications, 1991.

Haber, Francine, Kenneth R. Fuller and David N. Wetzel. *Robert S. Roeschlaub: Architect of the Emerging West, 1843–1923*. Denver: Colorado Historical Society, 1988.

Halaas, David Fridtjof. *Fairmount & Historic Colorado*. Denver, CO: Fairmount Cemetery Association, 1993. Originally published in 1976.

Hoffecker, John F. *Twenty-Seven Square Miles: Landscape and History at Rocky Mountain Arsenal National Wildlife Refuge*. Rev. ed. Walden, CO: Walden Press Inc., 2014.

Johnson, Charles A. *Denver's Mayor Speer*. Denver, CO: Green Mountain Press, 1969.

Kelly, George V. *The Old Gray Mayors of Denver*. Boulder, CO: Pruett Publishing, 1974.

Kerouac, Jack. *On the Road*. New York: Viking Press, 1957.

Kopp, Zack. *The Denver Beat Scene: The Mile-High Legacy of Kerouac, Cassady & Ginsberg*. Charleston, SC: The History Press, 2015.

Kreck, Dick. *Murder at the Brown Palace: A True Story of Seduction & Betrayal*. Golden, CO: Fulcrum Publishing, 2003.

———. *Rich People Behaving Badly*. Golden, CO: Fulcrum Publishing, 2016.

Laugen, R. Todd. *The Gospel of Progressivism: Moral Reform and Labor War in Colorado, 1900–1930*. Niwot: University Press of Colorado, 2010.

McCarthy, Sarah O. *Denver's Washington Park*. Charleston, SC: Arcadia Publishing, 2014.

McCartney, Laton. *The Teapot Dome Scandal*. New York: Random House, 2008.

McPhee, Mike. *Dana Crawford: 50 Years Saving the Soul of a City*. Denver, CO: Upper Gulch Publishing Company, 2015.

Mohr, Rob, and Leslie Mohr Krupa. *Golf in Denver*. Charleston, SC: Arcadia Publishing, 2011.

Nichols, R.E.D., and John Witty. *Holstory: Gunleather of the Twentieth Century*. N.p.: privately published, 2018.

Noel, Thomas J. *Buildings of Colorado*. New York: Oxford University Press, 1997.

———. *The City and the Saloon: Denver, 1858–1916*. Lincoln: University of Nebraska Press, 1982.

———. *Denver's Larimer Street: Main Street, Skid Row and Urban Renaissance*. Denver, CO: Historic Denver Inc., 1981.

Noel, Thomas J., and Amy B. Zimmer. *Showtime: Denver's Performing Arts, Convention Centers and Theatre District*. Denver, CO: City and County of Denver Division of Theatres and Arenas, 2008.

Noel, Thomas J., and Barbara S. Norgren. *Denver: The City Beautiful*. Denver, CO: Historic Denver Inc., 1987.

Noel, Thomas J., and Nicholas J. Wharton. *Denver Landmarks & Historic Districts*. 2nd ed. Boulder: University Press of Colorado, 2016.

Pearson, Michelle. *Historic Sacred Places of Denver*. Denver, CO: Historic Denver Inc., 2004.

Peters, Bette D. *Denver's Four Mile House*. Denver, CO: Golden Bell Press, 1980.

Price, Jeffrey C., Jeffrey S. Forrest and Shahn G. Sederberg. *Denver Airports from Stapleton to DIA.* Charleston, SC: Arcadia Publishing, 2018.

Pyle, Robert Michael. *The Thunder Tree: Lessons from an Urban Wildland.* New York: Houghton Mifflin, 1993.

Repplinger, Matthew Kasper, II. *Baseball in Denver.* Charleston, SC: Arcadia Publishing, 2013.

Robertson, Don, and Reverend W. Morris Cafky. *Denver's Street Railways.* Vol. 2, *1901–1950.* Denver CO: Sundance Publications Ltd., 2004.

Robertson, Don, Reverend W. Morris Cafky and E.J. Haley. *Denver's Street Railways.* Vol. 1, *1871–1900.* Denver, CO: Sundance Publications Ltd., 1999.

Snow, Shawn M. *Denver's City Park and Whittier Neighborhoods.* Charleston, SC: Arcadia Publishing, 2009.

———. *Southwest Denver.* Charleston, SC: Arcadia Publishing, 2016.

Ubbelohhde, Carl, Maxine Benson and Duane A. Smith. *A Colorado History.* 7th ed. Boulder, CO: Pruett Publishing, 1995.

Van Wyke, Millie. *The Town of South Denver.* Boulder, CO: Pruett Publishing, 1991.

West, William Allen. *Curtis Park: Denver's Oldest Neighborhood.* Denver, CO: Historic Denver Inc., 2002.

Widmann, Nancy L. *The East 7th Avenue Historic District.* Reprint, Denver, CO: Historic Denver Inc., 2006. Originally published in 1997.

Wommack, Linda R. *Our Ladies of the Tenderloin: Colorado's Legends in Lace.* Caldwell, ID: Caxton Press, 2005.

Wood, Richard E. *Here Lies Colorado: Fascinating Figures in Colorado History.* Helena, MT: Farcountry Press, 2005.

Wray, Diane. *The Arapahoe Acres Historic District.* Denver, CO: Historic Denver Inc., 2004.

Zimmer, Amy B. *Denver's Historic Homes.* Charleston, SC: Arcadia Publishing, 2013.

INDEX

E

University of Denver 95, 108–111, 137, 186, 223

V

Varian, Ernest P. 66, 77, 161
Varian, Lester E. 66, 161
Voorhies Memorial 121

W

Wagner, Stanley 172
Waite, Davis H. 15, 83
Walker, John Brisben 103, 123, 128, 206
Washington Park 132, 151, 158
Webb, Wellington E. 113, 126, 168, 178
Webb, Wilma 168, 178
Weil, Jack A. 46, 56
Wells Fargo Depot 44
West High School 134
White, Byron Raymond 64, 105, 190
White, Edward D., Jr. 183
Williamson, George Hebard 126, 140
Willison, Robert O. 25, 85, 213
Wilson, Woodrow 87, 192
Wings Over the Rockies Air & Space Museum 70, 200
Wolcott, Edward Oliver 69, 83
Wolcott, Henry Roger 69, 78, 82, 84
Woolley, Charles 41, 223
Wright, Frank Lloyd 34

Y

Yasui, Minoru 176

Z

Zang, Adolph 41, 145, 217
Zang, Philip 26, 217, 230
Zeckendorf, William 17, 92
Zietz, Henry H. 48
Zion Baptist Church 167, 178

ABOUT THE AUTHOR

Denver native Mark A. Barnhouse has been fascinated by his city's history from an early age, thanks to his mother's interest in old mansions. He remembers going with her to the grand opening of Ninth Street Historic Park on Colorado's 100th birthday, August 1, 1976. A graduate of the University of Colorado–Denver, he has been researching and writing about Denver's history for more than two decades. He is the author of *Lost Department Stores of Denver*; *Daniels and Fisher: Denver's Best Place to Shop*; *The Denver Dry Goods: Where Colorado Shopped with Confidence*; *Denver's Sixteenth Street*; *Lost Denver*; and *Northwest Denver*, all available from Arcadia Publishing/The History Press. He is available for talks to groups and for walking tours. He lives in northwest Denver and is a member of the Denver Posse of Westerners. You'll find him on Facebook at "Denver History Books by Mark A. Barnhouse."

Visit us at
www.historypress.com